Praise for Muckraker *by W. Sydney Robinson*

'A timely study of Britain's first investigative journalist … with impeccable research, Mr Robinson elegantly pieces together the backstory.'
– Tobias Grey, *Wall Street Journal*

'A lively and laconic biography.'
– John Pemble, *London Review of Books*

'I grew to quite dislike [Stead] as I read *Muckraker*, but that's because Robinson knows how to tell a story.'
– Jonathan Mirsky, *The Spectator*

'W. Sydney Robinson's admirably thoughtful and economical biography could hardly be better timed. Closely researched and briskly written, it does an excellent job of explaining one of the most extraordinary individuals in journalistic history.'
– Dominic Sandbrook, *Sunday Times*

'With a lovely eye for detail, a wry sense of irony and a fine grasp of character, it brings alive an age in which sensationalist papers went further in search of a story than even Rebekah Brooks would think appropriate.'
– *Prospect* magazine

'W. Sydney Robinson's energetic, thorough and hospitable new biography spares nothing.'
– Jonathan Barnes, *Times Literary Supplement*

'Robinson is a resourceful investigator and a connoisseur of human paradox.'
– *Irish Times*

'A timely, well-written biography of the brilliant, flawed Victorian journalist.'
– Bel Mooney, *Daily Mail*

'Tragically compelling.'
– Toby Thomas, *Literary Review*

'This is, quite simply, a marvellous book, the best I have read this year so far. Every politician and journalist should slip a copy of this slim, brilliantly written volume by a new young author into their holiday luggage this summer.'
– Lord Lexden, *The House*

'W. Sydney Robinson has produced an entertaining and clear-eyed introduction to an extraordinary life.'
– Robert Gray, *The Tablet*

'An engrossing biography.'
– *Times Higher Education*

'Gives a singular editor his rightful place in the history of journalism.'
– *Western Mail*

'An excellent account.'
– *The Oldie*

THE LAST VICTORIANS

A DARING REASSESSMENT OF
FOUR TWENTIETH-CENTURY ECCENTRICS:
SIR WILLIAM JOYNSON-HICKS;
DEAN INGE;
LORD REITH
&
SIR ARTHUR BRYANT

W. SYDNEY ROBINSON

The Robson Press

First published in Great Britain in 2014 by
The Robson Press (an imprint of Biteback Publishing Ltd)
Westminster Tower
3 Albert Embankment
London SE1 7SP
Copyright © W. Sydney Robinson 2014

ISBN 978-1-84954-716-1

10 9 8 7 6 5 4 3 2 1

A CIP catalogue record for this book is available from the British Library.

Set in Adobe Garamond Pro by 525 Graphic Design
Printed and bound in Great Britain by
CPI Group (UK) Ltd, Croydon CR0 4YY

Colonel Blimp and the Old School Tie, for whom Three Cheers.
J. M. Keynes, *New Statesman,* 14 October 1939

The oldest hath borne the most; we that are young
Shall never see so much, nor live so long.
Shakespeare, *King Lear*, Act V, Scene iii

CONTENTS

INTRODUCTION

When I used to daydream at the back of my classroom at school it was a habit of mine to examine something called 'The School's Chronology of World History', which hung upon the wall. Here, in a distance scarcely more than my youthful arms could reach, seemed to me a complete record of man's history on earth. Dissecting the timeline near the beginning were 'the Ancient Egyptians' with their flat faces and strange beards; then came 'the Greeks' with their airy temples and towel-clad philosophers; next were 'the Romans' with their fine bridges and beefy centurions; after them a slightly chaotic looking era called 'the Middle Ages', giving way at last to a montage of muskets, tobacco pipes and sheep enclosures. On the story rolled, past 'the Victorians' and the two world wars into 'the Present Day' – rather disturbingly represented, if I recall correctly, by a suited man grinning down upon me as if from the boardroom wall.

Even then, this all seemed too perfect. Was it possible that the Egyptians died out with Ptolemy XV in 30 BC? Or that the Romans sunk without trace in 455? Or that the Middle Ages ended with a whimper at Bosworth Field in 1485?

I did not think so. Many stalwarts of these old regimes must have lived on for decades – for some families, centuries perhaps – keeping up the same life while the world around them changed beyond recognition. With time against me, I resolved to find myself one of these living fossils: a real-life 'Victorian'. From that idea, hatched in my mind over twenty years ago, has emerged this book.

My first assistant in this audacious quest was my beloved grandfather, John Rossdale. Well can I remember his wry smile when I innocently asked if he could recall 'the olden days'. Born in the mid-1920s to an affluent professional family, he forgave my impertinence by describing some of the more exalted aspects of his parents' and grandparents' era: the grand houses, the starchy clothes and the libraries of French and German books which a dwindling number of the household could actually read. It all seemed so far away as we sat in his modest west London flat. He might as well have been telling me about the stories of the Old Testament.

It came as a shock, as it does in the life of any child, to realise that my grandfather was not the oldest creature alive upon this earth. Soon my investigations were throwing up elderly individuals twenty or thirty years his senior. They were of a very different sort to him. No indulgent smiles from them; no liking of children or amusements – many did not even own television sets. But there was something about them I found impossible not to hold in silent awe. They seemed to carry the treasure of a vanished age. And I can recall thinking, even in my extreme youth, that it would be my privilege to belong to the last generation which would – however dimly – remember them.

For about fifteen years these memories lay dormant in my mind. I then enrolled on a university history course and began to learn about the mysteries of the past in much more detail. Or so it seemed. The sense of connectedness I had previously felt with my frock-coated predecessors was rudely disillusioned when I discovered that a particular year – be it 1900, 1910 or 1914 – really had shattered Victorian civilisation, just as the School's Chronology had claimed all along. There was the evidence of *The Times* leader-writer who wrote upon the death of William Gladstone in 1898 'that with that honoured life there passes away not a man merely, but an epoch' – a sentiment echoed upon the demise of the revered queen three years later. There was also the more dramatic testimony of the novelist Virginia Woolf who opined in the early 1920s that 'on or about December 1910 human character changed'. And there was the brilliant attack of the magazine *Blast*, which enthused in the summer of 1914:

> Blast years 1837 to 1900! ... Blast their weeping whiskers, hirsute rhetoric of eunuch and stylist, sentimental hygienics, Rousseauisms (wild nature cranks) fraternizing with monkeys, DIABOLICS, raptures and roses of the erotic bookshelves culminating in purgatory of Putney.[1]

This was the sort of thing we undergraduates were expected to write about in our essays.

Which seemed to me ridiculous. The more independent reading that I did – not of dull textbooks, but masses of old newspapers, magazines and the like – suggested that at least until the 1960s and 1970s the 'Victorians', though silent and out of sight, were alive and kicking. They dwelt in places as various as Pall Mall clubs, dreary seaside cottages and chilly, unloved tenement blocks, emerging every so often to denounce the slide in manners and morals since their parents' day. Thousands of them nodded in restrained approval over their marmalade and toast as they read letters in the press from the likes of one Mrs Sheila Carter complaining that articles on contraception 'encourage[d] immorality among the younger generation'. Powerful figures such as *The Times* editor Sir William Rees-Mogg and his crusading ally Lord Longford threw their weight behind rearguard campaigns to slow the pace of change. Thousands of these lonely zealots, equally offended by the prevalence of 'filth' on television and in literature, joined the National Viewers' and Listeners' Association of Mary Whitehouse. Greater numbers yet lived out quiet but influential lives as magistrates, schoolmasters and policemen.[2]

It would be dangerous to lay down what exactly this mass of dissident opinion believed, let alone how much in common it had with the prudish morality of the Victorian watchdog of art and literature, 'Mrs Grundy'. It might be enough to say that those who objected to the rise of the permissive society in the 1960s were instinctively conservative, puritanical and parochial in outlook. Their story is an interesting one, worthy of a much longer book than this; it can only be treated incidentally here.

My defence is that there are still many prominent 'Victorian' figures from the last century who have suffered the same neglect of history as Mrs Whitehouse and her brigade. Any reader of the newspapers or magazines of the 1920s and 1930s, for instance, would be amazed to find little mention of the acknowledged greats of that era: T. S. Eliot, Evelyn Waugh, Roger Fry or – looking on a more European scale – Pablo Picasso. Instead he or she would find frequent mention of many characters often completely ignored in the standard textbooks published in more recent times. Four of these individuals, from the worlds of politics, religion, broad-casting and journalism respectively, make up the quartet of this group biography.

In this I have betrayed my sympathy for the now offensively Victorian 'great men' approach to history. For this I am unrepent-ant. So too, after all, was the greatest of all the debunkers of the Victorian era, Lytton Strachey. Like him, I have attempted to give a portrait of an age – in my case, the afterglow of an age – through the lives of four individuals who, despite being practically strangers to one another, seem to personify my theme. The four whom I have selected may not have been regarded by their contemporaries as giants in the way that Cardinal Manning, Dr Arnold, General Gordon and Florence Nightingale all were – beings, wrote one survivor into the new century, who seemed to 'live on islands segregated from the great human stream of life that poured itself into an ocean which they never saw'. They were more prosaically dismissed as 'pygmies'. In an age of satire and dirt-digging, their moral seriousness only served to make them seem ridiculous.[3]

The stock character invented by the inter-war journalist David Low to personify these figures was the bigoted and dim-witted retired staff officer Colonel Blimp. Wrapped in a towel in the Turkish bath of his club, he would explain to his bewildered companion that peace depended on militarism; that freedom was founded upon repression; that patriotism was the highest form of internationalism, and other examples of the counter-intuitive wisdom of the day. He symbolised the 'old men' who had allowed Britain to sleepwalk into a ruinous world war in 1914, and would continue to stand in the way of 'progress' long after. As I became more sympathetic towards my real-life Blimps, I felt increasingly like one of the 'descendants of Blimp' whom Low envisaged communing with his unloved creation 'in letters of fire on asbestos newspaper': 'Gad Sir,' I have occasionally sighed, 'you were right.'

THE LAST VICTORIANS

© Viscount Brentford

CHAPTER 1

THE POLICEMAN OF THE LORD: SIR WILLIAM JOYNSON-HICKS AT THE HOME OFFICE

A Puritan is such a one as loves God with all his soul, but hates his neighbour with all his heart.
– Seventeenth-century saying

Shortly after midnight on 21 April 1926, a rotund, thin-lipped figure, swinging an ebony and silver cane, arrived at the mansion of the Earl of Strathmore in Mayfair. Although dressed rather haphazardly in loose and comfortable clothing, his superior demeanour – proud to the point of brashness – suggested his high office. The gentleman was Sir William Joynson-Hicks, the Home Secretary. He had come to execute one of the most solemn and unusual duties known to the British state: the oversight of the birth of an heir to the throne, the future Queen Elizabeth II.

It was a highly apposite undertaking for a man of his disposition. Excessively grave, though possessing a wild and fanatical imagination, 'Jix' – as he was popularly known – took his role as inspector of royal warming-pans with the utmost seriousness. It was by means of one of these conveyances that a 'changeling' was believed to have been smuggled into the queen's bedroom during the confinement of James II's unhappy wife, Mary of Modena. No such subterfuge would occur under the eagle-eyed vigil of Home

Secretary Jix. For some three hours he sat in dignified silence with the child's father, the future George VI, until at last, the new-born princess was produced from behind a closed door. After congratulating the duke and bowing stiffly to the baby, Jix left the scene with haste. 'It would be indeed interesting', he mused to himself afterwards, 'if we once more had a Queen Elizabeth, but, alas, I shall be too old to play Lord Burghley to her!'[4]

Such thoughts came only too naturally to the man who had begun life, sixty-one years previously, as plain William Hicks, the eldest of four sons and two daughters of a pious Smithfield meat merchant, Henry Hicks, and his wife, Harriet. Yet the high regard with which he viewed himself was not entirely unjustified. Though born without any obvious advantages in life, Jix ended his days a Viscount, an ex-Cabinet minister and a national figure.

How had he managed it? Jix was more than happy to explain. 'I began life with nothing', he told one enquirer, 'and have worked hard for well over forty years – when I say hard, I mean really hard.'[5]

It was in his parents' modest Canonbury home that this tenacious character was forged. Even by the standards of 1865, the household was almost perversely antiquated – Victorian by date and Puritan in outlook. Hicks's mother, a prayerful though severe woman, believed implicitly in the literal truth of the Bible and sought to live in 'closest communion with the Creator'. Games and novels were as unfamiliar to her as the sound of uproarious laughter. And if any of her children strayed from his allotted path, her stern husband had 'no hesitation in resorting to a sound thrashing'. These strictures, however, were no encumbrance to the eldest of the brood. 'Though our amusements were simple,' he reflected in adulthood, 'they were sufficient, and led … to greater happiness than is achieved by the more pampered children of today.'[6]

The family worshipped twice every Sunday at a local Anglican church noted for its Evangelical leanings. It was here that the budding Spartan was brought, aged fourteen, to swear on the Bible that he would abstain from alcohol for the rest of his life. The pledge would be observed, like all other manifestations of self-denial, with extraordinary gleefulness. Even as the distinguished master of a City livery company, Jix would solemnly inform the wine waiters to keep him topped up with nothing more corrupting than ginger ale. Yet he was not without a sense of fun. When once accidentally replenished with champagne, the merry Puritan heartily congratulated his benefactor for introducing him to what he called an 'excellent new type' of his accustomed beverage.[7]

To contemporaries at the Merchant Taylors' School, where he was sent as a day boy in 1875, Hicks proved himself as neither a scholar nor a sportsman. But his abilities as an orator were soon acknowledged. The school magazine records victories in debates that would later be replayed with more formality, though scarcely less earnestness, from the dispatch box of the House of Commons. One motion he carried supported the death penalty; another called for the immediate retirement of the hero of the Liberal Party, William Gladstone.

Having briefly flirted with Liberalism himself, Hicks found his voice as a champion of conservative values. He spoke regularly on the platforms of the Church of England Temperance Society and a local Tory debating club. By his late teens he had become quite a well-known speaker, and boasted of having the 'most extensive acquaintance with Bishops of any layman' in the country.[8]

Success in the meat business allowed Hicks's father to move the family to a large house in Kent, Plaistow Hall, in 1885. But it was felt that the heir of this fortune should enter a profession straightaway rather than go up to university. So in 1881, aged sixteen, Hicks was articled to a prominent firm of Lincoln's Inn solicitors, Messrs. Monckton, Long and Gardiner, to study the law. This proved to be a turning point; but Hicks did not make an especially favourable impression on either his employer or his colleagues. On one occasion a burly clerk saw no way of terminating an unwanted sermon on morality than by throwing the speaker down a steep flight of stairs.

After completing his training, Hicks took the first of a number of seemingly bold and reckless steps by setting up his own practice. With what little money he had saved, the 21-year-old rented a shabby room in the Old Jewry chambers, where he sat at his desk each day from nine in the morning until six in the evening reading Gibbon's *Decline and Fall of the Roman Empire*, legal textbooks and 'other stiff volumes which prevented me from getting into mischief'. Characteristically, he also expended five shillings a week on an office boy, whom he instructed to make profitable use of the vacant hours by copying out old title deeds and contracts.[9]

Gradually, the situation became more favourable for Hicks. This was mostly due to his father becoming an associate director of the London General Omnibus Company, which brought him a modest number of cases relating to transport law. Phenomenal industry bolstered Hicks's good fortune. 'I rushed about London', he recalled, '…as enquiry agent, draughtsman, writer and subsequently prepared briefs for Counsel.' He even found time to prepare a sturdy reference book entitled *The Law of Light and Heavy Mechanical Traction on the Highways*, which established him as an early authority in the field.[10]

These efforts did not go unnoticed. By the end of his first year in practice Hicks had attracted a partner to his firm, and was already becoming well-known in the courts as a ferocious litigator. A letter from an early client gives the tenor of his methods: 'I hope you will pursue this man as relentlessly as you pursued me when you were acting against me.' On another occasion, a woman whom he was chasing for a debt declared that she would sooner hang herself in his office than pay up. 'Madam,' the beady young lawyer replied, 'there is only one personal favour I ask: if you must do this, please do it on a Wednesday – the night when the office cleaner comes.' The money was apparently soon forthcoming.[11]

A degree of success was now assured, but Hicks did not acquire the modesty or bonhomie required to reach the summit of his profession. When a much older and more distinguished lawyer, a King's Counsel, appeared to cut across him during a meeting with a client, young Hicks grandly resolved never to send him another brief. 'Let that be a useful warning', he seriously wrote in his memoirs, '...as to the treatment of young solicitors who do not wish to be put into the background in the presence of their clients.'[12]

Hicks could never tolerate being placed in the background. As he approached his thirtieth birthday he reflected that he had already achieved all that a lawyer possibly could. Now his ambition found its proper outlet – politics.

෩

The most significant event in the political career of the future Sir William Joynson-Hicks occurred in August 1894 at the home of a wealthy uncle living on the French Riviera. It was here that the rising solicitor was introduced to Grace Lynn Joynson, the shy and unassuming 21-year-old only child of a successful Manchester silk manufacturer and local Conservative Party figure named Richard Hampson Joynson.[13]

If there was something premeditated about this meeting, there was nothing particularly unusual about an ambitious young man seeking out an heiress. Even among the aristocracy, matches of this kind oiled the wheels of political power. What made Hicks's position different was his reluctance even to cloak this practical arrangement with the pretence of romance. Rather than trying to woo the young woman directly, he charmed her father, whom he claimed to have become enamoured with prior to noticing his daughter.

A remarkably swift courtship ensued. After a few supervised walks in the countryside surrounding Menton, Hicks proposed and was accepted. Satisfied with his speedy work, he continued with his holiday, sending Grace occasional proclamations of his affection from new destinations. These letters were to cease after their marriage early the following year, when Hicks incorporated her name into his own. On the day of the wedding, the groom thought nothing of spending the morning poring over legal documents at his office.

Joynson-Hicks, as he now became, seemed to have the world at his feet. Young, rich and increasingly well-connected, it was only a matter of time before his father-in-law secured his selection for a parliamentary seat. But the Manchester to which he was taken for his first political outing was no easy place for a Tory hopeful to make his reputation. Though selected to stand for Manchester North in 1898, the unknown candidate was defeated in the general election of 1900 by the eye-watering margin of twenty-six votes. At the next parliamentary contest, in 1906, he failed to secure what should have been the safe seat of Manchester North-West by a larger deficit of 1,241. Small was the consolation that his failure coincided with one of the worst nights in the party's history – even the Prime Minister, Arthur Balfour, lost his seat in the neighbouring constituency of Manchester East.

The victor of the Manchester North-West election was a young Tory renegade who had lately joined the Liberals in protest over the Tariff Reform (protectionism) agenda. His name was Winston Churchill. He had met his vanquished adversary two years previously at a dinner party hosted by his cousin, the Hon. Ivor Guest, whose legal affairs Joynson-Hicks handled. At the end of the meal, Churchill gently took the intemperate solicitor to one side and said: 'I am so sorry I am coming to Manchester to queer your pitch.' Needless to say, the listener was not amused. 'I noted at the time the calm assurance that he would succeed in doing so,' he recalled. Exactly two years after the disappointment of 1906, the thwarted parliamentarian had an opportunity to exact his revenge.[14]

His chance arose directly from Churchill's extraordinary success as a Liberal. At the outset of 1908 the future war leader was appointed President of the Board of Trade, which required him, due to a technicality in the law at the time, to offer himself for re-election. Convention dictated that no gentleman would upset this formality, but Joynson-Hicks felt no compunction in going

after what he called this 'guerrilla chieftain who was once a lieutenant of our party'. His fiery campaign, lasting almost three months,
attracted an unprecedented amount of press coverage. So distressed
were the leaders of the Liberal Party that the new Chancellor of
the Exchequer, David Lloyd George, was dispatched to the city
to make a surprise endorsement of his young colleague, while the
novelist H. G. Wells penned a bitter denunciation of Joynson-
Hicks as 'an obscure and ineffectual nobody ... [representing] the
worst element in British political life at the present time'.[15]

The abuse was not entirely undeserved. In his desperation to win
votes, Joynson-Hicks employed such extreme tactics that even the
leaders of his own party seemed reluctant to lend their support. In a
characteristically bombastic speech, afterwards printed and distributed to thousands of potential supporters, he accused Churchill
and his Liberal colleagues of a staggering array of crimes. 'In two
short years', he thundered, they had

> alienated our colonies, thrown away the fruits of the Transvaal war,
> attempted to gerrymander our Constitution, increased our taxation,
> flouted our religious convictions, let loose chaos and bloodshed in
> Ireland and are now setting out to attack every trade and institution
> not prepared to obey the rattle of the Radical drum.[16]

The candidate followed up this extraordinary onslaught by taking
issue with the new Licensing Act, ironically designed to promote
one of his most fanatical passions – sobriety. The problem,
complained Joynson-Hicks, was that the measure 'embodied in
naked form pure socialism'.

Although Churchill had been confident of victory right up to the close of the poll on 23 April, Joynson-Hicks achieved a huge swing of almost 10 per cent, winning by a majority of little more than 400 votes. Like Lord Byron before him, 'Jix' – as his supporters dubbed him – awoke to fame. In Manchester's Albert Square a vast crowd of 100,000 'packed [in] like sardines' to cheer on their new MP. None felt the enormity of the catastrophe more than Churchill, who lamented the outcome of what he described as 'one of the fiercest and most strenuously contested battles in the political history of our country'.[17]

Jix's victory was all the more amazing on account of the strong opposition of the entire Jewish community of Manchester, whose leaders opposed the Conservative-backed Aliens Act of 1905. This controversial piece of legislation had given the Home Secretary of the day powers to deport undesirable foreign nationals, placing the first significant restrictions on the rate of immigration in British history. Though popular with the majority of the electorate, the cosmopolitan nature of Manchester ensured that the issue weighted against the Tory candidate – Churchill had tactically opposed it. Foolishly, Jix allowed feelings of bitterness to outlive his sensational victory. Just a few days after his success, he had this to say to the members of a Jewish dining society:

If you like I could say smooth things. I could say that you are a delightful people, that the Jews are delightful opponents, that I am very pleased to receive the opposition of the Jewish community, and that, in spite of all, I am your very humble and obedient servant. I could say that if you like, but it would not be true in the slightest degree ... I have beaten you thoroughly and soundly, and I am no longer your servant.[18]

This was an outrageous statement for a newly elected Member of Parliament to make. Critics, unconvinced by Jix's explanation that his words had been justified by the vehemence of the campaign against him, took the gaffe as an early indication that he was not a man for practical politics. Regarded as fatally 'accident prone', it was said by the satirist and politician A. P. Herbert that whenever Jix opened his mouth there followed 'the gentle sound of dropping bricks'. The furore caused by his comments would live long in the memory of his constituents, blighting his chances of re-election and those of his party for many years to come. After losing his seat in the general election of 1910, the villain of the piece decamped to Brentford, which he represented in Parliament until 1918, when he transferred to the safe Conservative seat of Twickenham.[19]

An even more regrettable consequence of Jix's by-election victory was that he returned to Westminster in the manner of a triumphant Prime Minister. 'It was a mistake to win a spectacular by-election,' he later confessed, '...I am afraid that I thought I was a more important person than I really was.' A long and pompous maiden speech set the tone for a disappointing first decade in Parliament. But even if he had been able to show the humility and sensitivity required of a loyal backbencher, it is unlikely that he would have gone on to be offered a ministerial position. As well as facing a degree of prejudice about his obscure origins, Jix had a habit of attaching himself to hopeless causes, which – however righteous they may have been – distanced him from the respectable leadership of his party.[20]

The case of Brigadier General Reginald Dyer perfectly high-lighted this ambiguity. In April 1919, Dyer was dispatched to Amritsar, a Punjab city of 160,000 inhabitants, with orders to put down a violent nationalist insurrection. Accompanied by a small contingent of Sikh and Ghurkha riflemen, he paraded through the streets, warning the townsmen that martial law was in operation and that public meetings would be dispersed by force if necessary. On 13 April, in defiance of this proclamation, between 5,000 and 20,000 unarmed protesters gathered in Jallianwallah Bagh, a public square near the Golden Temple. Fearing the onset of a major rebellion, Dyer ordered his troops to open fire. After ten minutes of engagement, at least four hundred protesters lay dead and over one thousand more wounded. Dyer did nothing to help the injured and imposed a so-called 'crawling order' whereby any Indian seeking entrance to a street in which a female missionary had previously been assaulted had to proceed along it on all fours.[21]

On the face of it, this was a completely indefensible action, and Dyer was roundly condemned by liberal public opinion when news of the massacre reached England. A commission of inquiry found him to have shown a 'serious error of judgement', and he was duly cashiered from the army.

But to the British in India and their friends at home, Dyer was a hero. Jix eagerly took up their cause. In the hope of exonerating the disgraced officer, he made a three-month tour of the Punjab. The devastation he saw confirmed his suspicion that Dyer had been the scapegoat of an incompetent civilian government which had lost control of the region.

Upon his return to England, Jix joined forces with several other disaffected Tories to table a motion in the House of Commons calling for a reduction of £100 in the salary of the Liberal Secretary of State for India, Edwin Montagu. This canny exploitation of parliamentary procedure brilliantly circumvented the government's unwillingness to discuss the case of General Dyer. On the afternoon of 8 July 1920, the indefatigable MP for Twickenham arose to begin what was to become known as the Amritsar Debate.

Jix's performance in this historic onslaught upon the actions of a minister secured him a place in the pantheon of great backbench rebels. In sharp contrast to Montagu, whose attack on Dyer bordered on hysterical, Jix calmly asked his colleagues to consider the implications of Dyer's disgrace. What, he asked, would happen the next time senior British officers were faced with the spectre of rebellion?

> Are you going to tell them that this House of Commons has supported the action of the Army Council in the case of General Dyer, and are you going to tell them also that in the future in any action they may take they will not have the support of Great Britain? We must trust the men on the spot. We send out our best men to the Indian Civil Service and to the Army, and we have to trust them not once or twice, but at all times.[22]

With a populist touch, Jix closed his speech by reading extracts from a letter written to him by the English woman whose assault had precipitated the whole crisis.

At the end of the debate, the motion censuring Montagu was easily defeated, but the minister never fully recovered from the drubbing he had received. Dyer, who looked on with contentment from the public gallery, was later compensated with over £25,000 raised by a campaign launched by the *Morning Post*, to which Jix and his wife contributed generously.

No less controversial was Jix's opposition to the Government of Ireland Act, which effected the partition of that country the following year. Jix believed that an irrecoverable settlement of this kind would leave Protestant loyalists at the mercy of Republican extremists, and would also encourage nationalist intrigue elsewhere in the Empire. Although his Indian tour had prevented him from taking part in the second reading of the Bill, he explained his views on the subject of Ireland on many other occasions, both in the House of Commons and in appearances before his constituents. During a particularly heated debate in 1913, he asked the then Prime Minister, Herbert Asquith, in a tone more suited to his days as an abstinence crusader than a seasoned politician, to consider the possibility of unionist 'rebels' one day clashing with British troops:

> Behind them there are half a million women and children. Behind them is the whole Unionist [Conservative] Party in the House of Commons. Above them is the Lord God of Battles. In His name and under His protection I say to you, the Prime Minister, with your arms and with your batteries, fire! Fire, if you dare! Fire, and be damned![23]

This native outspokenness was given free rein during the troubled years of the First World War. Already personally loathed by the war leader for tabling almost 500 amendments to his 'People's Budget' of 1909, Jix harried Lloyd George and the ministers of his coalition government for not doing more to defeat the Germans. Once again, senior Tories could only blush at the vehemence of Jix's rhetoric. While they sidled up to their former opponents in the national interest and – less explicitly – to prevent the arrival of the first Labour administration, the meddlesome backbencher found his home among a rump of backward-looking Conservative MPs known as the 'diehards'.

In recognition of his role in forming two 'Footballers' Battalions' during the war, Jix was awarded a baronetcy by King George V at the end of 1919. The conflict had seriously delayed his rise to prominence, but he could at least be thankful that neither of his young sons, Richard and Lancelot, had been lost in battle. With a disappointing political career apparently behind him, Jix, a latter-day Cincinnatus, bought a modest country estate outside Norwich and contemplated taking up the plough in retirement. Nothing could have prepared him for the remarkable events of 1922–24 which would bring him to the brink of the highest office in the state.

℮℈

The coalition government headed up by David Lloyd George and the leader of the Conservative Party, Austen Chamberlain, seemed virtually impregnable at the outset of 1922. A lingering sense of wartime solidarity combined with industrial unrest and economic recession had convinced the majority within Parliament that party politics needed to be suspended. Yet outside Westminster, there was a widespread feeling that the coalition was a sham. It was to Jix and his fellow diehards that this silent majority looked for action.

Jix had campaigned against the government, in season and out, ever since its inception. Each time a senior Conservative indicated his dissent from one of his Liberal colleagues, he would fire off letters to the press predicting the imminent downfall of the government. This did little to improve Jix's political fortunes. When he was given the opportunity in April 1922 to propose a vote of 'no confidence' in the government, he was cut down to size by the cruel wit of the Tory leader. Pointing up to Jix, alone on his backbench, Chamberlain joked that this ridiculous figure was 'the alternative Prime Minister.' In a cutting reference to Jix's constituency, he went on to say that although 'For God, King and Empire' might be 'good enough for Twickenham', it did not pass muster in the House of Commons. The motion was easily defeated.[24]

A series of remarkable events in the summer of 1922 transformed the situation for Jix. In a climate in which the government was already divided by a bitter territory dispute involving Greece and Turkey, three sensational developments brought the coalition to its knees. First, on 22 June, an inveterate opponent of Lloyd George's Irish settlement, Field Marshal Sir Henry Wilson, was assassinated by Republican terrorists on the doorstep of his London home. A fortnight later Lloyd George's credibility was again shaken by a major cash-for-honours scandal which overnight destroyed his never particularly assured reputation as a man of integrity. To this formidable litany of misery was added the announcement by the Tory grandee Lord Salisbury that he henceforth considered himself to be the true leader of the 'whole Conservative and Unionist Party'. The diehards now had a banner around which to rally and a wounded quarry to pursue.

Jix moved quickly and silently in his intrigue. He made it his duty to gather together Conservatives from all wings of the party in order to effect a dramatic coup. Although by no means the only plotter, he made appearances at a greater number of clandestine meetings than any of his colleagues. This put him in an excellent position once the party voted to renounce Chamberlain and the coalition at a meeting held at the Carlton Club on the morning of 19 October.

Not for the first time, however, Jix's ambitions were thwarted. When the new Prime Minister, the dour Scots-Canadian ironmonger Andrew Bonar Law, offered to recompense him with a minor position at the Colonial Office, Jix seriously contemplated refusing in protest. It was his wife who wisely persuaded him to accept the offer, which she believed would lead to bigger and better things.

So it turned out. Following the premature departure and death of Bonar Law the following year, a new leader emerged who recognised Jix as a man of honesty and ability. Stanley Baldwin had relatively little ministerial experience, but was sufficiently popular with his colleagues to step easily into Bonar Law's shoes. His connection with Jix went back to the famous 1908 by-election, when he had journeyed up to Manchester to speak on the Tory candidate's behalf. Although the two men were of markedly different temperament, their shared love of the English countryside and uncomplicated approach to politics served as the basis for a friendship of sorts.

A series of modest ministerial positions were duly bestowed on Jix. In Baldwin's short-lived administration of 1923, he served successively as Paymaster General, Postmaster General, Financial Secretary to the Treasury and Minister of Health – offices made available by the rapid ascent of Austen Chamberlain's younger half-brother, Neville, who was included by Baldwin as a sop to the old regime.

As was all too apparent from the unpredictable reshuffles, Baldwin's government lacked both experience and political clout. Fears that the party had opted for the wrong course in abandoning the coalition seemed to be justified when Baldwin decided, after just one year in office, to call a snap election on the divisive issue of Tariff Reform.

Jix was among the first of Baldwin's colleagues to note the recklessness of this scheme, not least for the additional cost it would entail for self-made MPs such as himself. 'It would be most unpopular with our party in the House,' he warned his leader. 'They have all paid one thousand pounds to get there and their wives do not want to pay another thousand with the risk of being thrown out.'[25]

The result of the election more than justified this sombre warning – it led to a hung parliament and the first Labour administration in British history. In the diehard *Morning Post* there were howls of a 'terrible awakening' accompanied by tales of 'systematic violence and rowdyism' by Labour men. 'Can anyone be surprised', a gloomy editorial pronounced, 'that Italy should have found an answer in Fascism to the intolerable servitude of submission to such methods of conducting politics?'[26]

Jix flourished in this climate of hysteria. Week after week, in Parliament and at public meetings, he denounced the Labour administration and all its ways, prophesying the imminent breakdown of social order and constitutional government. In February 1924, just one month after the fall of Baldwin's ailing minority administration, he explained to the voters of Burnley that behind the 'milk-and-water' exterior of men like the Labour Prime Minister, Ramsay MacDonald, there were dark forces at work which would soon 'let loose the dogs of war' in Europe, creating 'mutiny, bloodshed, and red ruin in our land'. A week later he roused the Marylebone Constitutional Assembly with a cry that Labour 'interlopers' had undermined the Protestant work ethic by offering unemployment benefit as a solution to mass unemployment.[27]

Other speeches delivered during Jix's busy nine months out of office similarly captured the hopes and fears of his lower-middle class hinterland. In one oration he proposed to begin an emergency house-building programme; in another he clamoured for the cutting of red tape 'with a large pair of scissors', and in yet another fulmination he demanded that all road signage designed for health and safety purposes be torn down and sold for scrap.[28]

Jix reaped the rewards of his hard work in October 1924 when a 'Red Scare' forced MacDonald to call a general election. The crisis was precipitated by the decision of the Attorney General, Sir Patrick Hastings, to drop the prosecution of the left-wing journalist J. R. Campbell for calling upon soldiers to 'line up with your fellow workers … [to] attack … the exploiters and capitalists' in the event of a war or a major industrial dispute. Hastings's injudicious decision seemed to confirm Jix's suspicion that the Labour Party was little more than a cloak for international Bolshevism. The government's position was made even worse when the so-called 'Zinoviev letter' fell into the hands of the tabloid press just four days before votes were to be cast. This purported to be instructions from the leaders of the Soviet regime as to how a communist revolution could be effected in Britain. Though its authenticity was contested from the outset, and is now believed by some experts to have originated in Conservative Central Office itself, Jix used the letter further to tar the Labour government. As he nonchalantly explained to the children of the Orleans School, Twickenham: 'I have always said that the Bolshevist rulers of Russia are utterly untrustworthy and the kind of people that no loyal Englishman could have anything to do with.'[29]

Baldwin was the chief beneficiary of this sensation, but he did not share Jix's rabid hatred of socialism, and was disinclined to promote his fiery lieutenant from the Department of Health. Clearly, the restored Prime Minister had not reckoned with Jix's formidable powers of persuasion. As the process of 'Cabinet making' began, the First Lord of the Admiralty, Leo Amery, heard 'the most amazing stories' about Jix's 'pathetic' attempts to seek advancement in the new government. In similar vein, Austen Chamberlain wrote angrily to his sister that the political stripling was 'moving heaven and earth' to obtain favour. This seems to have included lobbying of the owner of the *Daily Express*, Lord Beaverbrook, who described Jix as a potential future leader of the party.[30]

These factors combined to persuade Baldwin to throw over his former Home Secretary, his close friend and ally William Bridgeman, in favour of Jix. Though recognised as a 'leap in the dark' by Baldwin's biographers, circumstances ensured that his bold decision was well received. According to the reporter from the *Daily News*, Jix took up his seat on the front bench of the new parliament in November 1924 as 'very nearly the most popular man in the House'. His time had come.[31]

❦

When Jix was asked by acquaintances to describe his new job, his reply was simple: 'It is I who am the ruler of England.' The boast was not completely unfounded. The powers of the Home Secretary, derived from those of the king's private secretary in the Middle Ages, were broad and extensive. Under his sway came every aspect of domestic governance not hived off to another department. In 1924 these powers included the exercise of the royal prerogative of mercy; the management of the criminal justice system; the supervision of the police force; the regulation of prisons; the control of immigration; the direction of the army during times of national emergency, and the implementation of censorship.

It was unfortunate that a man of Jix's stamp should have been accorded these enormous responsibilities at such a time. British society had been profoundly changed by the trauma of the war, but was still governed by the laws of a bygone era. Even the most liberal of Home Secretaries would have been compelled to become embroiled with aspects of law and order which he might have found repellent. What made Jix's position different was the gusto with which he discharged his duties.

Jix's first target for reform was the newest addition to the London entertainment scene: the nightclubs. Unknown to Edwardian England, these subterranean venues – 'haunts and hunting grounds of sharks and loose women', as Jix's allies in the London Public Morality Council deemed them – were the unintended consequence of wartime regulations forbidding the sale of alcohol beyond a certain hour in the evening. By masquerading as private houses, they largely avoided the notice of the police, admitting 'members', for a large premium, to drink and dance through to the small hours of the morning.[32]

From their earliest days, these clubs were loathed by officialdom. This was only partly because of their flagrant lawbreaking. Even the drugs and prostitutes which could readily be found therein were considered to be relatively minor peccadilloes compared to the effect they had on the social order. In the eyes of sardonic commentators such as Evelyn Waugh their tables attracted a motley crowd of baronets and whiskey salesmen, Oxbridge undergraduates and hardened blackmailers, army officers and pretty young 'hostesses'. To the Evangelical turn of mind, few crimes were greater than such upper-class incursion into the hedonistic *demi-monde*. It was tantamount to making sin respectable.

Jix wasted no time in commencing war with his unsuspecting enemies. Only two weeks after his appointment on 4 November, he wrote to the Commissioner of the Metropolitan Police, Brigadier General Sir William Horwood, asking for more details about several nightclubs recently brought to his attention. The long letter he received in reply indicated the Commissioner's delight in finally having a superior willing to address the issue. Of the six clubs then being investigated by the police, he explained, only one was 'at present thought to be well conducted'. The others were suspected of varying degrees of criminality, with afterhours drinking being the most persistent misdemeanour. The Commissioner's main complaint was that prosecution of the owners of such clubs was often ineffectual, as they simply paid a fine before reopening their premises under a different name. Horwood suggested that new legislation be introduced to prevent this 'farce' from continuing. Of especial importance, he said, was the need to be able to raid nightclubs without a warrant.[33]

At the time these letters were exchanged, the police had already paid a surprise visit to the most fashionable of all Soho clubs: the 'Forty-three' of 43 Gerrard Street, owned and managed by a notorious Irishwoman named Kate Meyrick. This entrepreneurial mother of eight, who had fled her husband in search of fortune after the war, personified the permissive spirit of 1920s London nightlife. Her club operated in a former storeroom of the Criterion restaurant, which she had redecorated in art deco style and furnished with a popular American jazz band. Through her activities she built up an enormous fortune of £150,000, and succeeded in marrying two of her daughters into the aristocracy.

Jix was adamant that such a woman should be punished. After being found guilty in November 1924 of selling intoxicating liquor after hours, she was duly sent to Holloway gaol for six months with hard labour – the most severe sentence yet handed down to a nightclub proprietor. Although Jix was not officially responsible for this decision, he was widely praised for curbing the excesses of what a friendly judge considered to be these 'disgusting sinks of iniquity at which young men of means are robbed, petted by prostitutes and filled with drink'.[34]

Not everyone, however, sided so forcibly with the minister. A defender of 'Merry England' complained in a letter to the *Daily Express* that the British public had an instinctive dislike of 'Puritanism and police'. Jix dutifully forwarded this contribution to his agents at Scotland Yard with a menacing note referring to its obscure author: 'Keep this with [the] night club file', he scrawled, 'and ... find out who or what Mr Michael Walsingham is.' Unfortunately, no record of the ensuing investigation has survived.[35]

Plans to tighten up the law relating to nightclubs were well underway by early 1925. In February of that year Jix pledged to the House of Commons that he would shortly be proposing a bill to remedy 'this great evil' of 'so-called nightclubs'. Yet he faced considerable opposition from his Cabinet colleagues, who discreetly pointed out that such a crusade might backfire. Not only was the total number of nightclubs negligible, many politicians followed the example of the Prince of Wales in frequenting them.[36]

Jix turned in disgust from such equivocation. Unaided by the new legislation he believed to be necessary, he made use of the un-repealed provisions of the wartime Defence of the Realm Act – 'DORA', as it was known – to secure six convictions for nightclub owners in the first half of 1925 alone. To circumvent the difficulty of obtaining evidence, he advised the police to infiltrate clubs dressed as revellers, only to arrest their unsuspecting hostesses when their orders for drinks were accepted.

For all Jix's zeal, however, his campaign lost momentum between 1926 and 1928. His contacts at Scotland Yard suggested that the nightclub owners had learnt their lesson and had mended their ways. It was said that most clubs had ceased serving alcohol; that they had become merely places were guests could dance and listen to music. The worst days seemed to be over.

Jix's natural suspicion of human nature did not allow these soothing testimonials to throw him off the scent. While ostensibly accepting the police's clean bill of health on nightclubs, he made several unchaperoned excursions into Soho to see for himself. Had it not been for the fact that he was spotted by a parliamentary colleague at the opening of the fashionable 'Kit-Kat Club', this curious fact might have gone unrecorded. Questioned on the matter in the House of Commons shortly afterwards, Jix meekly protested that he had been under the misapprehension that the said establishment was a restaurant. Jix and his wife, it should be noted, were not regular 'diner-outers'.[37]

The Kit-Kat Club incident provided much amusement for the press, but there was no reason why Jix should not have visited the clubs that his officers were supposed to be investigating. As he was wont to explain, he had no objection to clubs which were law-abiding – it was only the ones which insisted on serving alcohol after hours which roused his ire. For reputable club managers he had a certain degree of respect, even liking. After securing the deportation of a club owner named Victor Perosino in 1928, Jix received a letter from his victim suggesting that he visit his new club on the Continent. In his reply, Jix disarmingly wrote: 'I am glad to hear that you are starting in Paris, and when I am next there I shall do myself the pleasure of visiting.' The fact that the unused entrance tickets can be found among his private papers, however, suggests that Jix did not follow through with this surprising pledge.[38]

More disreputable nightclubs came to the Home Secretary's attention through conversations with parliamentary colleagues in the House of Lords. One peer with personal knowledge of the matter told him that Mrs Meyrick, now released from prison, was back to her old ways, having reopened the 'Forty-three' as the 'Richmond Club'. An enraged Jix immediately wrote to Commissioner Horwood that this club was a place 'of the most intense mischief and immorality, even to the extent of doped women and drunken men'. He closed his rather quaint letter by instructing the police to resume their surveillance programme with the utmost vigilance.[39]

It was not long before the cause of the police's inaction came to light. The officer assigned to monitor nightclubs in the Soho area, Sergeant George Goddard, was discovered to be taking enormous bribes from the club owners. On his humble salary of £6 per week, he was found to be maintaining a large freehold house, a private car and safe deposits amounting to over £12,000. He argued at his trial that his affluence stemmed from his wife's thrift and his own gambling successes, but he was duly sentenced, along with Mrs Meyrick, for a lengthy term of imprisonment.[40]

The scandal did much to undermine Jix's morality crusading. But it almost paled into insignificance beside the case of Sir Leo Chiozza Money, which blew up at practically the same time. Money, a 57-year-old former MP and government adviser, was caught late one evening in Hyde Park with his hand up the skirt of a young 'radio valve inspector' by the name of Irene Savidge. The miscreants were uncovered as a result of a parallel morality initiative formulated by Jix to make London's parks safe places for a man to 'take his daughters for a walk'. In pursuit of this end, Jix instructed Commissioner Horwood to deploy over sixty officers, at an annual cost of £25,000, to patrol these areas after dark. While dangerous parts of the city were left completely bereft of officers, this troop scoured the flowerbeds and shrubbery for evidence of illicit sexual activity.

The embarrassment of the scandal was exacerbated by the fact that the accused was well-known to Jix – he actually telephoned the Home Secretary from the police station on the night of his arrest.

At his trial, Money argued that he had only been sitting with Miss Savidge because they shared a mutual interest in economics. Jix was sympathetic to this improbable version of events and seems to have encouraged the trial judge to acquit Money owing to lack of evidence. An outcry inevitably ensued, but Jix refused to reopen the case; not even a note from the Public Prosecutor telling him of Sir Leo's well-documented predilections (ones which would ultimately lead to his downfall) stayed the minister's hand. As the Home Secretary told an incredulous House of Commons, 'It is not illegal for any young member of the community to take any equally young lady to Hyde Park to sit in the park, and it is not illegal to salute her with a chaste embrace.' A cartoon appeared in the press the following day showing this salutation, Jix in the guise of Cupid making a careful inspection assisted by two constables with torches.[41]

The incident highlighted the difficulty of Jix's attempt to reconcile his love of morality with a profound respect for the social hierarchy. Satirists found in him a hypocrite to mock, but there was no doubt that the tabloid sensationalism which accompanied high-profile cases such as Money's gave rise to separate misdemeanours. Many felt Jix to have been entirely justified in backing an Act of Parliament in 1926 which limited the reporting of such cases if they were likely to cause 'injury to public morals'.

But Jix was not quite in the clear. In order to spare Miss Savidge the ordeal of being cross-examined, the magistrate had not allowed her to be placed in the dock. This left the arresting officers open to the charge of perjury without ever having had the opportunity to put their case in open court. Guessing that senior officials at the Home Office would be unconcerned by this potential injustice, a chief inspector took it upon himself to have Miss Savidge 'voluntarily' brought to a police station and subjected to a five-hour interrogation. Although he and his colleagues eventually forced from her a full confession supporting the officers' account, a complaint was lodged and a full-scale public outcry rapidly ensued.

The affair was one of the greatest blunders of Jix's period at the Home Office, but the minister showed remarkable resourcefulness in deflecting criticism. Acknowledging the seriousness of Miss Savidge's grievance against the police, he established a parliamentary committee to examine the facts – though, once again, he stressed that the circumstances surrounding Money's arrest were not to be delved into. In response to the tribunal's findings, Jix amended the police code to ensure that a female officer would always be present when a woman was questioned about matters 'intimately affecting her morals'. He also mandated that no public prosecutions could be brought without the consent of his most trusted official, the Chief Commissioner.

Jix's faith in his hand-picked parliamentary committee was justified by the exoneration of the rogue officers, but an illusion of a new broom was afforded by the happy coincidence of Horwood's retirement later that year. As his replacement, Jix had the inspired idea of appointing a highly respected war hero, Field Marshal Viscount Byng, who began a series of reforms which stamped out the worst malpractices of the past. Jix deserved at least a glimmer of reflected glory. At the end of his five-year tenure at the Home Office, his portrait would be proudly hung in the entrance hall of the Metropolitan Police's headquarters in recognition of his services to law enforcement.

c/s

While Jix was thirsting for righteousness on the streets and in the clubs, matters were taking a rather different turn in the world of literature. In the works of authors such as James Joyce, D. H. Lawrence and Aldous Huxley aspects of life scarcely alluded to in the sentimental 'three-decker' novels of the Victorian age were treated with the utmost frankness.

No book to emerge from this circle compared to *Lady Chatterley's Lover*. Written by an acknowledged master of the English language, it is today hailed as one of the most original novels of all time. Yet when it was completed in 1928, the book's publisher could not bring it out in England. It could not even be posted into the country from abroad.[42]

It was the condemnation of a high-minded novel on the theme of lesbianism entitled *The Well of Loneliness* which sealed the book's fate. Its author, Radclyffe Hall, was a masculine and ostentatious woman of substantial private means who liked to be known as John. Partial to elegant men's suits and stodgy tomes on sexology, she spent the majority of her adult life touring the cathedrals of Europe with her lover, Lady Una Vicenzo Troubridge, whose attentions she had won from a disapproving admiral. Through the writings of her favourite sex theorist, Havelock Ellis, she became convinced that she was an 'invert' – by nature a man.

However much grey-bearded men enjoyed pouring scorn on Radclyffe Hall, there was nothing particularly explicit about her book. Not one of its 500 pages was sullied by the irksome four-letter words which so fired the creative genius of Lawrence. Her long-winded plot turns largely on the troubles of a distinctly autobiographical protagonist known as Stephen who is haunted by her attraction to heterosexual women. With sincere piety, she 'sacrifices' her lover by encouraging her to find happiness with a man. The raunchiest sex scene is confined to a half line: '…and that night they were not divided.'

By comparison to *Lady Chatterley* – with its depiction of sex as the 'ridiculous bouncing of the buttocks, and the wilting of the poor insignificant, moist little penis' – this was tame indeed. But to the Victorian turn of mind few themes were more dangerous or disgusting than homosexuality, particularly involving women. Though not quite illegal, lesbianism was regarded as a perverted attack on patriarchal society, and MPs had only recently contemplated extending the law to ensure that women, as well as men, could face prosecution for engaging in acts of 'gross indecency' with one another.

There was no obvious reason why Jix should have come into contact with the book. Since the relaxing of the printing laws in the seventeenth century, England had enjoyed one of the freest presses in the world. Publishers were at liberty to print what they wished; the only check being their foreknowledge that prosecution for defamation, sedition, breach of copyright or obscenity could follow. Members of the public who felt themselves aggrieved by any publication could either commence proceedings themselves or, if the case warranted government involvement, appeal to the Home Secretary to take action.

It was not long before this book became the subject of such a complaint. But it would be an exaggeration to say that it came from a disinterested member of the public. Only by a great stretch of the imagination could the novel be said to be of any public interest whatsoever. Bound in an anonymous black binding and priced well beyond the reach of the average reader, it was intended to appeal to a tiny coterie of progressive intellectuals to whom the subject matter was attractive. The publisher had not even thought to send review copies to the editors of the penny newspapers on the grounds that their readers would have no interest in the work.

These precautions did not prevent the most extravagant protest soon wafting up from the tabloid gutter. Beneath the screaming headline 'A Book That Must Be Suppressed', veteran commentator Jimmy Douglas drew on happy memories of the trial and conviction of Oscar Wilde in the 1890s to issue the following denunciation in the columns of the *Sunday Express*:

> I am well aware that sexual inversion and perversion are horrors which exist among us today. They flaunt themselves in public places with increasing effrontery and more insolently provocative bravado. The decadent apostles of the most hideous and most loathsome vices no longer conceal their degeneracy and their degradation … This pestilence is devastating the younger generation. It is wrecking young lives. It is defiling young souls.[43]

The writer closed this remarkable indictment by advising the Home Secretary to 'instruct the Director of Public Prosecutions to consider whether *The Well of Loneliness* is fit for circulation, and, if not, to take action to prevent its being further circulated'.

Jix had a copy of the book open on his octagonal writing desk at the Home Office by the following afternoon. It came directly from the book's publisher, Jonathan Cape, who, in a moment of ostensible folly, wondered if Jix might see the preposterousness of the newspaper's attack. As Havelock Ellis wrote to the incredulous author, who had not even been consulted on the matter: 'He [Cape] *invited* the Home Secretary's opinion – which he might have known beforehand!'[44]

It certainly seemed a reckless move. After wading through all 180,000 words of the *Well*, and conducting several 'long private conferences' with the Lord Chancellor and his own colleagues at the Home Department, Jix firmly planted himself on the side of the *Sunday Express*. In a letter to Cape sent only three days after receiving the book, he implicitly threatened the publisher with legal proceedings if he did not 'accept my decision and withdraw the book' at once. A memo to the Public Prosecutor made his position even clearer: the book, wrote Jix, was 'both obscene and indecent … If they decline [to withdraw it] proceed at once.'[45]

Solemn public apologies were duly offered up by Cape in *The Times* and several other national and regional newspapers. He said that he would strictly adhere to the Home Secretary's generous advice and would shortly be recalling every copy of the book for destruction. The effect was only too predictable – sales rocketed. All 5,000 copies of the book's second edition had flown off the shelves before a single volume could be reclaimed. Ever the canny business-man, Cape then arranged to publish further copies of the book in Paris so that he could profit from the heightened interest by export-ing them to England, thus avoiding the long arm of the law.

Or so he believed. By sending copies to private subscribers, Cape might avoid prosecution under the Obscene Publications Act of 1857, but he still had the even older Customs Consolidation Act of 1853 to contend with. This seldom enforced piece of legislation empowered the Head of Customs to impound any book likely to 'offend against public morals'. The idea of a modern government invoking such a draconian and antiquated provision filled every cultured man and woman with dread; but those with a sense of humour were also slightly amused. In his 1930 novel, *Vile Bodies*, Evelyn Waugh envisaged the following scene at the Customs and Excise counter:

'Books, eh?' he said. 'And what sort of books, may I ask?'

'Look for yourself.'

'Thank *you*, that's what I mean to do. *Books*, indeed.'

Adam wearily unstrapped and unlocked his suitcase.

'Yes,' said the Customs officer menacingly, as though his worst suspicions had been confirmed, 'I should just about say you had got some books.'

One by one he took the books out and piled them on the counter. A copy of Dante excited his especial disgust.

'French, eh?' he said. 'I guessed as much, and pretty dirty, too, I shouldn't wonder. Now just you wait while I look up these here *books*' – how he said it! – 'in my list. Particularly against books the Home Secretary is. If we can't stamp out literature in the country, we can at least stop its being brought in from outside. That's what he said the other day in Parliament, and I says 'Hear, hear...'[46]

Had Waugh known the truth about Jix's campaign against the *Well*, he might have spared the poor customs man. The real Head of Customs, Sir Charles Floud, actually found the book to be written with 'great literary skill and delicacy'. Contrary to Jix's advice, he suggested that the government leave the *Well* alone. '[I]t will be difficult to know where to stop,' he warned. If any book that referred to lesbianism was to be confiscated, then his men would have to seize even humorous works such as a recent satire by Compton Mackenzie entitled *Extraordinary Women*.[47]

Floud's opinion closely resembled that of his direct superior, the Chancellor of the Exchequer, Winston Churchill. Having returned to the Tories after the fall of the Lloyd George coalition, the future war leader had been appointed to this position as a reward for his renewed loyalty to the party. While Jix took great pains to befriend Churchill, the younger man nursed bitter memories of his 1908 defeat. 'Woe to the nightclubs! Confusion to all those naughty persons...' he wrote of 'the Puritan Home Secretary'. If Jix wished to condemn the *Well*, he could not expect for any help from this quarter.[48]

No matter. Apparently accepting Churchill's blank refusal to enforce the 1853 Act, Jix hatched a plan to suppress the *Well* by means of the 1857 Act instead. His methods pushed the law to its limit. By arrangement with his friend the Postmaster General it was agreed that every letter sent to and from the Parisian publisher of the book would be intercepted for the purpose of gathering evidence. Jix was encouraged in this line by further moralising articles by Douglas, who howled in his Sunday column that the *Well* was 'pouring into Britain and all over the world'.[49]

On 11 October 1928, the floodgates of reaction came crashing down. On that day Jix gave instructions to the Metropolitan Police to shadow a consignment of 250 copies of the book which had been released by Customs at Dover. A watch was kept on the bookshop to which they were headed 'in case the parcel is removed to any other address'. Similarly, four copies released in the same consignment were to be safely seen through the publisher's own letterbox. At both addresses the police were waiting with search warrants issued by the Chief Magistrate of Bow Street Police Court, Sir Charles Biron – a stalwart ally of the Home Secretary. Cape and the bookseller were duly summoned to explain why the *Well* should not be handed over to the common hangman for incineration, and themselves fined for possessing indecent matter.

Radclyffe Hall had every reason to feel persecuted. But not even her wildest conspiracy theories came close to discerning the full extent of the plot against her. Even the outcome of the trial had been fixed up in advance: Biron and Douglas had been given advance notice. On the same day that Jix had advised Cape to withdraw the book, the learned judge and the public moralist had been seen gossiping by Arnold Bennett at the all-male Garrick Club. This can hardly have been a coincidence. When Bennett went over to say a word in favour of his fellow author, he found the pair implacable: 'I set violently on Jimmy at once,' he wrote in his diary. 'Jimmy was very quiet and restrained,' he continued, 'but Biron defended Jimmy with *real* heat; so I went on attacking.'[50]

The battle lines were now drawn. In a dry-run of the famous 1960 Penguin trial of *Lady Chatterley*, Virginia Woolf, Desmond MacCarthy and E. M. Forster all agreed to testify to the book's literary merit. H. G. Wells, the Archbishop of York and Arthur Conan Doyle sent their best wishes. And George Bernard Shaw, although professing himself 'too immoral to have credibility', solemnly pledged his support.[51]

Jix was not to be outdone by these efforts. Not long after hearing of Radclyffe Hall's plan, he called upon the greatest survivor of the Victorian age, the poet Rudyard Kipling, to attest to the book's obscenity.

Incredibly, Kipling agreed. This was in contravention to his usual practice of disassociating himself from the transitory governments of the day, and his preference for abstaining from comment with regard to the works of his fellow authors. For Radclyffe Hall he was evidently prepared to make an exception. 'The whole point of the book', he wrote in fury to Jix, 'is that people with that peculiar taste should be made much of and received into general society with their "lovers".' More to the point, he objected to the book 'being sent to unmarried women'. 'That', he choked, 'gives the whole game away.'[52]

This was really getting to the heart of the matter. What appalled Jix and his allies was not the *Well's* inherent obscenity, but the effect *they* believed it would have on the mind of 'the young person'. 'The inconvenience of the young person', as Charles Dickens wrote in *Our Mutual Friend*, 'was that according to Mr Podsnap, she seemed always liable to burst into blushes when there was no need at all.'[53]

And yet the efforts of Jix and Radclyffe Hall were equally in vain. At both the magistrates' trial and the later County Court appeal – at which Kipling had actually been present – no 'expert' witnesses were allowed to be called. Biron was so alarmed by the lengthy list of luminaries summoned in defence of the novel that he cleared them from the court. '*I* am here to decide whether this book is obscene or not,' he thundered. After allowing only a few witnesses to testify, including the policeman responsible for raiding Cape's offices, he adjourned the court for one week to take stock of the situation over brandy with Jimmy Douglas at the Garrick.

On 16 November, Biron returned to pass judgment. With much gravity he explained from the bench that the 'horrible practices' referred to in the book constituted an obscene libel. 'Not merely that,' he revealingly continued, '…the actual physical acts of these women indulging in unnatural vices are described in the most alluring terms; their result is described as giving these women extraordinary rest, contentment and pleasure … it is actually put forward that it improves their mental balance and capacity.' He duly ordered the destruction of the book, and was upheld on appeal.

The verdict was greeted with whoops of joy in the tabloid press, where Jix was feted as a knight-errant of public morality. 'That is the kind of invigoratingly prompt and effective action that becomes a Government department', crowed Douglas. Only a handful of critics dared raise a voice in protest. In *Time and Tide*, author Hugh Walpole complained that Jix and his cronies had 'caused certain subjects to be discussed, inquired into and pleasingly investigated as never before in the history of this our hypocritical country'. No commentator, however, had any notion of the lengths to which Jix had gone to ban the book. Fewer still could have guessed that his meddling was not confined solely to the *Well*.[54]

Enter *Lady Chatterley's Lover*. Just two weeks after Biron's crushing verdict, Jix ordered his officials to look out for copies of this book being sent through the post. That was not all: Jix also decreed that any mere correspondence passing between the work's author and his English publisher should likewise be steamed open and copied for his perusal. In late November 1928, Lawrence, walled up in a hotel on the Continent, was informed that the typescript of his latest offering, a rude collection of poems entitled *Pansies*, was now being considered by the Home Secretary.

This was a new development in the history of censorship. But Jix once again found an ingenious way of circumventing criticism. In reply to a question on the matter put to him by a friend of Lawrence's in the House of Commons, the Home Secretary coolly explained that the offending material had only been opened as part of a routine check to ensure that the packet had been posted at the correct rate. When his officials had found the contents to be obscene, he explained, they had a legal obligation to prevent their circulation.

The only flaw in this brilliantly technical argument was that Lawrence had sent his manuscript by registered post – the stamp price could not have been in dispute. 'I *do* wish it could be shown', fumed Lawrence in disgust, 'that [Jix] is a *liar*, and he did open my sealed and registered *letter*.'[55]

No such accusation could be proved. But, as if to concede his error, Jix quietly arranged for Lawrence's file to be disposed of by his deputies at the Home Office.

The novelist waited two years to exact his revenge. He did so in a cruel pamphlet entitled *Pornography and Obscenity* in which he portrayed the former Home Secretary as a pervert and a hypocrite. In one of the most damning passages, Lawrence denounced Jix – that 'very sincere Puritan, grey, grey in every fibre' – as one of the 'grey elderly ones belong[ing] to the last century, the eunuch century, the century of the mealy-mouthed lie, the century that has tried to destroy humanity, the nineteenth century'. Like most of those earnest Victorians of yesteryear, he continued, Jix belonged to 'the great pornographical class ... They have the grey disease of sex-hatred, coupled with the yellow disease of dirt lust.'[56]

Lawrence ended this attack on the ex-minister by alleging that Jix had once castigated a novel for tempting a couple into having sex for the first time. '*One up to them!*' roared Lawrence. '...But the grey Guardian of British Morals seemed to think that if they had murdered one another, or worn each other to rags of nervous prostration, it would have been much better. The grey disease!'[57]

There may have been some truth in these charges, but Lawrence's tirade betrayed a misconception of Jix. For the late minister was not merely a petty tyrant and a kill-joy: he was also an idealist. In the closing lines of his trenchant defence of censorship, *Do We Need a Censor?*, published in the same series as Lawrence's polemic, Jix envisaged a world free from the Lord Chamberlain's blue pencil:

May I say one more word of the ideal which I have in mind? It is that by the spread of education and the extension of religion in the hearts of the people they will themselves learn to reject all forms of unpleasant conduct, literature, art – and beyond all, of personal thought. If the people learn, not merely to disregard, but to detest all these forms of indecency in thought, word and deed, the day will come when no form of censorship will be needed, when there will be no prosecutions for breaches of the law, and when Acts of Parliament will be a dead letter on the Statute Book, because the people themselves will have attained, by religion, by education and by personal thought, that cleanness of heart which alone can ensure a cleanness of thought and of action.[58]

∾

One of the most curious documents to be found among Jix's personal papers is a note written to Lieutenant Colonel J. F. Carter of New Scotland Yard's Special Branch. The letter concerned an alleged Soviet agent named McDonnell, who was said to have 'spoken in rather friendly terms about the Russian government' at the bar of Swanage Golf Club. The tip off came from the zealously anti-Bolshevist editor of the *Morning Post*, H. A. Gwynne, who kept the Home Secretary abreast of all matters Soviet related. Jix demanded that Carter make a thorough investigation of the matter.[59]

A month later came a laconic response from Carter's commanding officer, Major General Sir Wyndham Childs. He informed the Home Secretary that the suspect was unlikely to pose a serious threat to the state. Extensive investigations had revealed him to be none other than a former British vice-counsel and key negotiator of international trade contracts by the name of Aeneas Ronald MacDonnell, CBE. 'It is scarcely necessary to pursue further inquiries,' the official tartly concluded.

The exchange illustrates the extent to which Jix believed communism to have taken root in the country. If a revolution was being plotted in the smoking room of Swanage Golf Club, what hope was there for the constitution?

Jix wished to bring all such troublemakers before the courts. Only a short time after his appointment as Home Secretary, he persuaded the Attorney General, after personally lobbying the Lord Chancellor and even the King, to recommence proceedings against the most notorious of them all, J. R. Campbell, whose comments in the *Workers' Weekly* had helped bring down the first Labour government. The editor and eleven of his colleagues were duly arraigned before Jix's trusted accomplice Sir Chartres Biron at Bow Street before being sent up to the Old Bailey for trial. Here they were convicted under the eighteenth-century Incitement to Mutiny Act in one of the most sensational political trials of the inter-war years. Before sentencing, the judge sternly offered to spare five of the accused if they pledged to renounce their membership of the Communist Party. When they refused, he furiously ordered their incarceration.

Contemporaries found little to fault in the clearly prejudiced decision. As a stiff editorial in *The Times* explained, the Communist Party was not 'like any other party' – it was 'a branch of a widespread revolutionary and conspiratorial organisation which has never made any secret of its intention to work for the downfall of all states not organised on a Communistic basis'. Jix wholeheartedly endorsed this view. But he went further in seeing almost no distinction between communism, socialism and trade unionism. All were, in his eyes, part of the same malady.[60]

Jix's objection was moral. 'I fear that there has grown up in the hearts of the great mass of the English people', he lamented in his memoirs, 'a real disinclination to work hard, and a desire to get as much as they can without giving their utmost in return.'

In his view, there could be no return to 'better times' until the people regained 'the spirit of work for work's sake which is the only foundation of all real happiness and real prosperity'.[61]

Not since the days of Queen Victoria had such views been widespread. Crippled by a massive war debt and a stagnant world economy, Britain was not the booming industrial power she had once been. Jix's attempt to put the clock back might have been destined to fail, but he was not alone in his efforts. His colleague Churchill had used his first Budget as Chancellor to return Britain to the Gold Standard, fixing the Pound against the Dollar at its pre-war level. This was far too high a valuation, causing exports to dwindle, wages to fall and the cost of living to sky-rocket. In attempting to retreat into the past, the government had inadvertently sown the dragon's teeth of future unrest. A General Strike loomed.

At the heart of the matter were Britain's lacklustre coal mines. Once the pride of the nation and the driving force of the Industrial Revolution, they were now an embarrassment. Seams had run thin, and the ideas of the mine owners were looking even more depleted. Following the huge drop in the coal price after the war, the miners had been compelled to work for longer hours and to accept swingeing cuts in wages. In the face of this austerity, the Miners' Federation had formed a Triple Alliance with the unionised railwaymen and dock-workers to begin a fight-back. This triumvirate threatened to bring their members out on strike in April 1921 unless the government intervened to improve conditions. Desperate to avoid such a huge disruption, the coalition set up a Royal Commission to look into the matter. After rejecting its suggestion that the government partly nationalise the coal industry, Lloyd George offered a £10 million subsidy to the mine owners to get their house in order.

The task was beyond them. Four years later, when the subsidy expired, Baldwin found himself in an equally unsatisfactory position. In the face of strong opposition from Jix and several other hardliners in the Cabinet, he decided to renew the subsidy. In July 1925 another £10 million was splurged on the mine owners.

Jix was indignant. In the strongest terms he advised his colleagues against spending one penny of taxpayers' money in this way. He proposed instead to let the market take its course. If the miners had the temerity to strike, he suggested, the government should take action – and crush them.

Baldwin set himself firmly against this adversarial approach. Despite the majority of the country opposing the tactics of the unions, he warned Jix that the government was unprepared for such a major clash with industry. Grim forecasts of cities deprived of food and other essential supplies persuaded his colleagues to agree to the subsidy in spite of Jix's noisy protests. But to appease the Home Secretary and his fellow diehards, Baldwin asked a respected civil servant, Sir Herbert Samuel, to chair a new Royal Commission on the mining industry. Secret preparations were also set afoot to overcome the logistical challenge which a General Strike would present.

Jix was the ideal man to undertake this task. With his fierce loathing of communism and exceptional attention to detail, no member of the Cabinet rivalled his standing as the foremost opponent of Bolshevism. Baldwin duly appointed him director of the so-called 'Organisation for the Maintenance of Supplies': a secret quasi-governmental taskforce first established in 1923 to disguise the more military preparations which were to be the ultimate solution. In the style of a medieval king, Jix and his talented under-secretary, John Anderson, proceeded to divide the country into ten divisions, each to be overseen by a 'Civil Commissioner' with a staff of civil servants at his disposal. These Commissioners were instructed to recruit battalions of volunteers to act as strike breakers in the event of major disturbance. Although not an overtly political organisation, many of the recruits came from the far right – in Liverpool a group of British Fascists were appointed as Special Constables. On Jix's command (codeword 'Action!') these men were to come out to restore law and order by whatever means necessary.[62]

Throughout the latter half of 1925 and the beginning of 1926, the country waited anxiously for Baldwin's subsidy to expire. When the Samuel Commission issued its findings on 10 March, repeating many of the recommendations of the previous inquiry, the government found itself in exactly the position it had been in before. Negotiations with the miners, pit-owners and leaders of the labour movement were carried on throughout March and April, but to no avail. An abiding problem was the lack of co-ordination of the unions. The newly formed Trade Union Congress had delegated executive power to its General Council, but still retained a degree of power for itself. By contrast to Jix's slick, well-oiled machine at the Home Office, its processes were slow, cumbersome and unwieldy. This caused a major problem on the night of 1 May, when, in the midst of heated negotiations between the General Council and the government's most senior lawyer and lead negotiator, Lord Birkenhead, the union bosses sent an unauthorised telegram to their members instructing them to strike at midnight on 3 May.

Unaware of this development, Baldwin and the Lord Chancellor came to a provisional agreement with the General Council before adjourning at two o'clock in the morning.

This was the proposal put before the Cabinet at noon the following day. Once again, it fell to Jix to lead the assault on any compromise. He told his colleagues that he had heard from the Postmaster General that strike orders had already been sent out. He did not, however, add that these instructions had been contingent on no settlement being agreed between the General Council and Lord Birkenhead. At seven o'clock that evening, the General Council, realising the spectacular misunderstanding that had occurred, informed Baldwin that they had not been able to communicate with either the TUC leaders or the miners' representatives, who had returned home to the north of England. A desperate attempt was now made by the General Council to contact them and call off the strike. The Cabinet sat up late into the night anxiously awaiting news.

Just before midnight, a telephonist entered their room to inform the Home Secretary that someone from the *Daily Mail* wished to speak to him. Jix solemnly withdrew to take the call. Over a crackling line, he heard that the newspaper's compositors had refused to set to type a leading article entitled 'For King and Country', denouncing the proposed strike as illegal and unpatriotic. Jix's imagination now took over. Upon returning to his fellow ministers he gravely announced, on his own initiative, that the General Strike had begun. Credulously, Baldwin declared a state of emergency and authorised Jix to rouse his Civil Commissioners. When the unsuspecting General Council returned to the conference room a few hours later they found it dark and locked. As the *New Statesman* put it, 'The Cabinet had declared war and gone to bed.'[63]

There was no going back now. Jix had called the TUC's bluff: its members would have to go through with the strike whether they wanted to or not. In misleading his colleagues over the significance of the isolated *Daily Mail* incident, Jix had played a critical role in precipitating the crisis – but he was no less popular for it. Churchill, for one, believed it to have been Jix's finest hour: a masterstroke to overcome the 'wets' within the government. Even Lord Birkenhead was delighted. The long-awaited General Strike, desired by extremists on both sides of the political divide, was now underway.

For nine historic days, the veterans of the 1908 Manchester North-West by-election worked in harness to crush the insurrection. If anything, it was Churchill who was the more fanatical of the pair. While Jix's role was confined principally to organising the civilian response to the strike, Churchill assumed command of the military dimension. As he explained to Jix and the Minister for War, Sir Laming Worthington-Evans, 'I have done your job for four years, Jix, and yours for two, Worthy, so I had better unfold my plan.'[64]

His plan certainly lived up to Lord Beaverbrook's assertion that Churchill had in him 'the stuff of which tyrants are made'. His first move was to commandeer the offices of the *Morning Post* – willingly given up by Jix's loyal associate H. A. Gwynne – in order to put together a daily propaganda sheet entitled the *British Gazette*. This was a task for which Churchill, a journalist to his fingertips, was ideally suited. But Jix wisely restrained him from also taking command of the relatively new British Broadcasting Company.

Such a plan, he warned, would be 'fatal' to their purpose. Instead Jix negotiated with the company's general manager, John Reith, to be allowed to make a special broadcast calling for 50,000 volunteers to help distribute stockpiled supplies. As the more seasoned orator of the ministerial duo, this was certainly Jix's domain. On the evening of 5 May listeners heard his clipped, earnest voice calling upon the men who had lately given so unselfishly in the Great War to 'obey the call of their country' and help fight for 'their rights in order to preserve peace in our land'.[65]

Coming less than a decade after the brutal crushing of the Spartacist uprising in Berlin by the proto-fascist 'Freikorps', this was a worrying development, and Jix was widely taunted (not entirely to his disliking) as 'Mussolini Minor'. But beneath the veneer of extreme authoritarianism, Jix was more constitutionally minded than many of his enemies acknowledged. When Churchill proposed to arm their civilian cohort and merge them with units of the Territorial Army, Jix sounded a note of caution, suppressing a 'wild article' by Churchill advocating the policy. With greater deference to the laws of England, Jix suggested that they instead overcome the strike through ostentatious displays of 'British pluck'. Images of grinning office workers packed onto buses and milk vans controlled by hardy volunteers became an image of national solidarity. So too did the fleets of private motor cars put at Jix's disposal in recognition of his long association with the Automobile Association, over which he had presided from 1908 to 1923. 'To say that Britain was saved by the motor car', gloated Jix in his memoirs, 'is no idle boast.' The car owner, he said, would always be 'against the bitter selfishness of the striker'.[66]

The strike was also broken by Jix's creative use of the law. Yet again, the wartime DORA provisions were resurrected to put a stop to would-be rabble-rousers. With the assistance of a compliant judge of the High Court, Mr Justice Astbury, who declared the strike to be illegal, Jix ensured that the courts would be busy for many months to come. In Darlington a man was sentenced for three months imprisonment for throwing a stone at a car; in Birmingham a striker received six months with hard labour for assaulting a civilian assisting a police officer. Jix was also adamant that justice should be *seen* to be done. In Cardiff and Brighton, where rioting had accompanied the disturbances, prisoners travelling from cell to court were marched through the town in chains. Even MPs were not exempt. A fiery Indian communist named Shapurji Saklatvala, who sat on the Labour benches, was arraigned before Biron of Bow Street for making an impassioned May Day speech in Hyde Park on behalf of the miners. After being severely rebuked for his political opinions, he was bailed for the large sum of £200 and later sentenced to two months imprisonment at Wormwood Scrubs as a common felon.[67]

The combination of Jix's constitutional means of sapping the morale of the strikers and Churchill's more belligerent tactics was highly effective. Both men embraced the theatrical aspect of their undertaking, and were compared by one acid commentator to a pair of directors presiding over a film in which they were the heroes. The most spectacular demonstration of this was Churchill's insistence that they send in a division of tanks to break a picket line at a crucial East End dock. 'Winston was all for a tremendous display of force,' wrote the Chief Civil Commissioner, J. C. C. Davidson, 'machine guns hidden but there; tanks ... used in addition to armoured cars, and so on.' Reluctantly Jix agreed to this scheme, accepting a £5 bet from Davidson that not a single bullet would be fired – a wager he gladly lost. With greater foresight, Jix arranged for a submarine to be deployed beside the quay. When the dock lights were inevitably shut off by the thwarted unionists there was an alternative power supply on which to draw.[68]

By comparison to his zealous deputies, the Prime Minister appeared to be weak and indecisive throughout the strike. He was eager to negotiate with the unions, even hinting that he might implement the socialistic recommendations of the Samuel Commission as a means of ending the disruption. Jix, however, would allow no such thing. When the leaders of the TUC were invited to reopen discussions at Downing Street on 12 May, he wrote to Baldwin insisting that no meeting should take place until 'there has been an unconditional withdrawal of the General Strike'. Aware that the Prime Minister might not appreciate this lordly command, Jix forwarded his message to the more amenable permanent secretary at the Ministry of Labour, Sir Horace Wilson, who ensured that it was put into effect. The strategy worked brilliantly. Shortly after noon the TUC delegates abandoned the miners and instructed their members to return to work on the same conditions as before. The news was greeted with sighs of relief throughout the country.[69]

Jix had triumphed. He had shown that the unions could not act collectively to achieve their individual ends. In the *Sunday Express* he was proclaimed as the most universally respected member of the government besides the Prime Minister. Letters poured in from members of the public and high-profile admirers. The chairman of the London Underground, Lord Ashfield, commended him for his 'magnificent services to the state in the great crisis'. Even the veteran leader of the 1889 Dock Strike, Ben Tillett, signalled his grudging respect for the strike breaker.[70]

In the wave of euphoria which followed the government's victory, Jix helped pilot the controversial Trades Disputes and Trades Unions Act through Parliament as a means of preventing a General Strike from ever happening again. Although fiercely opposed by the Labour opposition as a vindictive piece of class legislation, the measure was not unreasonable in the context. As well as ensuring that trade unions would hereafter adhere to more democratic processes, it made illegal any strike 'designed or calculated to coerce the government either directly or by inflicting hardship upon the community'. The Act was easily passed in the House of Commons, and was seen through the Lords by the formidable diehard constitutional lawyer Lord Sumner, who dismissed critics of the bill as 'unworthy of the high position to which fortune had raised them'.[71]

Jix heartily concurred with that sentiment. For in spite of his intense loathing of socialism, and incessant blustering about threatened revolution, he was no mere stooge of the wealthy. One of his least publicised triumphs was to use DORA to prevent shopkeepers from reverting to the pre-war arrangement whereby their assistants could be forced to work until ten or eleven in the evening. Jix added to his radical credentials by advocating an elected House of Lords and by taking the initiative in the government's proposal to allow women to vote on the same terms as men at the next general election. Equally liberal-minded were his efforts in reforming the borstal system, which were remembered long after as among the most significant instances of penal reform of the era.

Even his record with regard to capital punishment was not nota-bly harsh by comparison with past and future Home Secretaries. Although averse to challenging lawful sentences, Jix once overruled his civil servants to grant a last-minute reprieve to three Brighton men convicted for a single murder. The non-political responsibility of dispensing mercy, he sincerely believed, was 'one of the most trying and painful tasks which can fall on the lot of any minister'.[72]

A truly paradoxical figure, Jix's greatest failing was his inability to know when to stop. Carried away by his strike-breaking activities, he soon ordered an unprecedented number of raids of premises suspected of fronting revolutionary cells. This policy came to an unfortunate climax in May 1927 when he instructed 150 police offic-ers to raid the London offices of the Soviet trade delegation, Arcos Ltd. Despite confiscating hundreds of boxes of papers and breaking into a large safe, no incriminating evidence could be found linking the organisation to British communists. As a young Conservative MP, Robert Boothby, later and rather unfairly remarked: 'A lot could have happened if we had developed the relationship [with Russia] – instead of which that idiot Sir William Joynson-Hicks raided the Arcos, seized their papers and generally wrecked our relationship with the Soviet Union.'[73]

At the end of 1926 the strain of work overtook Jix. For two years he had laboured for fourteen hours a day, seven days a week, in a ceaseless and often unrewarding quest to suppress every form of wrongdoing. While Lord Birkenhead was amazed at his incessant 'rushing here, there and everywhere', and other colleagues remarked upon his incredibly youthful appearance, he was already a relatively elderly man. Finally his health gave way. After being confined to his bed for several bleak days, Jix received a letter from the Prime Minister imploring him to take a proper holiday. 'Learn Italian,' he chaffed, 'or study rock plants, or Mussolini's police, or the art of sailing. And then Lady Jix will rise up and call you blessed (and me too!).'[74]

∞

In the months after his Continental sojourn, Jix began to enjoy life. Invitations to parties and dinners which had previously been responded to with a curt rejection were now accepted with relish. 'Why should I not enjoy these things?' he resolved. 'I know that the second I go out of office all that will come to an end.' In the same vein, Jix tried his hand at a little sport. As well as winning a gentlemanly golf tournament as the partner of Lady Margaret Hamilton Russell, the minister was frequently to be seen striding across rugged moorland with his shotgun and dazzling white stockings. A companion once remarked that no matter how many bogs he went through these garments never seemed to lose their splendour.[75]

These activities helped establish Jix as a member of high society. Although he once blundered by appearing at a Remembrance Day service dressed in his Ascot grey frock coat, he usually knew how to conduct himself, and basked in the company of the grand. This side of his character came out most strongly in his weekly letters to his octogenarian mother. In one, expressing thanks for a birthday cheque which he promised to spend on a 'beautiful new umbrella' and some 'fancy shirts', the Home Secretary slavishly minuted his 'career in mad society':

Yesterday we lunched with Sir George and Lady Maxwell. Princess Beatrice and any amount of swells were there. Then we went off to a garden party at the Prime Minister's. Lady Weigall asked us to dine. Princess Mary and her husband were also there. Today I lunched with the Grenfells ... Tonight I dine with Lord and Lady Salisbury. And I shall be seeing the King at Arthur Pageant's ... So you see we are keeping up the family reputation![76]

Jix was never quite as serious as he wished at these functions. He once admitted to laughing uncontrollably when a young peeress sitting beside him innocently asked the Shah of Persia, in French, if he was seeking an 'English mistress' to improve his linguistic skills.

So fond did Jix become of female company that some critics began to imagine that he too was having an affair. In a modern-dress production of Rutland Boughton's *Bethlehem*, staged towards the end of 1926, he was portrayed as a thinly disguised King Herod, complete with wife and mistress. But there is no evidence that any such relationship existed. A worldlier Cabinet colleague scoffed in his diary that Jix had eyes for one woman alone – 'DORA'.[77]

There was, however, at least one actual lady for whom Jix had a great regard. This was the King's austere but strangely playful consort, Queen Mary. Jix planned to detail his private discussions with this royal personage in no fewer than four chapters of his proposed autobiography. While this betrayed an exaggerated conception of their association, the acquaintanceship was certainly not without its moral hazards for Jix. One day, after a quiet lunch aboard the royal train, the queen casually offered him a cigarette. 'I confess that I was rather started,' wrote Jix. 'I did not know that Your Majesty smoked,' he haltingly responded; indeed, he thought she would be 'the last woman in the world to smoke'. Her reply was almost coquettish: 'Certainly,' she beamed – 'and why not, Sir William?' Jix cautiously took the proffered article and inhaled its toxic vapours for the first and only time in his life. The consort was kind enough not to mention this lapse to her husband; but Jix was almost eager to confess his peccadillo. Dining at Buckingham Palace shortly afterwards he overheard the monarch instruct a footman not to pass the cigars to the Home Secretary on account of his being 'no good – he neither smokes nor drinks'. Jix instantly became the darling of the Royal Household by interjecting, 'I beg your pardon. I always smoke – with queens!'[78]

Clearly there was a time for fun, but Jix remained a staunch Puritan to his core. As if to reaffirm his credentials, he was soon to launch his final, and most characteristic, crusade: a defence of the seventeenth-century Book of Common Prayer.

The tortuous journey of the Revised Prayer Book had begun twenty years previously, when a Royal Commission found there to be inconsistencies in the form of worship observed in the Church of England. In some parishes it was considered that the clergy had adopted practices which leaned too heavily in a 'Romeward' direction. The bishops were instructed to take decisive action to ensure greater liturgical uniformity.

There were two obvious ways that this could be achieved: to prosecute errant clergymen under draconian Victorian ecclesiastical laws, or to loosen up the prayer rubrics themselves. The first of these options could not be seriously contemplated. Not since the days of Jix's great predecessor at the Home Office, Sir William Harcourt – 'Old Morality', as he was known – in the 1880s had a member of the clergy been imprisoned for celebrating the Eucharist in a manner contrary to the Prayer Book. Such action had, in any case, only given fresh impetus to those within the Church calling themselves 'Anglo-Catholics' – disciples of Cardinal Newman believing in the compatibility of Catholic and Anglican doctrine. Many congregations had followed this celebrated apostle into the Catholic fold, but the majority still sought reconciliation with their fellow Anglicans. Seeking a compromise, the bishops offered their brethren a settlement. For the first time since 1662, they proposed to modify the Prayer Book of Thomas Cranmer.

Parliament bent over backwards to assist the work of the bishops. By the Enabling Act of 1919 the leaders of the Church were given command of an ecclesiastical directorate, the Church Assembly, with powers to amend and reform whatever aspects of religious life its members resolved. For eight years the Upper and Lower Houses of Convocation debated the issue of the Prayer Book. Ultimately, by an overwhelming majority, it was agreed that certain practices, hitherto illegal, would now be permitted on the understanding that there would be clear boundaries, and that the changes would signify no alteration in doctrine. Those receiving the sacrament would hereafter be allowed to kneel, just like Roman Catholics; not because they were worshipping the 'Real Presence' in the bread and wine, but because they wished to show their humility. Likewise, the sacrament was now to be 'reserved' (kept in a tabernacle to one side of the church); not to be worshipped, but for a practical reason – so that it could be administered to the sick. And so on, and so on.

This compromise was nothing short of astounding. Years of in-fighting had apparently been ended by the shrewd diplomacy of the eighty-year-old Archbishop of Canterbury, Randall Davidson, whose efforts had satisfied everyone except the extreme elements of the Anglo-Catholic and Evangelical lobbies. All that remained was for Parliament to rubber stamp the resolution of the Church Assembly under the auspices of the Elizabethan Act of Supremacy.

Nothing should have been simpler. Only Jix and a handful of other hardliners had voiced any disapproval of the archbishop's compromise. The vast majority within both Houses of Parliament were resolved not even to vote on the measure, as they believed the Enabling Act to have effectively removed the legislature's ancient right to moderate the practices of the Church. Jix made it his business to remind them of their historic obligations.

His efforts extended many months prior to the fateful parliamentary showdown. His first action had been to write personally to Archbishop Davidson warning of future difficulties. With a lawyer's eye for inconsistency, he asked the Primate how the bishops would discipline those clergy who continued to flout the rules of the Church, even under the new, more liberal rubrics. The archbishop responded with a friendly letter explaining that 'once the new Book has been legalised I do not think that we shall experience the same difficulty as hitherto'.[79]

This was insufficient for Jix. In a chilly reply to the archbishop he stated that he and his fellow Evangelicals had only been willing to accept the new Book on the strict understanding that those who persisted in adopting overtly Roman Catholic practices would be punished. 'I am deeply sorry,' he concluded. 'I thought there might have been … a hope for peace in the Church, but as I write it seems to me to recede into the distance.'[80]

In a characteristic gesture, Jix unilaterally forwarded the entire correspondence to the editor of *The Times*, and began a nationwide campaign against the new Prayer Book.

Jix was well placed to lead such a crusade. As the president of the National Church League and the Tyndale Bible Society he was already one of the foremost spokesmen of the Evangelical Party. Through his powerful oratory and ceaseless flow of open letters and pamphlets – not officially issued in his capacity as a government minister – he encouraged armies of previously uninterested members of the public to write to their MPs and to sign a scourging petition which he helped draft. Although he never said or wrote anything expressly hostile to Catholics, a large contingent of his followers were driven by the same bigotry which had inspired the reaction to the arrest of Guy Fawkes and, almost two centuries later, the infamous Gordon Riots of 1780. It was a body of fanatics denounced by the Bishop of Durham, Dr Hensley Henson, as the 'Protestant Underworld' – 'illiterates generalled by octogenarians'.[81]

The supporters of the new Book were far more respectable than this cohort. They included nearly all of the bishops and senior churchmen; practically every highbrow newspaper and periodical, and the vast majority of both the Cabinet and the House of Lords. But these moderates gravely misjudged the fervour of their lowly opponents.

When the measure came before the House of Commons on 15 December 1927, Baldwin diplomatically allowed a free vote to take place. Only Jix and two other, less high-ranking, government ministers joined a collection of obscure backbenchers in opposing

the resolution. A majority of at least 100 was confidently anticipated by the sage pundits of Fleet Street.

At four o'clock the First Lord of the Admiralty, William
Bridgeman, rose to begin the debate. A Christian gentleman and
avowed man of toleration, he was the ideal person to dampen the
fanaticism which had flared up outside Parliament. To a packed
chamber, he explained that the opinion of the Archbishop of
Canterbury must 'certainly carry greater weight than' – turning to
Jix – 'his'. Amid cheers and laughter he went on to wonder if the
historically minded Home Secretary would 'feel happier if he was
obliged to hang a man for sheep stealing?'[82]

Jix endured these insults without any sign of emotion. Then, at
half past four, a hush fell as he rose to make his reply. He began
in a slow, measured and respectful tone. He wished to say nothing
against any Church or sect which believed in transubstantiation,
or vestments, or prayers for the dead. Nor was it his intention to
cause distress to his 'friend', the archbishop, who sat listening in the
gallery. All he wanted, he said, was to emphasise to his fellow MPs
that the new Prayer Book was not an improvement on the 1662
version – a book sacred to 'hundreds of thousands ... second only
to their Bible' – but a transparent bribe to those whose sympathies
properly lay outside the national Church. As his speech reached
its climax, his sentences were punctuated by bursts of spontaneous
applause from the backbenches. Dismissing the result in the House
of Lords, he reminded his audience that

the final appeal which the Protestants, the old-fashioned believers
in the Church of England, make today is to this House of Commons.

I am told that some Honourable Members do not wish to vote in this matter because they are not members of the Church of England. I say to those Members: 'You are not sent here as Nonconformists, you are sent here as Members of Parliament. You have no right in, perhaps, the most difficult and dangerous vote that this House has ever given, to disenfranchise your constituents.' Vote against me if you wish, vote for the new Prayer Book if you wish, but every Member who comes to this House has a bounden duty to consider for himself the great issues which are put before him and to decide those issues in what he believes to be the interests of right and justice.[83]

As Jix returned to his seat the elderly archbishop was seen to bury his face in his hands. A woman beside him began to sob loudly. After an even more vitriolic speech by Jix's unlikely ally, the Labour back-bencher Rosslyn Mitchell, the tide had turned decisively against the new Book. Not even an earnest plea from the Prime Minister towards the end of the seven-hour debate had any effect. When the tellers announced a narrow majority of thirty-three against the Revised Prayer Book shortly before midnight, the chamber reverberated with cheers. 'Half the members rose to their feet,' exulted the reporter from the *Daily Express*. 'Shouts rent the air. A number of members were almost hysterical.' Jix had done it again.[84]

It was the 'speech of his life'. He had, said *The Spectator*, 'swept the House off its feet', and after he was finished 'the issue was never really in doubt'. Even Churchill, who found the entire spectacle 'strange … and rather repellent', admitted that the oration was 'a speech for its substance, its sincerity and its command, [which] ranks among the best specimens of modern Parliamentary art'.[85]

Tributes poured in from hundreds of less exalted admirers. One postcard carried the single sentence: 'A Lancashire lass is proud o' ye today, sir.' A shop assistant scrawled a similar accolade on the reverse of a blank receipt. And yet another correspondent related how, on visiting a famous English cathedral, the verger had held up a portrait of Jix pasted on the flyleaf of his diary and declared: 'I am glad we've got a man like that!'[86]

But not everyone was so enthused. A 'disgusted fellow churchman' residing in the Netherlands wrote to explain that there was 'something positively disgusting in reading of your doings in the House of Commons'. 'You may belong to the strictest sect of Pharisees,' he bemoaned, 'but you are certainly not a Christian ... Why boastest thou thyself, thou Tyrant, that thou canst do mischief?'[87]

Jix accepted such criticism with the same equanimity that he received praise. In his reply he simply wrote: 'Thank you so much for your kind letter ... I like to feel that though we are separated even by bounds of country, we are united in Christian fellowship.'

Such magnanimity did not prevent Jix's opponents from regrouping shortly after his sensational victory. Convinced that the triumph had been a fluke, the bishops made some minor amendments to the new rubrics and re-submitted them to Parliament for approval. Jix inwardly groaned. For several months he carried on with his reactionary campaign, inviting reporters up to his new country home at Newick, East Sussex, to restate his position surrounded by calves and sucking pigs. Many felt him to be posing as an old Reformer of bygone days, but his conviction shone through. 'Since that wonderful moment when an enthusiastic journalist compared him with Oliver Cromwell,' a disapproving editorial in *The Times* observed, '…he has never ceased to live and move and have his being as a strong, if not silent, leader of men.'[88]

The second Prayer Book debate was even more grandiose than the first. In the hope of allaying the excitement of the previous encounter, Baldwin allocated an incredible two days to the debate, with the stipulation that Jix should not speak until the first night was safely through. But those who believed the Home Secretary to be spoiling for a fight were well wide of the mark. A colleague who saw him in Palace Yard shortly before the debate was in no doubt of his sincerity. 'His face was white and his eyes looked anguished,' he wrote. 'I walked to meet him. He seemed a little dazed and kept my hand in his as we walked. Suddenly he burst out: "How can I carry this load of responsibility? How can I find words? There is no more to say; I have said it already."'[89]

Jix did not employ the same high rhetoric as he did in his first speech. But it was no less of a masterpiece of its kind. The combination of fervour and sincerity carried as many of his listeners as before. At the end of the debate the new Prayer Book was once again rejected, and this time by an even greater majority.

That, however, was still not the end of the story. Twelve months later the humiliated Church hierarchy resolved to introduce the new Book in spite of Parliament's rejection. Jix, now retired from active politics, took the opportunity to denounce the bishops for their defiance in a full-blooded article in the *Evening Standard*. With the confidence of a man who was of no doubt as to the answer, he asked his readers: 'Have I ever tried to score over the defeated party? Have I not for the whole of the year remained silent on Church questions in order that no word of mine should add to the bitterness of the subject?' He strongly objected to the Church's proposal to flout the law, which he believed in 'these revolutionary days' would set a dangerous example to the public at large. 'All laws are not pleasant,' he ended, 'but England allows no man to revoke laws for his own pleasure: therein lies the road to anarchy.'[90]

Unfortunately for Jix, there were to be no prosecutions. Somehow the public had lost its interest in the Prayer Book. Within a few years the issue would seem as remote to them as the ecclesiastical controversies of the later Middle Ages. As so often, the great Puritan's victory had been in vain.

☙

Jix's final years in office were not his happiest. Increasingly disappointed by the laxity of his colleagues, he cut a lonely and rather sad figure on the front bench. Unauthorised outbursts in favour of votes for women and protectionism furthered his insularity. As the parliamentary session of 1928 drew to its close, he decided that it was time to call it a day.

It was a good time to quit. The fortunes of the Conservative Party were at a low ebb; the landslide of 1924 seemed far away. With unemployment still rife, and the government hugely unpopular, Labour candidates were set to make considerable gains. But Jix was not content merely to return to his farm to die in obscurity. In a brazen letter to Baldwin shortly before the general election of 1929, he suggested that the time had come for him to take up a seat in the House of Lords. He cited three justifications for his presumptuous request: first, his failing health; second, his long service to the party; and, finally – and most boldly – his objection to the policies of his colleagues. Rather than condoning Churchill's plan to appeal to Labour voters, Jix pledged to attack the socialists 'every day and all day'. This, he feared, might cause embarrassment to the party.[91]

Was it blackmail? Baldwin did not think so. Although he often disapproved of Jix, he did not begrudge him his reward. 'He may have said many foolish things,' he later reflected, 'but he rarely did one.' In the Dissolution Honours list, the outgoing premier asked the King to elevate his elderly colleague to the fourth highest rank of the nobility. Viscount Brentford of Newick Jix became.[92]

His political career was now over. For the remaining three years of his life, Jix devoted himself to gardening projects at Newick; his only real contribution to public life being the occasional philippic in the *Morning Post*. After a tour of the West Indies with his wife early in 1932, he returned to England with congested lungs and a weakened heart. On 8 June of that year he died at his home in St James's Square while awaiting the arrival of a doctor.

છ

Jix's career defies easy assessment. At one level, he was simply a prig and a busybody: 'a miserable creature', growled one adversary – 'a shop-walker attempting to pose as a strong man'. And yet there were sides to his character which were truly inspiring. One or two of his warnings even turned out to be prophetic.[93]

At a time when statesmen were becoming increasingly professionalised and overly cautious in their choice of words, Jix stood up for the old-fashioned politics of personality. His outbursts, though often tactless and inflammatory, spiced the tedium of mechanical parliamentary government. 'He made great blunders and he made mistakes,' recalled a young Labour MP, 'but he was not a man for whom you could feel any malice whatever.'[94]

The fact that the young MP in question was Sir Oswald Mosley, later to become leader of the British Union of Fascists, cannot be dismissed as incidental. But even one of Jix's harshest modern critics has concluded that he was 'no fascist'. This verdict has been expanded upon by Professor W. D. Rubinstein of the University of Aberystwyth, who, in a favourable reassessment of Jix's career, has comprehensively refuted the charge that he was an anti-Semite – 'he was nothing of the sort', he has written. These findings suggest that however cold and belligerent Jix could be as an individual, he was not an enemy of human dignity. He would likely have found Nazism as abhorrent and unchristian as he found Communism. As with so many of his contemporaries, it is possible that he would have tolerated its existence in Germany, but it is inconceivable he would have endorsed such policies in his native land.[95]

The principal reason why Jix's reputation has fared so badly is not far to seek. Within only a few decades of his death the rise of the permissive society consigned his worldview to history. That movement's legislative architect, Roy Jenkins, accused his late, unlamented predecessor at the Home Office of launching their department 'upon a course of dour obscurantism from which it took three or four decades to recover'. But in the wake of global terrorism and the rise of the internet, Home Secretaries are once again seeking to employ similar methods of surveillance and censorship to Jix. Future governments may yet find it necessary to roll back the frontiers of civil liberties still further.[96]

Jix had his faults. He was certainly neither an intellectual nor a man with an attuned sense of 'the art of the possible'. He spoke his mind too freely for that. And he was too pompous and conscious of his own virtue to rank among the true greats. But, overall, he was a brave if sometimes unscrupulous crusader for righteousness, who gave his entire life to furthering the causes in which he believed. Had he entered Parliament a few decades earlier, or been born slightly earlier in the nineteenth century, his ambition might well have carried him to the highest office. It was his bad luck to be born out of season, making him often seem a ludicrous and outmoded figure. As his colleague Churchill splendidly put it: 'The worst that can be said about him is that he runs the risk of being most humorous when he wishes to be most serious ... [but] by the canons established in the reign of Queen Victoria ... he was always a very good man.'[97]

St Paul's Cathedral

CHAPTER 2

THE GLOOMY DEAN:
DR INGE OF ST PAUL'S

I am sane in a world of lunatics.

– 'The Elder', *Too True to be Good*, Act III, Scene i

There have been eight Deans of St Paul's Cathedral since the retirement of the Very Rev. Dr William Ralph Inge ('rhymes with sting') in 1934. Not one of them, it is fair to say, has come close to matching his notoriety. Doomsayer, scholar and eugenicist, he was for over thirty years the most discussed clergyman in the English-speaking world. Sporting an outlandish top hat and a greasy dog collar, he would speak cheerfully of such horrors as sterilising the unfit and, in lighter moods, throwing adulterers into jail. While critics viewed him as a Nazi apologist and a cloying hypocrite, his loyal adherents celebrated him as the bravest and most insightful defender of Victorian values there ever was.

How does one approach such a man? His own judgement was frank. 'It is plain that there has been a kink in my make-up,' he confessed in old age. 'If a Lytton Strachey ever got hold of my diaries, he could make me the laughing stock of the whole country.' All he hoped was that such a chronicler would find in him 'some good mixed with the bad'...[98]

ᕫ

William Ralph Inge – known as Ralph to his intimates – never forgot that he belonged to a large and distinguished family. A forebear on his father's side was Lord Chief Justice in the reign of Edward II; other illustrious predecessors included the architect of London's Guildhall and a Lord Chancellor of Ireland. Around the time of the English Civil War the clan settled near the Staffordshire village of Alrewas, prospering for many generations as successful landowners, soldiers and clerics. For over a century the head of the family appointed the vicar of the nearby parish of Berkswich.

The future Dean's own father, another William Inge, was the eldest of five sons in this long line of Inges. Educated at Charterhouse and Christ Church, Oxford, he was a Christian gentleman redolent of the era of Jane Austen. After obtaining a first-class degree and a cap in the university cricket eleven, he migrated to Yorkshire, where he became tutor to the male children of the scholarly Archdeacon of Cleveland and Rector of Crayke, Dr Edward Churton. 'There must be very few now alive', opined the eminent Dean nearly eighty years later, 'who can remember what that atmosphere was.' Steeped in the Anglo-Catholic traditions of the early Victorian Oxford Movement, these long-bearded gentlemen shared a devotion to the memory of 'King Charles the Martyr', a 'loyalty to the old Anglican tradition', an 'ingrained conservatism' and a 'horror of dissent and of every kind of theological liberalism'. After five years of proselytising these doctrines, the tutor married the archdeacon's cold but likeminded daughter, Susanna.[99]

According to custom, William was duly appointed curate to his father-in-law, and the newlyweds moved into a large house beside the Rectory known as The Cottage. It was here that their first child, the future Dean of St Paul's Cathedral, was born on 6 June 1860. He was followed in the ensuing eight years by two brothers and two sisters, of whom Ralph formed close relationships particularly with his nearest siblings, Sophy and Edward. The latter's death in infancy greatly affected the sensitive and 'wayward' eldest child; all the more so on account of his parents' strict instruction that he and his sister were not to mourn the tragedy excessively. Such an imposition, however, proved too great for young Ralph. Only a few days after a restrained funeral service presided over by his grandfather, the boy was found cowering behind a sofa with a photograph of his brother's corpse pressed to his lips, kissing it 'again and again'. 'Seeing that I saw him,' his mother wrote archly to her husband, 'he said "that was my little secret, Mama", and then came with a glowing face to give me such a hug.'[100]

This was only one of many childhood experiences which would have been of great interest to the Dean's noted contemporary Sigmund Freud. As well as his evident attachment to his mother, young Inge soon developed a pronounced sadistic streak – one playmate was almost killed after being locked for several hours in a disused rabbit hutch. Yet in adulthood Inge never tired of denouncing the 'nauseous rubbish' of 'the unpleasant Doctor Freud'. Only in moments of chilling self-realisation did the Dean privately concede that the father of psychoanalysis might have been 'right after all'. 'My parents did not understand me at all,' he soliloquised in his brief memoir, *Vale*. 'My father, who had the placid and healthy temperament of a family of athletes, could only say, "Remember good Bishop Hacket's motto – Serve God and be cheerful." Alas! How could I be, with a legion of devils waiting for me in my unoccupied moments?'[101]

The 'unpleasant Doctor Freud' might have looked no further than the Dean's mother to explain these torturing apparitions. Described by Inge's school contemporary Arthur Benson as 'a grim mixture of saint and fanatic, utterly hard and cruel, with all the hideous strength of virtue unbesmirched', Susanna taught her son to think always upon the Judgment Day. If he hesitated over his Latin grammar, or misconstrued his Greek, she would beat him; if he wanted to play, she would set him in a corner with a hoop. 'Mother really loves me,' the shy young man would reassure himself in later years. He was never really sure.[102]

Work was the rod which gave structure to the young boy's life. His ambitious schooling, entirely overseen by his commanding parents, was designed to prepare him for the intellectual rigours of the Eton scholarship examination. The family's confidence in his aptitude was vindicated when Inge won the second top scholarship to that establishment in 1874; but the triumph came at a heavy price to the boy's social and emotional development. Remembered by fellow pupils as an 'eccentric and passionate' youth, he was an easy target for bullies, especially of the predatory kind. A friend in the scholar's house had to be removed after becoming the 'evil plaything' of the senior boys, and it seems likely that Ralph, too, fell victim to unwanted advances. In later years he would become furious when school friends retailed salacious details of those days. One feels there were incidents he thought best forgotten about.[103]

This was not without justification. During his first year at Eton Inge fell under the spell of one of the most controversial masters in the school's history, Oscar Browning. This notorious Eton 'character' was shortly to be dismissed on suspicion of carrying on an illicit affair with the future viceroy of India, fifteen-year-old Lord Curzon. The scandal highlighted the culture of snobbery and pederasty then prevalent at the school – 'I have found that he is a lord,' wrote 'O. B.' of another protégé, 'but I loved him before.' Inge was among the many bright and attentive junior boys invited to Browning's rooms each week to discuss the virtues of Hellenic culture and – more dubiously – 'Greek love'. But there is no indication that anything harmful came of these meetings; indeed, Inge remained on friendly terms with Browning long after the master's disgrace. Both men's passion for the ancient world was tempered by a correcting, if sometimes contradictory, obsession with chastity and sexual morality.[104]

Bereft of O. B.'s guidance and protection, young Inge returned to the pattern of life to which he was accustomed: unrelenting study. At a time when the workload of the average Etonian was said to be practically insurmountable, he grandly dismissed the entire classical curriculum as 'child's play'. His only recorded act of defiance was to make a small bonfire out of blotting paper, for which he and an accomplice, Benson, received a 'gentle caning' from a member of Sixth Form. Academically, the boy was in a league of his own. 'Excellent in all respects,' one tutor purred, 'work up to a high standard. Ought to become a distinguished scholar.'[105]

In his final term at Eton Inge won the coveted Newcastle Scholarship, awarded annually to the most accomplished pupil in the school. It was no surprise that he was also offered the top scholarship to the school's sister institution, King's College, Cambridge, where he continued to win major prizes and awards with seeming ease until his graduation with a double first in 'Greats' (classics, philosophy and ancient history) in 1883.

Looking back upon this outstanding scholastic record, Inge had a single regret: he had made virtually no friends. 'I found myself completely isolated', he privately complained, 'and only escaped the sense of failure by grimly setting myself to become the best classicist of my year, a project which, as it succeeded, seemed to have been undertaken voluntarily.'[106]

Contemporaries recalled this angular, nervous young man as an 'intellectual freak', scurrying between lecture hall and library. Yet behind the bookish veneer there were already the first stirrings of the naïve arrogance which would mar so many of the future Dean's fine achievements. 'Very easily first,' he gloated to his father of his examination results. '921 marks to the next man's 802.' No one doubted, however, that a great future lay before him.[107]

The missing ingredient, so Inge believed, was ambition. While lesser contemporaries walked effortlessly into politics and the civil service, he fell complacently into the life of a schoolmaster. This would never do. After a few unsatisfactory years teaching at Harrow, Winchester and Eton, he found himself pining for greater things. 'I have wasted a vast amount of time', he upbraided himself at the end of his return to Eton, 'in daydreaming – mostly of ambition or avarice.' There were other problems, too – 'wayward thoughts', as Inge quaintly called them. These mostly involved a first-year Eton boy called Calvert, whom Inge was fond of taking to the school's nude bathing area. 'How angelic Calvert looked at the top of the steep bank,' he wrote on revisiting the scene in his mind's eye years later, 'his straw hat on the back of his head looking like an aureole, and his eyes dancing like two sunbeams. It was the prettiest sight I ever saw or shall see...'[108]

There is no evidence that this attraction was anything except platonic. But, just like Oscar Browning before him, Inge was evidently concerned about the state of his morals. He had the added disadvantage of being pathologically incapable of keeping control in the classroom. Cursed with a short temper and a surprising degree of credulity, he once released a class of boys who tricked him into believing that mice were gnawing through the ceiling. These factors combined to make Inge exceedingly anxious about his future. He had no interest in becoming a clergyman – at Cambridge he had objected so strongly to the 'elaborate choral services' that he actually refused to attend chapel. This may have partially contributed to his surprising failure to obtain a teaching position at his former university upon his graduation.[109]

It was, then, with some reluctance that the 28-year-old attempted to follow in the family tradition by taking Holy Orders towards the end of 1888. Only his fortuitous election as a Fellow of Hertford College, Oxford, prevented him from carrying through with his unhappy design to find a parish. Almost certainly he owed his salvation to his increasingly distinguished father, who had lately been appointed Provost of nearby Worcester College.

Oxford was a crucible for Inge. Conscious of his growing status in the world, he resolved to keep a diary. Towards the end of his long life he would immodestly compare this wandering daily record to the journals of the Georgian politician and court gossip Thomas Creevey. There is no hint, however, that this was Inge's

model in the late 1880s. 'I am getting very lazy about work', wrote
the young don wrote in one entry, 'and am generally remiss, losing
self-control, thoughts wandering … This is serious, and must be
mended speedily. Will keep a record a bit.'[110]

Life in college proved less congenial than Inge had envisaged.
Hertford was not an old or an especially prestigious institution,
and the undergraduates were notoriously wild. He regarded the
founder's son, Godfrey Baring, lately expelled from Harrow, as 'a
desperate character who ought to be in jail'. Talent in the senior
common room was only marginally better in Inge's lofty opinion,
but he certainly benefited from contact with at least two eminent
colleagues: the theologian Hastings Rashdall and the political
thinker the Hon. Hugh Cecil, son of the Prime Minister, Lord
Salisbury. To the former, Inge owed his conversion to the study
of philosophy; to the latter his increasing interest in conservative
politics. For, at this stage in life, Inge considered himself something
of a liberal.[111]

Inge's Oxford diaries make for dismal reading. They give the
impression of a man thoroughly dissatisfied with his lot, often
literally praying for death. 'One cannot do much to resist strong
marked hereditary mental weakness,' he wrote in May 1896, 'there
is a maggot in my brain which *must* spoil my life as it has spoilt
those of Uncle Willie and Uncle Harry' (his mother's dour brothers). Undoubtedly sexual thoughts continued to loom large, but
Inge remained above any taint of impropriety. 'I *must* not lose my
self control and self respect,' he wrote a little later, 'or else I shall
end my life in a lunatic asylum.'[112]

At the close of his fifth year at Hertford, Inge took stock of his situation:

> I suppose every year is likely to be uneventful to me, until that one which shall remove me from this phase of existence. How do I like the prospect? Fifteen years or so of routine work at Oxford – delivering the same lectures, discoursing on the same compositions, eating the same dinners, playing the same games of whist in Common Room: and then retirement, with a house and a hobby – and the shades of ignoble leisure for an unknown number of years?[113]

A broken engagement with a young lady he met while holidaying in Italy spurred Inge on to turn things around. He dabbled with the idea of transforming himself into a popular man of letters or going in for 'a headmastership or high office in the Church'. Progress was slow – agonisingly so – but Inge persevered. 'I shall have my *revanche* eventually,' he predicted, 'but meanwhile I need all the courage and determination I can muster.'[114]

Inge's first taste of success was modest: he was invited to preach the university sermon. Few eyebrows were raised when he chose 'sin' as his theme – in later years the Dean would need little provocation to wax upon 'special temptations which come upon many boys and young men'. This small triumph gave rise to fresh opportunities for Inge to expand his intellectual horizon. In preference to an impressive list of distinguished ecclesiastics, he was selected in 1899 to deliver the prestigious Bampton Lectures, a major event in the life of Victorian Oxford. His series, published as *Christian Mysticism*, proved highly successful, selling several thousand copies, and establishing the young author as a popular authority on religion.[115]

Aside from demonstrating his mastery of a wide range of ancient and medieval sources, the lectures revealed Inge's patent lack of orthodoxy. To the regret of his High Church parents, especially his mother – who 'never really forgave' him – Inge publicly declared a belief in an inner religion, free from dogma, ritual and superstition. It was perhaps the faith of a scholar and a sceptic rather than a fervent Anglican, but it was of little importance to the world at large. He was, after all, not yet entrusted with the care of souls.[116]

It was the sudden death of Inge's father in 1903 which changed this situation. He decided to marry. 'I *must*', he oddly resolved, 'find someone to love and marry to fill the great gap in my life left by the loss of a father's affection.' But precious few young women were interested in his romantic overtures. Although blessed with handsome features and a healthy bank balance, Inge was painfully lacking in the less tangible attributes required to attract a spouse. The 'perfectly idiotic' females whom he met at college garden parties were liable to find him arrogant and bad-tempered.[117]

But Inge knew at least one girl for whom he felt real affection. This was his cousin, Kitty Spooner. Rich and vivacious, she was the daughter of the Archdeacon of Maidstone and the niece of the Warden of New College, Dr William Spooner (creator of the 'spoonerism'). They met at the Staffordshire home of Inge's uncle George, who was married to Kitty's great-aunt. At forty-two, the lonely scholar was nearly twice her age, but this was not a barrier in their social circle. 'She is a very bright clever girl,' recorded Inge in his diary, 'rather mature for her years, which I guess to be about 21 or 22.' When they met the following year at Canterbury, he wrote: 'If Kitty Spooner were rather older, or I rather younger I should try my luck.' After a little encouragement, he did.[118]

The couple's unlikely travelling companion George Bernard Shaw would later joke that their relationship was one-sided and a failure. He put into the mouth of a character clearly based on Inge: 'My wife has died cursing me. I do not know how to live without her: we were unhappy together for forty years.' There was certainly some truth in this. On meeting her future husband, Kitty described him as a 'very odd man', and Inge would prove strangely inept at such basic tasks as fetching a doctor when she went into labour – the dangers of childbirth, he was fond of saying, were 'enormously exaggerated'. But he was clearly devoted to her, and counted the marriage as the greatest blessing of his life.[119]

In the all-male world of post-Victorian Oxford, Inge was aware that his marriage would mean the end of his fellowship. So shortly before proposing by letter to Kitty he applied to become the vicar of the fashionable west London parish of All Saints, Ennismore Gardens. Inge's reputation as a theologian made him a credible, if rather unsuitable, candidate for this wealthy parish, where the pew-rents alone amounted to £1,350 – over five times the value of his Oxford salary. The living also came with a large house in one of the smartest squares in Kensington, Rutland Gate. Yet Inge still worried that pastoral work would not be to his liking. Imploring him to accept the offer, the Dean of Westminster, Dr Hensley Henson, stressed the advantages. 'The congregation', he explained, '…is aristocratic: there are no poor save a few hangers-on (coachmen and stable boys etc.) belonging to the well-to-do residents.'[120]

That was encouragement enough for the snobbish Inge. At the mature age of forty-four, this shy and awkward scholar launched what he called his 'crazy little skiff' into the world. He expected to make many blunders, but, with a beautiful young wife and a formidable academic reputation behind him, he knew – at last – that he was not destined to be one of life's gifted failures.[121]

೧೧

The Inges were married, as befitted the scions of two clerical dynasties, by the Archbishop of Canterbury, Randall Davidson, at Canterbury on 3 May 1905. The best man, Arthur Benson, himself the son of a former Primate and Inge's only remaining school friend, signed the register along with the sons and grandsons of an assortment of other eminent figures of the Victorian church.

Inge was lucky to have even made it to the ceremony. After a sumptuous lunch at the Dean's house, he and Benson had incautiously withdrawn from the party to discuss intellectual matters. They believed that Davidson would reappear shortly before the service to lead them through the precincts, but they were mistaken. Just as Inge was reaching the climax of a venomous attack on Catholic theology, Benson became aware that the house was unusually still. 'I pulled out my watch,' he wrote. 'It was 2.12 and the wedding was at 2.15.' The pair had to run around the west front of the cathedral, barging their way through a large crowd blocking the north aisle. Inge made it to his place just as his bride reached the end of her slow procession. It was an inauspicious beginning to married life.[122]

After the service, the couple returned to 34 Rutland Gate, where Inge had been living since the previous year. It was an extremely commodious house, requiring a small army of servants, a world away from the poky rooms Inge had occupied at Hertford College. Their neighbours were suitably distinguished. As well as the arch-conservative former Lord Chancellor, Lord Halsbury, they included the elderly population theorist Sir Francis Galton, who lived only a few doors away. Both of these eminent men would become close acquaintances of their new vicar, especially Galton, whom Inge had coincidently met in connection with his first attempt at marriage – he was the young lady's great-uncle.

Inge would later describe Galton as 'one of the best and wisest men whom I have known personally'. A first cousin of Charles Darwin, he was the inventor of the pseudo-science of eugenics. In a monument of learned folly, he expounded the theory that intelligence, as well as physical attributes, were transferred entirely genetically. Now at the end of a long career stretching back to the mid-nineteenth century, his work had given rise to a major politi-cal movement calling for state-incentives to encourage the well-educated to breed – and for the mentally or physically 'unfit' to be forcibly sterilised. His grim doctrine appealed directly to Inge's innate sense of uniqueness. 'Talent and peculiarities of character', wrote Galton, 'are found in the children, when they have existed in either of the parents, to an extent beyond all question greater than in the children of ordinary parents.' Inge soon joined the Eugenics Society, of which he remained a committed member right up until the Second World War, when he resigned in disgust – not, however, in protest of Hitler's sinister application of the doctrine, but because the society had invited the father of the welfare state, Sir William Beveridge, to deliver its annual lecture. 'It was enough to make my honoured friend, Sir Francis Galton, turn in his grave,' fumed Inge in his letter to the secretary.[123]

As parish priest, Inge was, by his own admission, a complete failure. The healthy congregation which he inherited from a jovial predecessor slowly withered in the face of his demanding sermons on theology and, unusually, politics. Inge could not understand why the smart ladies of Kensington did not care for Marcus Aurelius or why, when he made his pastoral visits, their 'supercilious butlers' showed him condescension. In all likelihood, Inge was regarded as a snob and a toady; a suspicion which his diary – replete with overexcited details of lavish society weddings and parties – more than vindicates. In a typical entry he recounts an evening with a noble lady: 'A party of five in a doll's house,' he sniffed, 'dinner very badly served. The other two guests a young German who wanted to talk to me about immortality, and a middle-aged lady with black hair, who smoked.' Inge did *not* approve.[124]

The decline of his congregation had a disastrous effect on the offertories – the parish takings – which furnished an important part of his income. Although Inge's stipend was one of the largest in London, he found it insufficient for his domestic needs. 'And it was for this that I gave up the secure happy congenial life at Oxford!' the scholar bemoaned. When news reached him that a professorship was soon to become available at Cambridge, Inge inexpertly held himself out for election. As he told a friend on the selection panel, he would not put himself forward as a candidate, but if they chose him he would accept. Such equivocation was not appreciated, and the professorship went to another applicant, much to Inge's annoyance.[125]

A second opportunity to return to the comfortable world of academia arose just one year later. This time Inge made sure. After receiving a 'kind note' from the same source, he put himself forward for election as the Lady Margaret Professor of Divinity, one of the most highly regarded positions in the university at the time. Kitty was not minded to leave London after so short a stay, but when an envelope arrived a few days later addressed to 'Professor Inge' there was no question of their remaining. Although Inge had enjoyed his taste of cosmopolitan life, he was happy to return to a place where he would be respected, if not necessarily liked.

The terms of the professorship were exceedingly generous. Inge was required to give only two lecture courses a year, and was under no obligation to publish anything whatsoever. Even with this manage-able workload, the new professor dispensed with the customary inaugural lecture. But at his first appearance in the Divinity Schools there was a large crowd; over seventy undergraduates gave in their names to hear him discuss 'Faith and its Psychology'. In the Easter term, however, only sixty were present at his first lecture on the theology of St John. Later, Inge complained of addressing empty lecture halls. He attributed this failure, with stubborn confidence, to the intellectual incapacity of the 'dull undergraduates'. Most of them, he complained, were mere 'Passmen who want certificates for Ordination'. 'I have been reduced almost to tears', he wrote of these novitiates, 'to find, in the terminal examination, that the large majority seem to have assimilated absolutely nothing.' Yet there were signs, too, that Inge was learning the gentle art of appealing to the masses: 'I must try and find out what the undergraduates like, and give it to them.'[126]

The Inges had by this time grown to four. While at Rutland Gate, Kitty had given birth to their first son, Craufurd, who was now followed by Edward. Their father initially showed little interest in them, but he was fond of playing with them once they could talk. In line with his eugenic beliefs, he and his wife went on to have three more children: Catharine, Richard and Paula.

Although Inge had fled London to escape the travails of parish work, he was soon complaining that Cambridge was 'disappointingly provincial'. For practically the first time in his life, he began to show an interest in the world outside his study. He read the newspapers, wrote letters for publication and jockeyed for favour among important ecclesiastics. Two significant political events in particular galvanised him in this unlikely direction: the proposed Education Act of 1908 and the ruling in the landmark case of *Thompson* v. *Dibdin*.[127]

The Education Act was intended as a reward to the Liberal government's large contingent of Nonconformist and Catholic supporters, who resented the monopoly of Anglican clergy over religious instruction in free schools. Many English bishops, eager to seem reasonable and popular, came out strongly in support of the government. Not so Professor Inge. In a vitriolic letter to *The Times* he denounced those who favoured sectarian teaching as a 'well-organised minority who wish to turn the Church of England into a pseudo-Catholic sect'. After being excoriated in the columns of the *Manchester Guardian* and the *Church Times*, he admitted in his diary that he had perhaps 'made the characteristic mistake of expressing myself too strongly'.[128]

Inge's reaction to the *Thompson* ruling was equally forthright. The case arose from another instance of the Liberal government's reform of the law: the Deceased Wife's Sister's Marriage Act of 1907. This largely self-explanatory measure allowed certain marriages to take place which had previously been illegal. Although the legislation was strongly resisted by the laity and most of the clergy, Archbishop Davidson accepted it on the basis that individual ministers would still be allowed to refuse to conduct such ceremonies on grounds of conscience. The question in *Thompson* was whether a disapproving clergyman could subsequently withhold communion from the parties to one of these marriages. The appeal court thought not.

Inge was outraged. The judges, he thundered in another intemperate letter printed in *The Times*, had 'based their decision on a principle which must be intolerable to all Churchmen' – that the clergy could not, if they so pleased, publicly anathematise lawabiding citizens as 'notorious evil livers'. Although Davidson (incorrectly) reassured him that the offending passages in the judgment were merely *obiter dicta*, with no binding force, Inge foresaw that *Thompson* marked the beginning of the end of the high-minded Victorian church. Future governments, he warned, would use the ruling to 'coerce the clergy in matters even more offensive to our conscience'. And so they would.[129]

After years of obscurity, Inge was slowly becoming a public figure. He was asked to preach all over the country, and started to wonder, rather hopefully, if he might not be offered an important position in the Church. The deanery of Lincoln was for some time in his sights, and he scoured the columns of the newspapers each morning to see if, by some miracle, he had been appointed. But he was not such a prig as to fail to see his own ridiculousness. 'I am being made painfully conscious', he wrote in his diary, 'of my moral weakness and silliness.' He might have added 'perverse ambition' to his list.[130]

For there was little chance that such a position would ever be offered to him. Not only had Inge established himself as a radical and an excessively combative figure, unsuited to the nuanced politics of a Cathedral Chapter; he was also beginning to go quite badly deaf. He first became aware of this affliction while at Oxford, where he took 'illogical satisfaction' at being so effectively able to shut himself off, both physically and mentally, from the unpleasantness of reality. There was little trace of such stoicism now: he spent a small fortune having the condition treated, but to no avail.[131]

An even greater reason why Inge was unlikely to progress in the Church was that the institution was moving in a markedly different direction to his own. The era of the gentlemanly clergyman, contemptuous of fanaticism and piety alike, was coming to an end. It was no longer possible for a senior cleric completely to ignore, as did Inge, the lives of 95 per cent of the population. Not even Inge's crowd-pleasing anti-Catholicism was likely to mitigate this perceived failing. Only a small number of lonely and eccentric figures such as his ally Dean Henson shared his controversial views. The pair would spend many long evenings at Dean's Yard, Westminster, lamenting the decline of their beloved church – its Anglo-Catholic tendencies, the prevalence of 'ardent young seminarians', and the impossibility of men with their ideas gaining promotion. 'I feel that it is bad for me to talk with him', wrote

Inge after a short stay in May 1910, 'because he aggravates my own tendency to pessimism … I cannot deny his arguments – there is far too much truth in them.'[132]

Ironically, a major source of agreement between Inge and Henson was that St Paul's Cathedral had become a sink of High Church fanaticism and superstition. Solemnly presided over by the nonagenarian Dean Gregory, it was a bastion of Anglo-Catholicism, with elaborate services, extravagant decor and a famous choir. When one of its canons came to stay with the Inges in Cambridge to give a talk to students about the 'Real Presence' (transubstantiation), the professor could scarcely conceal his condescension. 'He asked me to come and preach during his residence,' wrote Inge, 'for which I tried to appear grateful, though I dislike preaching there, and have no love for the place or the services.'[133]

The Prime Minister, Herbert Asquith, knew nothing of these theological hang-ups. One of the most intellectual premiers in history, he regarded Inge primarily as a great scholar: a man who might 'restore the traditions of scholarship and culture associated with the Deanery in the past'. On 17 April 1911, he unexpectedly wrote to Inge asking if he would succeed Dean Gregory.[134]

Before accepting, Inge sought the counsel of his friends and family. The responses were not encouraging. His widowed mother, living quietly in a large house in Oxford, explained that she had 'no opinions or wishes to give' whatsoever, before adding that she thought St Paul's would be a 'very far from attractive, and even distasteful' proposition for a man of his pronounced views. As though that was not cold water enough, Archbishop Davidson weighed in with further doubts. 'To even be *offered*', he discouragingly began, 'is a big thing for any man.' The Primate went on to list four reasons why Inge should refuse. 'Consider,' he wrote:

(1) The almost unique position that you hold in the university…

(2) The opportunity you have of being a teacher to whom men listen day by day or week by week…

(3) The harmony of your surroundings…

(4) The fact that you have not yet been very long in the saddle…[13]

Even if some of these points were partially accepted by Inge, the archbishop's mealy-mouthed reservations were hardly sufficient for him to turn down one of the greatest positions in the Church. The office was not in Davidson's patronage anyhow: it was the Prime Minister's decision, and his alone. But it is significant that Inge's great leap into the Church was opposed at the outset by the ecclesiastical hierarchy. Even in outlining the supposed advantages of accepting Asquith's offer, Davidson could scarcely conceal his worries. As Dean, he explained, Inge would have the dubious privilege of playing a leading role in Convocation – 'how far that would be congenial, or possible, for you I cannot tell'. And as for the splendid opportunity of 'offering guidance and leadership' on the form of worship at the cathedral – 'it would be perilous to interfere too much'. 'Nobody who looks fairly at the Church life of London today', he concluded, 'can doubt that the reasonable and restrained High Churchmanship which marks St Paul's should be retained there as a distinctive feature.'

Inge, it was clear, was expected to send Asquith a courteous 'no, thank you' and retire to his library.

But Inge was not one to take instructions from archbishops. 'If the Prime Minister', he wrote in his diary, 'singles out a man who has never stirred a finger for preferment, who has no friends in high places, who is not even a political supporter, it means that he deliberately thinks that this man is the right man for the post, and it is rather a fine thing…'

'All the humiliations' of the past were forgotten. Dean Inge had arrived.[136]

꙳

There is a story that Queen Mary, on taking her leave from St Paul's, once remarked to the Dean that it must be a great privilege for him to hear such wonderful services. 'I can assure you, ma'am,' the long-faced clergyman replied, 'I find it most irksome.'[137]

It matters little if the words were actually said – they reflected the Dean's views accurately enough. But at the outset of his career at St Paul's, Inge was not quite so despondent. His only grievance at that time was Asquith's decision to allow his predecessor to remain in possession of the Deanery until his death. This made life rather complicated for the Inges. After much discussion they decided to keep their Cambridge home, and that the Dean would commute regularly by train to London, staying whenever necessary at an expensive hotel near the cathedral. After a few months of this arrangement they decided instead to rent a large house in Bedford Square – 'a most beautiful old mansion', gushed Inge, 'half as big again as 34 Rutland Gate'. Fortunately, however, Dean Gregory died just before the lease began, allowing the Inges to move straightaway into their impressive official residence at Dean's Court, adjacent to the cathedral.[138]

As with his professorship, Inge's responsibilities as Dean were not especially onerous. The cathedral, as his critics liked to remind him, was not exactly 'his': it was the seat of the Bishop of London, Arthur Winnington-Ingram – a High Churchman for whom Inge took a strong and instant dislike. As Dean it only fell to him to deliver a sermon about five times a year. His main responsibility was the upkeep and day-to-day running of the church, and also to determine how its ample funds and patronage were to be distributed. He was supposed to be assisted in these functions by the canons, who, with himself presiding, constituted the Chapter. St Paul's was unlike other cathedrals in that the Dean did not have a casting vote. Inge compared his position to 'a mouse watched by four cats'.[139]

These 'cats' were men of widely different temperament to his own. Three of them had little interest in the affairs of the world, devoting all their time to piety and good works. Inge had nothing but contempt for such persons: the first time he met one prospective canon he sustained a twenty-minute silence before letting it be known, through the medium of his wife, that the meeting had been 'a *great* success'. The only canon who rivalled Inge as an aspiring man of the world was the cathedral treasurer, Sidney Alexander. The two men completely despised each other at sight: they were too alike. It was said by one mutual friend that Alexander was 'shrivelled by the blistering acidity' of the Dean, who did not see in him 'the kindly Christian scholar with a deep affection for the Church, but only the vain and ambitious churchman'. Inge made a point of never appearing at public functions alongside him. Apologising for the absence of his senior canon at a Saturday dinner party, he regretfully announced that 'tonight is his bath night'.[140]

It was soon clear that however gratifying it was to be the Dean of St Paul's, the experience was not going to be pleasant for Inge. After his first Sunday in office, the new incumbent recounted his impressions in his diary:

> *May 28.* Spent nearly the whole day in church, 8–9; 10.30–1.15; 3.15–4.45; 7–8.30. I have never before had work to do which wounded my conscience, but these services seem to me a criminal waste of time. I have held different views at different times about the character and nature of the Creator of the Universe; but never at any time have I thought it at all probable that he is the kind of person who enjoys being serenaded![141]

Inge saw a novel way to improve the situation. 'I believe', he continued, 'that I can, without giving offence, pursue my theological studies in my stall.' This scandalous idea was not as easy as he envisaged. As well as being in full view of the choir and congregation, Inge found that it was not possible to concentrate on his reading. 'The noise gets on my nerves', he complained of the hymns, 'and interferes with consecutive thought.' Many came to the conclusion that he would rather not be there at all. They were not far wrong. Within a few months of commencing his tenure at St Paul's, Inge was 'conscious of [a] growing irritation and dislike of the Cathedral', and began to wonder if 'a year hence I should not decide to give it up'.[142]

Yet it was not all bad. Inge admitted to enjoying being 'Mr Dean', 'a person of consideration ... in the middle of things' and he gladly accepted the many dinner invitations which soon came his way. Although he was at first reluctant to draw attention upon himself, it was not long before he developed a reputation as a shy but amusing after-dinner speaker. A ditty in *Punch* highlighted his increasingly unconventional status: 'Though I never heard him preach,' it ran, 'I've known him make a funny speech.' His wit and wisdom were usually most effective when he was the only clergyman present. At a banquet hosted by the London School of Economics shortly after the war, he amused the university's left-wing professor, Harold Laski, with the 'quiet complacency with which he accepted the very obvious decline in religious belief'; at another party he outraged a fellow theologian by casually remarking that 'we must drop the idea of the brass band at the day of Judgment'. But no clergyman was ever further in temperament from the garrulous Sydney Smith than Dean Inge. One dinner companion recalled him 'addressing his plate'. Equally disconcerting was his slowness in answering questions. 'Yes, *I* heard,' he snapped on another occasion. 'I was thinking.'[143]

Inge's growing reputation for the good life did little to endear him to the grassroots of the Church. 'I have enemies,' he recounted in his diary. Foremost among these early critics was the saintly journalist G. K. Chesterton, who claimed to have converted to Catholicism in protest against the heresies of the Dean of St Paul's. No less disapproving was the high-minded editor of the *Church Times*, Sidney Dark, who complained that this worldly cleric was too 'popular with the City magnates': an objectionable throw-back to the dark days of the eighteenth century. But neither Chesterton – whose scriptures Inge once dismissed as the 'elephantine capers of an obese mountebank' – nor the pious editor recognised that Inge had no great love of mere feasting. After an eight course banquet with the Worshipful Company of Curriers, he resolved to 'have a previous engagement' should they ask him again. His hosts, he grandly complained, were 'aggressively vulgar – quite like the conventional aldermen of fiction'.[144]

A more congenial dining companion for Inge was the Minister for War, Lord Haldane. The pair met shortly after Inge's return to London at a dinner hosted by the distinguished judge Lord Macnaghten and would remain in close touch until Haldane's death nearly twenty years later. A typical evening would involve the two men sitting comfortably in Inge's large study smoking and discussing German metaphysics. Although not a natural host, Inge could always lay on the best quality goods. 'Dean,' the astonished minister once interposed, 'these are very good cigars.' They were, explained his slightly embarrassed companion, a gift from an American admirer.[145]

Neither Inge, still less Haldane, suspected that this comfortable Edwardian world was about to be shattered by a ruinous war with Germany. Far more important in 1913 seemed the suffragette agitation. Inge believed this 'feminist outbreak' to be the 'most appalling example of epidemic moral insanity that our age has witnessed'. He was furious to learn that senior members of his own Church actually supported both the cause and the illegal methods employed by many of its advocates. In a series of indignant letters published in *The Times*, Inge castigated these characters as 'foolish and mischievous clergy': they might as well have encouraged the Pankhurst family's mob of 'criminal anarchists' to 'burn the Bodleian Library as a protest against Welsh disestablishment'. 'Such opinions', the Dean concluded, 'would disgrace Bedlam at full moon.'[146]

It was another instance of Inge 'expressing himself a little too strongly'. The following Sunday he was confronted by 'forty hussies' banging on the door of his cathedral. One of these women planted a dummy bomb beneath his stall.[147]

While misogyny undoubtedly played a part in the Dean's objections to the women's cause, his opposition was rooted in a far greater hatred – for democracy. In his first months at St Pauls, Inge spoke out against this method of governance as 'the silliest of all fetishes that are seriously worshipped among us'. To incredulous liberals, supposing 'the voice of the people to be the voice of God', he was fond of mentioning 'the famous occasion when the voice of the people cried "Crucify Him!"'. Rather than granting votes to women, he would have much preferred if a great many fewer males were accorded this privilege. When Parliament finally agreed to electoral reform after the war, Inge dryly commented that there was 'something to be said for extending an absurdity to its logical conclusion'.[148]

These contrarian views fast made Inge a target of abuse in the popular press. Only a few months after his arrival at St Paul's, he was placarded all over London as the 'Gloomy Dean' for suggesting that the high birth rate among the working-class population of the city would have catastrophic implications for the future of the British people. At his most extreme, he was not above suggesting that the government of the day should look seriously into the possibility of exterminating some of the 'surplus' population.

'The horror of taking life under any circumstances', he once dropped into a lecture, 'seems to me unnatural, and probably only temporary. The state of the future, I believe, will kill mercifully but freely.'[149]

And yet Inge always maintained that he was not gloomy. He preferred to see himself as a realist: the one man willing to say that civilisation as it had been known to rich white men like himself for the past 200 years was about to be obliterated by feminism and socialism. Certainly, the world, as he saw it from St Paul's, was a dark, unhappy place. 'It is a period', he wrote in October 1908, 'when clear sighted people *must* be pessimistic unless they can live in the sphere of eternal ideas. The social and political outlook for this country is one of unrelieved gloom.' Many agreed with him, but Inge merely took the occasional 'fan letters' he received as evidence that 'freedom of speech is already becoming dangerous in England – as it certainly will be if the thoroughly tyrannical labour movement acquires much more strength'.[150]

When disaster struck in August 1914, Inge was desolate. 'We are now back in the Dark Ages,' he lamented, 'without the piety and fear of God which tempered the ferocity of Goths and Franks.' In the early months of the conflict he joined the rest of the establishment in preaching a gospel of hatred against the 'Prussians', who were widely believed to have crucified babies and butchered entire towns in Belgium. Later, however, Inge bravely spoke out against the 'insane' clamour for victory 'at any price'. 'We cherish three impossible hopes,' he frankly told the public in December 1917,

(1) that we can destroy German militarism. We cannot; they will only live for revenge.

(2) A restoration of the balance of power. This means a mad competition in armaments and the suicide of Europe.

(3) That we can force Germany to adopt our democratic system.
They do not want government by mass-bribery, and will prefer
military dictatorship.[151]

These startlingly prescient warnings brought further obloquy upon
Inge both in the press and in letters from private citizens. 'I am
praying for your death,' wrote one lady. 'I have been very successful
in two other cases.'[152]

Such controversies were the exception for Inge during the war.
Sick with reality, he turned inwards, devoting his leisure time to
a long-planned study of the third-century philosopher Plotinus.
His choice of subject was not as arbitrary as it may appear. Like
Inge, Plotinus was a cerebral man – 'the one great genius in an age
singularly barren of greatness' – who found happiness in abstract
thought while civilisation crumbled around him. The author's
self-identification was not lost on contemporaries such as Bertrand
Russell, who aptly described Plotinus as a 'melancholy optimist'.
Inge's two-volume study of this neglected figure was his final
contribution to scholarship, and probably his most enduring.[153]

The Dean was lecturing on Plotinus at St Andrews when the
Armistice was declared. It was just as well that he was far from
the celebrations which engulfed the capital: he saw no cause for
triumphalism. 'Europe is ruined for my lifetime and longer,' he
soberly wrote in his diary. 'Nearly one-fifth of the upper and middle
class of military age – the public school and university men ... are
dead.' 'Half the continent', he continued,

is devastated by famine, anarchy, and utter misery. The horrors in Russia are indescribable, and the Austrians are starving and despairing. At home, the country is seething with revolutionary unrest, and the government has no remedy except the payment of unlimited blackmail. The class to which I belong is marked out for spoliation and ruin.[154]

A man holding such views could not keep silent for long. Already, while the war was still raging, Inge had set himself to write a book about modern-day problems. 'It is to be a discussion', he explained, 'of the present conditions and future prospects of religion and social organisation, showing the importance of machinery and the necessity of accepting the Christian standard of values.' The result was a collection of articles and lectures entitled *Outspoken Essays*, published in October 1919. It formed the keynote of Inge's grim social and political outlook, which he would enlarge upon remorselessly for the remainder of his life. A few characteristic quotations give a picture of the whole:

Of public opinion: 'A vulgar, impertinent, anonymous tyrant who deliberately makes life unpleasant for anyone who is not content to be the average man.'

Of the state: 'A Russian under the Tsars was far less interfered with than an Englishman or American or Australian.'

Of utopia: 'The present ideal of the masses seems to be the greatest idleness to the greatest number.'

Of modern state finance: 'Mortgaging the industry of the future to protect the prosperity of the present.'

Of post-war England: 'A chaos of factories and mean streets, reeking of smoke, millionaires, and paupers.'

Of political patriotism: 'Devil-worship remains what it was, even when the idol is draped in the national flag.'

Of feminism: 'It does not seem to have occurred to any young lady of the early nineteenth century to ask Scott or Wordsworth what they were doing during the war.'

Of contraception: 'A *pis aller* which high-minded married persons should avoid if they can practise self-restraint.'

And of the Church of England:

> In the sixteenth century it proclaimed Henry VIII the Supreme Head of the Church; in the seventeenth century it passionately upheld the 'right divine of kings to govern wrong'; in the eighteenth and nineteenth it was the obsequious supporter of the squirearchy and plutocracy; and now it grovels before the working-man, and supports every scheme of plundering the minority.[155]

The result of this daring book was that Inge became an overnight sensation. Even the socialist George Bernard Shaw found it delightful. In a four-column laudation of 'Our Great Dean' he praised Inge for 'his intellect, his character, his courage, and – speaking professionally, as one author to another – his technique'. 'In the Church,' he went on, 'Dr Inge is like a refiner's fire: he puts it to its purgation and purification as no atheist could.'[156]

Offers to write in the press now flowed thick and fast. The editors of the *Sunday Express*, *Morning Post*, *Manchester Guardian* and *Evening Standard* competed with each other to fasten him to their columns. 'It looks as if I might make several hundred a year in this way,' the Dean wrote smugly in his diary. But he was worth every penny. His first series of eight articles for the *Sunday Express* on 'Utopian Dreams', 'Democracy in Danger', and other kindred themes, led to an offer from the editor of the *Evening Standard* to write a column each week. This would be continued, with occasional lapses, almost until his death thirty-three years later. The paper's owner, Lord Beaverbrook, regarded the Dean's column as one of the best features in his entire newspaper empire, a fact borne out by the exceptional remuneration that Inge received – up to £40 per article at a time when 'penny-a-liners' were still common in Fleet Street.

'At last,' the delighted sixty-year-old exulted, 'the poor little prophet is beginning to have honour in his own country.'[157]

∽

It would be hard to exaggerate how much offence was caused, over the years, by the Dean's flood of journalism. Few sacred cows or special interests were spared from his mordant pen. But what really characterised his many articles, as one perceptive critic observed, was his uncanny ability to write 'in the style of a man who is in touch with the public, while the [subject] matter is that of a man who is utterly out of touch with it'.[158]

A classic example of Inge's haughty populism was an early attempt entitled 'The Servant Problem'. 'How many happy homes', the Dean seriously asked post-war London, 'have been broken up, not by poverty or marital infidelity, but because the mistress simply cannot keep a servant?' 'The plight of the middle class', he wrote another time, 'is a world-wide tragedy. The sufferings of the poor professional man and his family are piteous in this country; in parts of the Continent they are terrible beyond description.'[159]

That Inge assumed his audience to be of the same social group as his own was only part of the problem. It was his apparent contempt of the other nine-tenths of humanity which proved so controversial. One article in particular secured his reputation as a public enemy. Entitled 'Gentlemen's Schools', it took to task the entire notion of state education. 'In the past,' wrote Inge,

> the public school man has been exposed only to the natural competition
> of his own class, recruited very sparingly from below. But now our sons
> have to meet the artificial competition deliberately created by the govern-
> ment, who are educating the children of the working man, *at our expense*,
> in order that they may take the bread out of our children's mouths.[160]

The outrage which resulted from these remarks was unprecedented. A large meeting of workmen from the Woolwich Arsenal petitioned Archbishop Davidson to rebuke the Dean; he did so, with some circumspection, in the columns of the same newspaper. Even the former headmaster of Eton, the Rev. and Hon. Edward Lyttelton, condemned the remarks as undemocratic and contrary to the principle of free competition. Inge regarded the commotion as 'most unfair and improper', but took solace in the fact that at least his editor stood nobly by him. 'We do not want a regiment of Dean Inges,' boomed a leading article the following day,

> any more than we want to live on tonics. But it is a great asset
> to any generation to possess at least one man who says exactly what

he believes concerning things in general, and for the moment we can only look for such a man in the Deanery of St Paul's.[161]

In response to the more general criticism that a clergyman had no place in the columns of a tabloid newspaper, the editor went on to observe that Inge introduced spiritual ideas to 'hundreds of thousands of eager readers who are seldom seen in a church'. But this was not enough to placate the increasingly exasperated archbishop – especially when Inge began to parody some of the most sacred beliefs of their Anglo-Catholic brethren. In the most offensive of these contributions, the star columnist took a swipe at two cherished dogmas in a single paragraph: that the Virgin Mary gave birth without damaging her hymen, and that her son emerged full-clothed from his tomb:

> Let the reader suppose that he is privileged to assist at the accouche-ment of the Virgin Mary, in the stable at Bethlehem, and to satisfy himself by ocular demonstration that her physical condition was not that of other married women … Let him suppose that he is watching the Saviour clambering out of His grave, and then putting on the clothes which the angels brought with them; for we know that the grave-clothes remained in the tomb.[162]

Protestant England was not amused. In a letter of complaint signed by many erstwhile admirers, including Inge's former colleague Lord Hugh Cecil and his occasional dining companion Sir William Joynson-Hicks, the leaders of the House of Laity expressed to Archbishop Davidson 'the general feelings of Christians throughout the country ... that Dr Inge's language is most unfit for the pen of any member of the Church, and specially offensive when uttered by one holding such a position as that of the Dean of St Paul's'. After much pressure, Davidson again agreed to reprimand his wayward lieutenant, with the greatest courtesy, for 'culpably bad taste rather than ... heretical utterances'. But Inge stood his ground. He complained in a testy reply to the archbishop that the signatories must be 'very ignorant of Catholic theology', and although he was 'very sorry that these people have worried his Grace', he was 'still more [sorry] that you half agree with them'.[163]

It is surprising that the writer of this letter was not an intellectual 'debunker' of the school of Lytton Strachey, but a deeply conservative figure, proud to identify himself with his Victorian forebears. Yet Inge's scorn for the new age was sincere. Defying the 'literary impertinence' of the day, he frequently cast his mind back to the 'healthy and happy' time of Queen Victoria's reign, when both politics and religion were properly conducted. It was a time, he once wrote, when 'the choice lay between Mr Gladstone and Mr Disraeli, one of whom proposed to abolish the income-tax altogether, and the other fixed it at threepence in the pound'. Throughout the inter-war years Inge elaborated upon these increasingly untenable propositions. 'The nineteenth century', he declared in his Romanes Lecture of 1920, 'was the most wonderful century in human history.' It was an era, he continued, when 'society was well ordered, under its wisest men'; when 'those who paid the taxes were also those who imposed them', and in which there was no 'large half-educated class which now dominates all public discussion'. To the charge that the Victorians were overly materialistic and blindly attached to the idea of progress, Inge riposted that these were largely modern-day fixations. 'There was a shadow of apprehension over everything,' he recalled, 'never glad confident morning again.'[164]

While Inge's Victorian nostalgia made him both deeply unpopular and unfashionable, his powers of persuasion were uncommon. In November 1922 well over three hundred members of the Oxford Union backed his ultimately unsuccessful proposition that 'This House would welcome a return to Victorian Ideals'.[165]

For a journalist as prolific as Inge, it is equally remarkable that so few of his contributions were expressly autobiographical. Much of his output, however, was suggestive of his temperament and character. Although occasionally photographed in the press sitting happily beside his wife at her piano, Inge was not fond of spending quiet evenings alone with his family. 'We are to make a habit of relaxation,' he wrote with contempt of modern psychotherapy. 'Sit in your most comfortable armchair, stretch out your arms and legs in the easiest posture, be very careful to think of nothing and wish for nothing, and wait for the subconscious to manifest itself.' In a similar article lambasting the theory that happiness is essential for good health he declared: 'It would be unfortunate if I said, "I wish to be the happiest man in England", and promptly found myself locked up in an asylum, a cheerful lunatic who believed himself to be the Emperor of China.'[166]

The Dean's serious approach to life often made him seem a hard and unsympathetic father. When one of his young children accidently knocked over a pot of ink in the nursery the culprit was heard to enquire 'what the Gloomy Dean would say'. But the Inge children were balanced by a healthy streak of naughtiness and rebelliousness – a favourite pastime of theirs was a game called 'smack the Dean of St Paul's'. Their father's attitude towards these antics is not known, but he was evidently no great disciplinarian. Several of the children's governesses found it necessary to hand in their notices on account of their charges' impossible behaviour. Of greater concern to Inge was the apparent intellectual backwardness of his three sons. Only Richard succeeded in following him to Eton, but not as a scholar. Inge could not understand it, 'their four grandparents being who they were'. Eugenics had failed.[167]

Inge was less exacting when it came to his daughters. His youngest, Paula, was his favourite, and he was devastated to learn at the end of 1921 that she was diabetic. In the days before insulin, this was likely to be fatal to an eleven-year-old child, and the Dean prepared himself for the worst. After a year of unsuccessful treatment, during which Inge spent more time with his children than ever before, she told him that it had been 'the happiest year' of her life. Her brief existence ended on Maundy Thursday 1923, shortly after asking her nurse to place flowers on the war memorial as her Easter penance. Her father celebrated her life in a special service at the cathedral, calling her 'one of God's saints'. Afterwards the cortege proceeded to Oxford, passing crowds of mourners that lined Ludgate Hill from top to bottom. 'Paula was buried like a princess,' wrote her father of the occasion.[168]

The tragedy reminded Inge of what he had. Almost immediately he became less preoccupied and began caring for his wife and his surviving children to a greater extent than ever before. He took them for more holidays, including a two-week trip to stay with cousins living near Shrewsbury, where he enjoyed his first games of tennis since Oxford days. Before long the Inges were going further afield, on trips to Cornwall, the Isle of Wight, Switzerland and Norway; mostly for pleasure but also so that the Dean could see more of the world.

Inge's warm reception abroad soon led him to venture to the United States. It was the second time that he had crossed the Atlantic, but this time was very different to the scholarly pilgrimage he had made to Yale in 1906. The Dean summarised his experiences thus:

> This has been the most extraordinary experience of our lives. I am being boomed like a first-class celebrity. At the railway stations I am surrounded by reporters and photographers, and I believe I have been filmed for the 'movies' more than once when I was not aware of it. The Americans say themselves that possibly Bernard Shaw or Kipling would be received in the same way, but nobody else.[169]

While grumblers at home moaned that Inge's incautious proclamations about democracy and eugenics might harm trans-Atlantic relations, the American public were thrilled by his witty commentary on their country. Asked by a reporter what he thought of Prohibition, the Dean explained that he was 'quite willing to stick it for three weeks, but, since you ask me, I think cold water, with which the Psalmist says wild asses quench their thirst, is a poor beverage to offer to a human being'. Similarly, when asked about 'the morals of the modern flapper as compared with those of her grandmother', the sage proclaimed: 'The early indiscretions of the flapper's grandmother I neither witnessed nor shared.' It was said

that by the end of his lecture tour he and his wife had been photographed 23,000 times, while many of his sermons appeared on the
front pages of the newspapers.[170]

The trip was also highly lucrative for the Dean: a lecture series
at Baltimore alone netted him an impressive $1,000. These profits
were boosted by the fact that he and his wife rarely had to meet
any of their travel expenses. The owner of their cruise-liner generously upgraded them to a first-class berth, and friends in New York
provided them with a large apartment on Fifth Avenue in which to
stay. Curious to know something of American prices, Inge learnt
from the lift operator that the rents in the block ranged between
$15,000 and $25,000 per annum: a spectacular sum of money at
the time. Inge was impressed. He confidently predicted that the
future belonged to countries such as the USA where the demands
of the workforce were reasonable and the management of industry autocratic. By contrast to Britain, with its burgeoning labour
movement and mounting government debt, he told reporters that
the United States was a nation with a great future.

Inge's negative remarks about Britain were noted in *The Times*
as 'extraordinarily foolish', but the Dean was only warming to his
theme. Upon his return to London he expanded on his thoughts
in his first bestseller: *England*. This timely book was the culmination of months of silent brooding about the great crisis which had
briefly paralysed the country during the General Strike of May
1926. Superficially the text reads like a parody of Inge's journalism: 'There is still much gross gluttony among the middle class,'
he wrote in one passage, 'especially in the north of England, and
among miners.' In another chapter he dismissed the 'new type

of Labour member' as 'a drunken blackguard', and went on to complain that the Irish had no better justification of disliking the English 'than that Cromwell exercised the laws of war somewhat severely against the Irish rebels, and that William III won the battle of the Boyne'. But the book had a serious point, too. Ahead of academic opinion, Inge explained that the most serious problem facing the country was what was to become known as the 'revolution of rising expectations'. As Inge put it, 'It has become more and more difficult to earn enough to pay for the comfort and amusements which the worker expects, especially as he demands a shorter working day in order to enjoy his improved conditions.' In a globalised economy, he predicted, these expectations would prove unsustainable.[171]

Inge saw two potential solutions to this challenge. Either the state could provide doles to millions of countrymen who would be unable to find work even at the best of times; or a serious attempt could be made by future governments to reduce the population to a sustainable level. Inge did not pretend that either option could maintain Britain as a leading world power. Nor did he deny that many ancient rights would have to be dispensed with. But he saw no alternatives. His favouring of eugenics was not irrational. Being somewhat prejudiced against the poor, it was inconceivable to him that the country could survive if hundreds of thousands of its citizens had to be paid to remain idle. Better, he thought, to focus on nurturing 'quality over quantity'. Lowering the birth rate would not be easy – there would be a massive reduction in the average standard of living – but every man and woman would have work to do for which they could feel proud. Inge felt it essential that the reduction was shared proportionately between the classes, and that the reduced numbers were not countered by an influx of immigrants.

∾

Inge's growing reputation as a controversialist naturally soured his relations with the Chapter. Meetings were by this time unbearable. Increasingly deaf and bored by parochial matters, Inge would sit silently in his tall-backed chair, solemnly scribbling on a piece of paper what his colleagues assumed to be his latest journalistic offering. When discussion became too heated, he was prone to leave the canons to it; on one occasion he actually had to force his way out of their meeting room. No wonder a newly appointed member of the Chapter complained of the 'backbiting and bad spirit in Amen Court'. Inge curtly dismissed this man as a 'whinger'. 'A Minor Canonry', he later added, 'is not a man's job.'[172]

High on the Chapter's agenda throughout these years was the fabric of the cathedral. Concerns had been raised as long ago as the late nineteenth century that the eight load-bearing piers, which supported the dome, were in need of extensive restoration and improvement. Little was done until 1912, when an extension of the London Underground was proposed to pass beneath the east end of the cathedral. Surveyors found that Sir Christopher Wren's great church was not as secure as many had supposed.

Inge was foremost among the opponents of any restoration works. As well as objecting to the cost and unwanted publicity implied by such a project, Inge worried that the cathedral would have to be closed for a lengthy time – one expert proposed a period as long as eight years. Such an encumbrance would be intolerable for the Dean.

Strongly opposed to Inge's stance was his scheming adversary, the cathedral treasurer, Canon Alexander. On his own instigation this enemy launched two public appeals for funds; but without the backing of the Dean and the Corporation of London there was little that could be achieved. Nevertheless, money slowly trickled in, and some preliminary works were commenced just before the First World War. Inge's involvement was limited to supporting an abatement of traffic around the cathedral; the vibrations upset him, and he worried that he might one day get knocked down by a bus. A favourite Latin joke of his, derived from Wren's famous epitaph, was, 'If you don't want your name on a tombstone, look out!'

On Christmas Eve 1924, the joking stopped. The Surveyor of the City of London issued a 'Dangerous Structure' notice upon the cathedral. For the first time Inge accepted that something had to be done. A huge public campaign was launched by Canon Alexander and *The Times*, raising £400,000 by the end of the following year. There was some suggestion at one stage of having the entire dome temporarily removed, but a less complex solution was ultimately resolved upon.

Inge followed these happenings with lazy indifference. While touring America the great industrialist John D. Rockefeller had offered him as much money as was required for the project; but Inge was not one to play the role of fund-raiser. He replied that the agitation was a mere 'newspaper stunt', and that no further contributions were needed.[173]

Annoyingly for Inge, much of the cathedral was soon screened off, and major work commenced on the piers. The Dean's nonchalance about the project can largely be attributed to his personal dislike of Canon Alexander, whom he suspected of using the campaign to further his career. This uncharitable view was given some support by the influential Tory wire-puller, David Lindsay, 27th Earl of Crawford, who gave the following account of a meeting with the embittered treasurer:

The subject of our conversation was the structural stability of St Paul's, but I very soon discovered that he is absorbed in one problem and one only, namely his chance of succeeding Inge ... His hatred of the Dean is frank and avowed. He looks upon him as an unbeliever, dislikes his habit of reading more or less secular books all through divine service, but most of all Canon Alexander is indignant at Inge's refusal, maintained I suppose for fifteen or twenty years, to raise a finger to fight the battle of the cathedral structure. The whole of this he left to Alexander, who got uncommonly little help from other members of the Chapter. Meanwhile Inge pursues his cynical journalism, and cultivates his hobby of eating and drinking. He can attend public dinners five nights in a week, and often enough does so, without apparent ill effects, though for the last year or two somnolence added to deafness has made this untidy, ill-kempt churchman a very poor colleague in conference.[174]

Events were approaching a crisis. It was impossible for Inge to fulfil his duties when there was such open and vitriolic animosity between himself and the senior canon. In a letter to the popular former vicar of St Martin-in-the-Fields, the Rev. Dick Sheppard, Inge described Alexander as 'insane'. 'He is a poisonous reptile,' he wrote, 'poisoned at last by his own venom.'[175]

Relations with the canons were not improved by Inge's erratic invitations to controversial ecclesiastics to preach in the cathedral. None of these visitors caused greater offence than Dr Ernest Barnes, the outspoken Bishop of Birmingham, whom Inge invited in October 1927 to deliver one of his so-called 'gorilla sermons' celebrating the advances of modern science.

The Bishop of London had by this time had enough of Inge. He tried to prevent a repetition of the outcry caused when Barnes had preached in Westminster Abbey a few weeks previously, during the course of which he had declared that 'Darwin's triumph has destroyed the whole theological scheme'. This alleged sacrilege was compounded by a sermon in Barnes's own diocese a week later in which he challenged any devotee to tell the difference between a consecrated and an unconsecrated loaf. Bishop Winnington-Ingram had to make do with a solemn pledge from Inge that Dr Barnes would not repeat these provocations at St Paul's.

In the context of the acrimonious Prayer Book debate, which was now reaching its climax in Parliament, this pledge was redundant. Even Inge's old ally Hensley Henson, now Bishop of Durham, pleaded with him to avoid antagonising their Anglo-Catholic brethren. To do so, he warned, might lead to the disestablishment of the Church: a cataclysm wanted only by their enemies – socialists and atheists. Unmoved, Inge now dismissed his former associate as 'a double turncoat' and seldom communicated with him again.[176]

But Inge might have listened to Henson. As Dr Barnes ascended
the steps of the pulpit on 17 October, the congregation witnessed
one of the most unedifying scenes in the cathedral's history. As the
reporter from the *Church Times* recounts:

> It was in no 'quiet mind' that I took up my place on Sunday morning last
> in St Paul's Cathedral, but troubled with a sense of undefined foreboding ... The crowded congregation had listened to a beautiful rendering
> of the Introit, 'Jesu, Star of Consolation' (Macpherson), and the service
> had proceeded in the customary reverent way to the Declaration of
> Faith made by all assembled in reciting the Nicene Creed. During the
> singing of this I was struck by the unusual number of worshippers who
> made their humble acknowledgement of the Divine condescension by
> kneeling at the *Incarnatus* and by making the Holy Sign at the end of
> the Creed ... And then came the not unexpected, but highly dramatic
> interruption! Dr Barnes was mounting the steps of the pulpit, and the
> Dean had begun to give out a notice of some kind, when a small procession – Canon Bullock-Webster, vested in surplice, hood, and stole, and
> supported by four stalwart laymen ... advanced to the barrier dividing
> the nave from the temporary sanctuary. The Dean paused; there was a
> momentary silence, while the congregation waited in tense expectancy,
> wondering what was going to happen. Then Canon Bullock-Webster,
> after bowing to the altar, to the Dean, and to the preacher, with what
> can only be described as superb courage, turned to the congregation
> and proceeded to read the following protest.[177]

The protest was a sharply worded admonition of Bishop Barnes and
the Dean of St Paul's for promoting 'false and heretical teaching'.

After calling upon the Bishop of London to put an end to this 'scandal and offence', he invited the entire congregation to join him in marching out of the cathedral 'lest our ears should be defiled with fresh profanities'.

Inge was understandably livid. During the course of the lengthy denunciation, he signalled frantically to the organist to drown out the protester – but it appears that he, too, was in on the conspiracy. When the unrepentant canon, a rector of a City church and ironically a distant cousin of Dr Barnes's wife, sent Inge a formal copy of his protest the next day, the Dean responded with his usual asperity: 'Since you have had the impertinence to write to me,' he wrote, '…I must reply that until I receive from you a full and proper apology for your scandalous and disgraceful behaviour in brawling in the Cathedral, I refuse to have any communication with you whatever.' 'Brawling', as both men were aware, was a criminal offence under the Public Worship Act of 1874.[178]

This unseemly row ensued for several weeks in the columns of the press. Open letters were issued with a vengeance by Inge, Dr Barnes and the two archbishops, while thousands of indignant parishioners called upon the clerical authorities either to anathematise the canon or the Bishop of Birmingham, depending on their viewpoint. As ever, Inge reserved his most stinging comments for his weekly causerie in the *Evening Standard*. Entitled 'The Latest Heresy Hunt', the Dean used this contribution to liken himself and Dr Barnes to that other great philosopher set-upon by unlettered fanatics, Socrates. 'These little dogs', he wrote of the Anglo-Catholic lobby, 'are very ill-bred and ill-tempered animals, who keep up a vociferous chorus until they are called off. It is an unpleasant experience for the victim, and it is a little difficult to remain in charity with all men when each day brings a shower of insults.'[179]

Yet the agitation was not without a heroic aspect. With the exception of the Bishop of Norwich, Bertram Pollock, not a single bishop joined Inge in his fearless support of Dr Barnes, whose faith in reconciling science and religion was as brave as it was divisive. Eager to persuade others of his opinion that rejection of scientific discovery would make it impossible for anyone except 'a dunce, a liar or a bigot' to remain a member of the Church of England, Inge implored his fellow Christians to renounce fanaticism, superstition and fundamentalism altogether. For those unwilling to share this progressive view, Inge was unsparing in his criticism – even of the most senior members of the Church. At the height of the Dr Barnes controversy he wrote in columns of the *Church of England Newspaper*, with unmistakable reference to Archbishop Davidson and his heir-presumptive, the Archbishop of York, Dr Cosmo Lang: 'My chival-rous feelings are revolted when I see archbishops and bishops joining a mob of guttersnipes in pelting one of their own order.'[180]

With no friends among the Chapter or the episcopate, Inge slowly began to wind down as Dean. Although he boasted of being 'in the prime of life' at seventy-four, it was resolved shortly after the Dr Barnes controversy that Deans should henceforth retire during their seventy-fifth year. The snub was transparent. Inge continued gloomily with his journalism until 1931, though he did not think it was of the same standard as before. He was perhaps too harsh a critic of himself. One of his last articles as Dean coined a memorable expression: 'All young people with soft hearts tend to be Socialists at 21; only those with soft heads are Socialists 20 years

later.' He was also invited to contribute to the BBC series 'What I
would do with the world' alongside H. G. Wells and an assortment
of other hypothetical dictators. In his 'queer, unpleasing' voice, the
Dean advocated the forcible disarmament of the Soviet Union,
the reduction of domestic taxation and the mandatory wearing of
an 'ignominious badge' by 'the idle rich, tramps and others of no
occupation'. Parliament he envisaged supplanted by an unelected
senate 'consisting mainly of elderly men who have served their
country with distinction'; prisons he would have abolished, preferring a more liberal employment of the death penalty, and gambling
he proposed to put down 'with a strong hand' – all before his 'assas-
sination, long overdue'.[181]

Rumours of his early resignation spread throughout the late '20s
and early '30s, not least because of the Dean's own indiscretions.
At a dinner party hosted by London University in the summer
of 1934, he neglected the presence of the owner of the *News of the
World*, Lord Riddell, when asking his companions to recommend
a suitable village in Oxfordshire for his retirement. As soon as he
reasonably could, complained Inge, the press lord 'hurried off to
the office of his disreputable rag' to file the story. The Dean was
disturbed by reporters all the following day. It took several weeks
of further speculation for Inge finally to announce his intention
to leave the Deanery slightly ahead of schedule. He and his wife
bought a large manor house in the village of Brightwell on the
border of Oxfordshire and Berkshire and looked ahead to 'a quiet
old age in real retirement'.[182]

His impending departure from the Deanery did not prevent
Inge from making the most of his remaining dining opportunities.

His diary for his final months in office bristles with entries such as the following:

> *October 18.* I preached at Bow Church for the Royal College of Physicians. My sermon pleased Lord Dawson and Lord Horder, who want it to be printed. I dined with the College, and spoke after Sir Austen Chamberlain, who was too long, and dull. The College has a wonderful collection of old printed books, including one or two Caxtons.
>
> *November 9.* Guildhall banquet. As it was my last appearance, I was heartily cheered as I walked up the room. Ramsay MacDonald talked for nearly forty-five minutes and bored everybody.
>
> *November 29.* Royal Society banquet. I sat between Lord Sumner and Sir Henry McGowan. An excellent dinner and pleasant company, but the speeches were dismally long and dreary. I murmured to my neighbour, *'Scientia longa, vita brevis'* ['knowledge is long, life is short'].[183]

On 23 September 1934, Inge preached his final sermon in the cathedral. Press photographers captured him, gaunt and expressionless, ascending the famous steps for the last time. In the newspapers there were numerous 'obituaries' dissecting his lengthy career. But Inge was uninterested in these. He recorded the official close of his working life abruptly: 'I went back into trousers.'[184]

જી

If Inge had intended retirement to signal the end of his active involvement in the world, he betrayed a profound misunderstanding of himself. He might have been an old man, but he remained remarkably fresh-looking and active. At the time of his appointment as Dean the Prime Minister's wife, Margot Asquith, had declared, 'When I saw his beautiful face I said, "I mean to have that man as my friend."' In his later years, Inge lost neither his youthful appearance nor his powerful intellect.[185]

His routine remained relentless. Each day he would rise before dawn, do some reading or writing, and then either catch the train to London or pay a visit to a neighbour. He and his wife were themselves prolific hosts, entertaining an average of a hundred guests a year in the first decade of their retirement. But there were occasional holidays, too. Since 1930 the pair had taken an annual Mediterranean cruise, during the course of which they had become friendly with the famous playwright George Bernard Shaw.

The friendship would be consummated by Shaw's decision in 1932 to create a character based upon the Dean. 'The Elder' in *Too True to be Good* was a brilliant and kindly caricature of the distinguished controversialist. Making use of Inge's angry lamentation that his eldest son had recently become a socialist, Shaw began the third act of the play with the Elder sitting amid the ruins of St Paul's cursing the world. 'My son,' he roars,

> whom I brought up to be an incorruptible God-fearing atheist, has become a thief and a scoundrel, and I can say nothing to him but, 'Go, boy: perish in your villainy; for neither your father nor anyone else can now give you a good reason for being a man of honour.'

Inge's real-life relationship with Craufurd was little better. With reference to his son's career in the petrol industry, Inge complained: 'He never reads my books, preferring very light literature, and I know nothing of oil, music or gardening.'[186]

One reason why Shaw may have taken so strongly to Inge was his unconcealed admiration for Kitty. When Shaw visited Lenin's mausoleum in 1938 he explained to her that the great revolutionary was 'a delicate blonde who might have been your twin'. It seems that the pair shared many a joke unobserved by her increasingly deaf and unperceptive husband. In a letter to Inge not long after the war, the playwright indicated a desire for him to pass on his salutations to Kitty 'as affectionate as she can stand'. Another time Shaw gifted Kitty a signed copy of his Inge-inspired play using a cautionary alias – 'the Tempter'.[187]

But adultery could never have defiled the Inge marital bed. Both the Dean and his wife had pronounced views on the subject. They regarded infidelity as a 'disease … almost as bad as "boozing"', which had been lamentably encouraged by profane modern literature. 'Those squalid tales', explained Inge, 'of adultery are not life in Paris or anywhere, except in a very narrow circle of what is called "the smart set".' To combat these developments, Inge frequently advocated the criminalisation of both 'trashy' novels and the elopements to which they supposedly gave rise. Those who persisted in committing adultery, he implored, should either be sent to prison or forbidden from ever remarrying.[188]

Such high-mindedness put Inge in a troublesome position with regard to King Edward VIII. When the former Dean heard rumours of this monarch's liaison with the American divorcee Mrs

Wallis Simpson towards the end of 1936, he wrote with alarm to Bishop Henson that 'the people will not stand this sort of thing in these days'. But Inge displayed his Victorian taboo of sex by refusing to make any public statement on the matter. At the height of the sensation he devoted his usually outspoken *Evening Standard* column to a medieval saint. A few months later he attempted to put off a hopeful biographer of the ex-king with the advice that he should attempt to pass discreetly over the matter of the abdication.[189]

Of greater importance to Inge in retirement was his ambition to revive his tarnished reputation as a scholar. This was largely motivated by his desire to overturn the popular jibe that he had begun his career as 'a pillar of the Church and ended it as two columns in the *Evening Standard*'. But the would-be masterpieces which fell from his desk in the years either side of his departure from St Paul's were not particularly well received. Both *God and the Astronomers* and an unpublished supplementary volume to his *Plotinus* seemed dated and overwrought. No one could have imagined that their author had once been a popular journalist. Nor could the public have anticipated that he was shortly to re-emerge as a major commentator on world affairs.

But he did. At the behest of Lord Beaverbrook, Inge resumed his *Evening Standard* column during the summer of 1935. He would continue it intermittently until his ninety-second year. Unlike his earlier articles, which focused mainly on domestic and political issues, these contributions were remarkably wide-ranging. This was hardly surprising. The world had changed a great deal since the inward-looking days of the 1920s: Hitler had come to power. And Inge, described by Bernard Shaw as 'the last Whig', was well-placed to speak out against those wishing to see Britain allied with France against a resurgent Germany. Lifelong pacifist and Francophobe that he was, he became one of the chief spokesmen of Lord Beaverbrook's policy of appeasement and isolationism. Although this resulted in Inge later being denounced as one of the so-called 'Guilty Men', responsible for encouraging Hitler, his views had probably never chimed so much with public opinion.

The former Dean's first article on Nazism appeared in July 1935. It was a startlingly wise and far-sighted delineation of the ideology. Featured in a series entitled 'Substitutes for Religion', Inge explained that Nazism was no more than a 'cult of hatred'. While he could marvel at Hitler's ability to dissolve every trade union in Germany in a single day, he found it impossible to subscribe to the regime's 'absurd' theories on race. Nor could he admire the stifling of intellectual freedom. 'I am neither pro-German nor anti-German,' he declared. 'I like fair play and decent generosity.' He recognised that neither could thrive beneath the Nazi jackboot.[190]

It was typical of Inge to hold the victorious Allies of the last war largely responsible for the rise of Hitler. The gross triumphalism of the Treaty of Versailles, as he regarded it, had been a gift to exactly those elements which were now in power. Yet in his attempt to make the public comprehend the evil of Nazism, Inge could be remarkably tactless. His association with *The Church of England Newspaper* came to an abrupt end when he submitted an article in 1944 describing Martin Luther 'as the spiritual father of Nazism'. On other occasions he went so far as to compare the German leaders to Jesuits or – more chillingly – Jews. Some critics, remembering a sermon he had once preached contrasting the 'higher' patriotism of the English with the 'lower' patriotism of Judaism, began to wonder if the former Dean might not himself be an anti-Semite.[191]

The Board of Deputies of British Jews did not count itself among these accusers. In response to a letter complaining that the 'doddering old fool' was going about the country accusing the Jews of plotting the Russian Revolution and repeating similar atrocities in Britain, the chairman recalled the Dean's good services in years past. As well as publishing what he called a 'devastating' review of Hilaire Belloc's anti-Semitic diatribe *The Jews* (1922), which the Board had distributed in pamphlet form, Inge had also used one of his last sermons as Dean to denounce Nazi persecution. 'It is rather distressing', he told his congregation in 1933,

> that the Jewish nation, a nation which has done so much for the world, should even now be hated and persecuted. Why the new German government should behave in that strange manner I cannot even guess. It is foolish as well as wrong, for the Jews have stood by the graves of all their oppressors in turn.[192]

Later the former Dean expressed amazement that the citizens of Austria could 'stand by and witness such disgraceful treatment of their peaceful neighbours, with some of whom they must have been on friendly terms'. His objection to taking up arms to put an end to the 'disgusting' persecution stemmed from his engrained suspicion of 'indignation … worked up for political reasons'. He preferred to assume that the German people would see reason for themselves.[193]

This muted toleration of Nazism was based neither on anti-Semitism nor cowardice. Like his favourite modern-day politician, Neville Chamberlain, Inge simply did not find it credible that, so soon after the horror of the First World War, the rulers of Europe could again plunge the continent into catastrophe. 'Is there any Frenchman or German outside a lunatic asylum', he asked his readers in October 1936, 'who seriously wishes to exterminate the population of Berlin or Paris, and reduce those great cities to ashes, apart from the high probability that his own capital would share the same fate? I cannot believe it.'[194]

A major source of derision for Inge throughout these years was the League of Nations. 'It is useless', he memorably quipped, 'for the sheep to pass resolutions in favour of vegetarianism while the wolf remains of a different opinion.' He felt his pessimism to have been vindicated when the League stood helplessly by as Mussolini pillaged Abyssinia – a travesty he denounced in his weekly column as 'the blackest outrage in our time'. The League had been 'murdered'. 'Never again', the veteran commentator lamented, 'will a weak nation feel the slightest confidence that by belonging to [the League] it will be protected against wanton aggression.'[195]

There was, however, a great difference between this position and the stance of those who advocated the deployment of British troops to protect the faraway peoples of Europe. After the Munich peace summit, at which Chamberlain had wrung a promise from Hitler that Bohemia would be his last territorial acquisition in Europe, Inge joined the chorus of praise for the triumphant premier. In an article entitled 'Face the Facts' he observed that Britain was not ready or willing to make an enemy of the most belligerent country in Europe. 'We escaped by the skin of our teeth', he wrote, 'from a disaster which might have wrecked European civilisation for a hundred years, and which would probably have ended finally the position of this country as one of the great powers.' 'No one would have known what we were fighting for,' he contended, 'and in spite of patriotic assertions to the contrary, nine out of ten Englishmen were strongly opposed to war.'[196]

It took courage to persist in this view once war was declared in September 1939. Inge was allowed to carry on with his column for a time, but it was clear that his new editor, the future Labour leader and co-author of *Guilty Men*, Michael Foot, was no friend. Along with Beaverbrook, who soon joined Churchill's War Cabinet, Foot threw the weight of the paper vigorously behind the government. Only Inge held out in lonely isolation. He regarded Churchill as a heavy drinker, a 'war-monger' and a 'squandermaniac' who would ultimately preside over the ruin of the country. When Inge expressed some of these contrarian views in a collection of his *Evening Standard* articles entitled *A Pacifist in Trouble* at the end of 1939, he was excoriated as a defeatist and a traitor. Foot later suppressed his contributions and ultimately enforced a lengthy sabbatical upon his unlamented columnist.[197]

Inge did not entirely regret this. He was not proud to be of the opinion that Britain could not win the war after the intensification of the German offensive in June 1941. Nor did he wish to publicise his view that Britain had 'played into the hands of a greater blackguard than Hitler' – Stalin. In one of his last public comments on the crisis, made in response to a fierce denunciation of his ideas by Field Marshal Lord Milne, Inge argued that Britain 'would have done the same' as Germany had the Kaiser won the last war and 'stripped us of our colonies and given Ulster, half of Lancashire (including Liverpool) to [the Irish leader Éamon] De Valera'.[198]

Few readers were persuaded. Aware of his growing pariah status, Inge, as in his university days, resolved to confide his worries to his diary. At the outset of 1940 he began yet another volume of that tortured narrative in the mood of a weary and melancholy man:

> So begins what I sometimes hope will be my last year on earth, for the England into which I was born, in which I have lived and which I have loved, is mortally wounded by the folly of our politicians and by the crimes of foreign nations. I think this war will end in the destruction of the British Empire; it will certainly end our position as a World Power, and ruin all who have anything to lose. I seem to be entirely out of touch with the younger generation, who, like our [son] Edward, are enlisting joyfully in this suicidal struggle, and are apparently indifferent to the financial ruin which will engulf all the upper and middle class. I can see no ray of hope anywhere.[199]

Later the same year he wrote: 'May God help me, during the short and sad closing days of my long life, to set my affections on things above, and not to think too much of the ruin of earthly hopes. Our countrymen are not degenerate, and most of them are still full of high spirits.'[200]

In April 1941 the Inges learnt that their son Richard had been killed in a training accident. 'He and Paula were the most purely good and sweet characters I have ever known,' he wrote. 'The devil seemed to have forgotten them.' He and his wife went into an extended period of mourning, rarely venturing out of Brightwell until the end of the conflict.

After the war, Inge made noticeably few public utterances. But he did cause one final controversy. It resulted from an article he had written on the Nuremberg Trials in his resumed *Evening Standard* column. Under the heading 'Should We Hang Them?', Inge boldly suggested that the Allies were setting an undesirable precedent in executing the Nazi leaders, especially when it was remembered that an American atomic bomb had recently killed over one hundred thousand residents of the cities of Hiroshima and Nagasaki. 'I hope that I shall not be accused of being a pro-Nazi or a Fascist', ventured Inge, 'when I suggest that the tribunal should issue a calm and well-documented statement of their crimes, and should then let them go with the brand of Cain on their foreheads. Perhaps the Jew-Baiter [Julius Streicher] and one or two others should be executed but not the majority.' Inge called for a 'general amnesty', believing the most effective way of rebuilding Germany would be to allow certain patriotic though misguided Nazis to reintegrate into civil society.[201]

Although this view was shared by many enlightened contemporaries, including the respected military historian Captain Sir Basil Liddell Hart, the former Cabinet Secretary Lord Hankey, and General Smuts of South Africa, Inge was roundly condemned by public opinion. The charge against him was led by the populist 'Red Dean' of Canterbury, Dr Hewlett Johnson, who thundered in a special article for the *Evening Standard*: 'What sentimentality, what class bias, or what inadequate sense of justice, begs a reprieve for those who stand at the apex of all human crime?' [202]

Inge only gave brief mention to this 'little commotion' in his diary. But a few days later the 86-year-old continued: 'In fact I think I have been sacked.'[203]

When Kitty died in 1949, Inge felt he had little left to live for. The future seemed bleaker than ever; but he was not without a grain of optimism. He envisaged that small, self-supporting communities would soon be established all over Britain in order to 'keep the torch of learning, science and art burning through the age of vulgarity which ... is coming upon us'. During the war he had corresponded with the ex-Kaiser about the tragedy of Europe's ruin at the hands of demagogues and fanatics, and he remained an occasional addition to the 'new releases' announced by booksellers; as late as his ninety-third year he penned a new introduction to *England* which had all the energy and flair of his younger self. The titles of his later works were, however, suggestive of his increasingly resigned outlook: *A Rustic Moralist* (1937), *The Fall of the Idols* (1940) and *The End of an Age* (1948). He felt that his 'hand had lost its cunning', and the sales of these last books did not rival the phenomenal success enjoyed by younger rivals such as the lay theologian C. S. Lewis, whom Inge bracketed with his lifelong adversary G. K. Chesterton as 'overrated' and 'not worth reading'.[204]

For a further five years Inge continued, as he put it, 'cumbering the ground' – reading, thinking and tending to his apple trees. When asked, on the occasion of his ninetieth birthday, what hopes he held for the future, he predicted that civilisation was approaching 'another Dark Age' – and then he chuckled to himself. Four years later, still mentally active and physically fit, the grand old man, unhappy and alone, died at Brightwell. His last recorded words were

characteristic: 'I have no vision of "heaven" or a "welcoming God".
I do not know what I shall find … I do not love the human race.
I have loved just a few of them. The rest are a pretty mixed lot.'[205]

⁓

Few lamented the passing of what one newspaper tactfully called
'the last of the Victorians' – an unenviable distinction in the eyes
of many residents of post-war Britain. A new world had already
come into being. It had no place for the likes of Dean Inge. But the
eminent old clergyman had achieved something far greater than
mere popularity – honour. In a leading article in *The Times* he was
favourably compared to his most famous predecessor at St Paul's,
John Donne, as a man whose personality had 'projected on a wider
than an exclusively ecclesiastical screen'. While the editor acknowledged the Dean's tendency towards exaggeration and paradox, he
conceded that it would be 'wrong to dismiss him as a Blimp in a
dog collar'. For Inge was not merely the bane of reformers and
'wounded progressives': he was also, on occasion, the scourge of
conservatives and reactionaries as well.[206]

Inge's actual contemporaries, nearly all of whom were long dead,
had already passed their dissenting judgements. Bishop Henson,
writing in 1939, thought him to have possessed 'an odd mixture of
real greatness and … perverse wrongheadedness'. He vehemently
disapproved of his friendship with the likes of George Bernard
Shaw, and could not accept the famous playwright's verdict that he
was 'the greatest intellectual asset of the Church of England'. Still
less so could the late editor of the *Church Times*, Sidney Dark, who

denounced his still-living adversary in 1941 as 'the most mischievous enemy of true religion of his generation'.[207]

Such views have since become part of received wisdom. In an authoritative study of English Christianity published in 1985 Inge is curtly dismissed as 'an immensely self-satisfied column writer ... exemplific [sic] of almost all the defects from which the Church of England was then suffering'. 'Despite his great cleverness', the book's author concludes, '[he] was plainly rather silly ... [he] belonged to no school and was at the end of the day merely one man who gained a temporary notoriety and was then quickly forgotten.'[208]

No one could entirely dispute this. But the backlash against Inge has been just as exaggerated as his own miscalculations. He may have been an extremely difficult colleague, a stunningly insensitive commentator, an egomaniac and a fanatical anti-Communist, but he was more than merely a freak or a showman. If he belonged to a privileged elite, disdainful of populism and democracy alike, at least he had the courage to say so. 'Floating with the stream', he was fond of saying of his more mercurial contemporaries, 'is a feat which any dead dog can accomplish.' No one ever accused Inge of that.[209]

In an era of resurgent fanaticism, in which radicalism and populism are often mistaken for religious conviction, the world needs more rationalist clerics like Dean Inge. Whatever his imperfections, he never failed to make the public think. And while so many of his contemporaries attempted to play politics with religion, Inge never claimed to speak on behalf of the Deity. His hatred of the twentieth century, cold and superior though it was, had its roots in a genuine love of his country and a desire to repopulate it with the large, well-educated families of his youth. As his modern reap-praiser A. N. Wilson has observed, 'He could have no conception, even dying in 1954, of the degradation and ruination which was to come upon England in the latter half of the twentieth century: a degradation which is partly due to the fact that cultivated, civilised people are in an ever decreasing minority in our world.'[210]

Today his cathedral is more a museum than a church. Worshippers struggle to appreciate the majesty of their surroundings, the quality of the preaching, or even the beauty of the music amid the droves of ogling, baseball-capped tourists, who often make up the bulk of the transitory congregation. Only the death of a major public figure or – at the other extreme – a chaotic vigil by leisured protesters, briefly regains the cathedral its former prominence. Set in a sea of Babylonian towers, Wren's great church can barely even be considered a major landmark. Deans have not lived in the valu-able Old Deanery for well over forty years.

Although something of a precursor of Thatcherism, Inge would have regretted these symptoms of the liberal economic revolution of the later twentieth century. He represented a bygone Toryism which placed its faith not only in profits and the free market, but also in culture, patriotism and spiritualism. His chief failure was to believe that the Church of England – or Christianity in general – could purge itself of 'superstition' without alienating the majority of its less intellectually inclined devotees.

Aside from a modest plaque at the east end of the crypt and a small bust in the cathedral library, there are no monuments to Dean Inge. But he would have been silently amused by a back-handed compliment paid to him by his immediate successor at the Deanery, Dr W. R. Matthews. Travelling by bus up Ludgate Hill one afternoon during the early 1960s, this affable clergyman found himself in conversation with an elderly gentleman. 'Ah,' the stranger declared,

'there's St Paul's. What's happened to old Inge?'

'I'm afraid he's dead,' I answered.

'Poor old Inge', he said, 'used to write some spicy articles in the *Evening Standard*: every Thursday, I think. Who's there now?'

'A fellow named Matthews, I think,' I replied.

'Ah, don't hear much about him, do we?' he said.

'No', I answered. 'Rather a dim type if you ask me'.

This 'remarkable and enigmatic' figure disembarked at the next stop leaving the Dean to his reflections. 'They were humiliating,' he wrote. 'Here have I been Dean of St Paul's for nearly thirty years, writing and speaking all the time, and there are intelligent people who are under the impression that Dr Inge had no successor.'[211]

What finer monument could the Gloomy Dean have wished for?

CHAPTER 3

LORD PROTECTOR OF THE AIRWAVES: THE PARALLEL LIVES OF LORD REITH OF STONEHAVEN

Where I am not, nothing but folly is committed.
– Napoleon

Young Dawn Mackay returned home from a dance in the summer of 1961 to the sound of the telephone ringing. As it was two o'clock in the morning, there was no doubt of the caller's identity. It was her 'godfather', the first Director General of the BBC and acclaimed pioneer of British broadcasting, Lord Reith of Stonehaven. The great man was feeling down. His life, he angrily explained, had been a failure. His talents had been wasted; his dreams unrealised. Even God had in the end forsaken him. With unconvincing finality he declared that he had no option left but to end it all by means of the loaded revolver he clasped in his bony spare hand. After standing two hours of this dreary monologue, the young woman broke in: 'Well, if that's what you want to do, it's perfectly easy – just pull the trigger.' There followed a deafening crash and then nothing but the sound of the night. His lordship had thrown both gun and receiver to the ground and stalked off to his bedroom.[212]

No single event so perfectly captures the restless, selfish and intolerably ambitious spirit that was Reith of the BBC. For all his

remarkable accomplishments, this giant both in stature and reputation shared many of the characteristics of a spoilt child.

It was the only flaw in his personality that Reith ever acknowledged. 'I am an odd fellow,' he once admitted to himself. 'There are
some respects in which I haven't grown up.' The self-analysis was
uncharacteristically sound. The keeper of a secret 'hate list' and a
bully in the eyes of many an employee and family member, Reith
appeared to have progressed from the nursery to the summit of
worldly power without ever thinking to reform his behaviour. As
his daughter Marista gently put it: he seemed 'as if he had had bad
news in 1889 and had not got over it'.[213]

John Charles Walsham Reith was born prematurely on 20 July
of that year in the Kincardineshire resort of Stonehaven, where his
parents were taking a short seaside holiday. The youngest of the
family by almost ten years, the infant entered the world with a
vague sense that he was predestined to be forever alone. His 47-year-
old father, Dr George Reith, Presbyterian minister of the College
Church, Glasgow, would add to this childhood superstition a belief
that his soul might also be marked out for eternal damnation. Both
Dr Reith and his already middle-aged wife, Adah – the daughter of
a ruined London stockbroker – took a highly serious view of life,
ostentatiously shunning the pleasures of the world and imploring
their seven children to do likewise.

Reith was not particularly close to any of his siblings. 'I did not
get on with my brothers and sisters', he told one friend, 'and two or
three of them I deeply disliked.' All members of the family shared a
remarkable tendency to irritability, preferring to devote themselves
to earnest prayer and study in their respective bedrooms rather than

partaking in a convivial family life. The eldest, Archie, broke away from their father's unbending Presbyterianism by being ordained as a clergyman of the Church of England. Ernest, meanwhile, went insane in his early thirties and was little heard of again. Reith was always haunted by the tragic memory of the day the men from the Crichton Institute arrived at the manse to take him away. 'This evening was a terrible experience,' he wrote of the event in his diary.

> Of course he did not want to go and wanted me to help him to keep the men off. I went to see him off at the station. I had almost given him a chance of getting off down my fire escape earlier in the evening, but I knew that it was my duty to resist natural inclinations.[214]

The trauma deeply affected the future Lord Reith, at the time a man in his early twenties; but he seldom referred to the incident again. Like so many difficult aspects of his youth and adolescence, he chose simply to ignore it. Ernest barely saw his father and mother thereafter, and was not mentioned by name in either of his youngest brother's narcissistic two volumes of autobiography.

Accepted family members fared little better. Of his sisters, Reith admitted to having a close affinity with Beta, who left the manse when he was eight to become a nurse in Edinburgh. The only member of the family still living at home after that time was his nearest sister, Jean, whose permanently locked door was believed to represent an intense loathing for her youngest sibling. Another one of the brothers, Robert, an engineer on Clydeside, proved to be more accommodating. As well as encouraging John to exercise greater organisation and academic discipline, he gave the impressionable boy a glimpse of a flashier world. 'I admired his style of living,' he recalled years after, 'hansom cabs, first-class travelling and so forth.' Yet Reith's only real friend among his brothers and sisters was his nearest in age, Douglas, who went on to become a missionary in India. 'He was serious and pious,' recalled Reith, 'but was decent to me, and however little he may have known of the world, tried to help.'[215]

With the exception of Archie, the family belonged to the Free Church of Scotland, whose dour adherents spoke fondly of the great 'Disruption' of 1843 as though it were a recent occurrence. It was this event which had unshackled them from the more latitudinarian Presbyterians of the Church of Scotland, who had conceded the right of the state to appoint certain ministers. Dr Reith and his brethren had to pay a heavy penalty for their forebears' conviction that earthly governments should exercise no authority over spiritual affairs. In a well-orchestrated act of defiance, over two thousand of them had walked out of their manses to set up their own Church, entirely controlled – at least in theory – by their congregations. Ministers had to be provided with homes and stipends, sometimes taking to dank rooms above noisy pubs in place of their confiscated churches. These fervent Puritans were said to be the nineteenth century's equivalent of the rabidly anti-Catholic Covenanters of the seventeenth – and the comparison was supposed to be flattering.[216]

From an early age Reith was in awe of his father. He was 'the last of his caste', a man of unquestioned virtue and scruple who found ready comparison in the person of Moses. 'In magnificence of presence I have not met his equal,' recorded his son. 'His countenance in repose was austere, but his ready smile [was] not just benign – itself a benediction.' A graduate of the Free Church's prestigious New

College in Edinburgh, Dr Reith was a highly cultivated individual, lecturing from time to time on themes as weighty as Savonarola, Leonardo da Vinci, Michelangelo and John Ruskin. His eminence as a theologian was equally assured, though his views often brought him into conflict with his Free Church confreres. An argument with the New College's disagreeable principal, Dr Robert Rainy, over the possibility of rejoining the Church of Scotland – provided certain terms were agreed to – gave rise to much acrimony. Dr Reith believed that the Church of Scotland need not be financially independent of the state in order to be spiritually free; a doctrine known as 'antidisestablishmentarianism'. An unpopular standpoint in the eyes of most Presbyterians, this prevented Dr Reith from obtaining high office in the Free Church until the last years of his life, when he was, at the age of seventy-three, appointed Moderator of the United Free Church Assembly in 1915. Had he lived a further decade he would have seen his dream of an independent state church partially realised by the reunion of the Free Church and the Church of Scotland in 1929.[217]

Although Dr Reith was not a wealthy man, his congregation included some of the richest men in Glasgow. Merchants, bankers and the great industrialists of the city all thronged to hear him. It is hard to say whether this or his father's preaching had a greater impact on his youngest son. Distinguishable from his elder siblings by the derisive nickname 'Lord Walsham', John adopted a grand manner almost before he could talk. His first recorded act was to command his nurse to pick some flowers for him on the grounds that he was too large to stoop down himself. Shortly afterwards he amazed a distinguished friend of his father's by casually instructing him to make payment for an iced bun he had purloined from a shop they had visited together.

Few of Dr Reith's sermons have survived, but it is clear that a favourite theme was the story of Samson. The tale of this Hebrew titan reduced to slavery in punishment for his fatal attraction to the Philistine Delilah would be of lifelong interest to John Reith. 'He is a child of many prayers', the minister intoned one Sabbath,

> whose godly parents received him as a special gift from God's hand, who, before his birth, was consecrated to His service. Yet he ends his restless and troubled life in a Philistine prison, a wreck, his eyes put out, chained to the handle of a millstone, and grinding corn for his enemies.[218]

Like Samson, it was not long until Reith also found himself at odds with his parents. Unaccompanied for long stretches of the day while they attended to various good works, the lonely child began to show signs of dissatisfaction. 'I had a violent temper', he later admitted, 'and was disrespectful to my father and mother.' Most painful of all was the emotional detachment which slowly began to develop between himself and his mother, who accorded her youngest child only one hour a week of personal contact. In adulthood Reith would recall this precious Sunday visit 'with gratitude and emotion', regretting that his mother had been too preoccupied with the 'alien, manifold and exacting duties of the lady of a Scottish manse' to attend more fully to his needs. Although Adah succeeded in teaching John the hymns and Psalms which were to prove such a solace in his maturity, her main focus came to be the work of the

Glasgow Kyrle Society, which sought to improve the spiritual and material life of the poorest residents of the city. It was occasionally remarked that her famous son's much-vaunted Christian values never inspired him to help the disadvantaged in this way. 'I am a poor practitioner,' he was wont to mutter in riposte.[219]

The Reiths' concern for their youngest child grew in the years after he began attending the famous Glasgow Academy in 1896. Following four ambitious brothers, all of whom had excelled both academically and on the games fields, was never going to be easy, but John's failure to achieve even a modicum of success at the school was mostly down to his own indolence. He was, by his own admission, 'undistinguished, unsatisfactory', yet still felt 'a kind of intellectual superiority over others'. His father in particular implored him to mend his ways. 'You are growing to be a big boy now', he wrote on the occasion of the child's ninth birthday, 'and will need to gather sense and wisdom, patience and self-restraint.' But the boy remained 'a problem'. After two classmates were found to have absconded on account of his bullying, the Reiths were asked to remove the fifteen-year-old from the school. Dr Reith was furious. It seemed, he thundered, as if John 'would have to live on a desert island'. One brother unkindly suggested packing him off for a career in the Merchant Navy.[220]

Reith was instead sent away to Gresham's School, a small English public school near the Norfolk parish of his eldest brother, Archie. It was here that the future Lord Reith had his first taste of 'the establishment': that warm coterie of wealthy and well-educated men to whom he was to be so inexorably drawn. Whatever his later predilections, however, it could not be said that he took to it with ease.

Gresham's was, after all, a strange choice for his parents to have made. Being the only Scot and, worse, only Presbyterian in the school – and a late-comer at that – he was instantly cast in the role of misfit. Reith did not make his life any easier by, as he grandly explained, subjecting 'the ordered procedure of this establishment … to some strain'. With 'unprecedented effrontery' he dared 'question and resist' some of his elders' 'principles of management'. This rapidly brought him into conflict with the school's belligerent Victorian headmaster, G. W. S. Howson, whose dislike Reith 'cordially reciprocated'. 'I was entirely moral,' he elucidated, 'but otherwise vexatious and difficult.' During his second term he attempted escape by bicycling to his brother's vicarage, but was soon recaptured and given one of his intermittent childhood beatings.[221]

Towards the end of his fourth term at the school a small but important transformation occurred. Having made his peace with Howson, Reith won the school German prize and laid the foundations of a lifetime's love of classical tags by receiving a commendation for his attempts at Latin prose. In extra-curricular activities he went further, winning promotion to the rank of sergeant in the school Rifle Corps. Reith's impressive 'word of command' was similarly attested on the rugby field, where he achieved the crowning glory of any public school career by being selected for the First XV. He played a season at fullback, where his towering height (eventually to reach 6ft 6in.) assisted him in guarding the Gresham's try-line with courage and distinction.

For all his accomplishments, however, Reith remained essentially a loner. Years later he would recall walking across the moors at Bisley during an inter-school shooting competition wishing he had someone to accompany him. 'Always this longing for a real friend,' he painfully recollected. Thankfully he soon found one. Like so many of his companions in later life, this ally was considerably junior to himself and something of a hero-worshipper. He was called John Valentine Betts; 'an exceedingly good-looking boy', thought Reith, 'as much my inferior mentally as he was my superior at games'. As Betts also happened to be one of the most popular boys in their house, Reith was surprised that he wished to spend so much time with him. 'Strange to say,' he continued in reverie, 'the more fond he grew of me the less fond I grew of him.' They occupied beds next to each other for two terms and would talk quietly to all hours of the night.[222]

These earnest dormitory conversations inevitably touched upon what was to happen after Gresham's. Reith was already adamant that an Oxbridge career beckoned – 'classics, philosophy, physics, literature, history – almost anything', he wistfully recalled. But it was not to be. At the end of his second year at the school, the seventeen-year-old had the greatest shock of his life so far. He was not going up to Oxford or Cambridge – he was not even going to be rejoining Betts. For on the first day of his summer holiday in 1906 his father called him into his study 'for a talk'. This never boded well, but he was completely unprepared for what was to follow. The minister handed him a slip of paper. It was a report delivered to him by Mr Howson. 'You will not be continuing your studies,' the old man unexpectedly announced. 'That is perfectly clear.' There had been no 'special signs of scholarship', and any further outlay on his education would simply be a waste. He must begin a career at once, as an engineer.[223]

Reith's Wagnerian sense of drama would lead him in later years to confuse where exactly he passed the remainder of that gloomy summer. He claimed that he had been 'roaming the Rothiemurchus forest and climbing the Cairngorm mountains', but his father's notebook reveals the prosaic fact that the family holidayed at the small east-coast golfing resort of Carnoustie that year. No matter. Wherever he was, Reith was straining his ears just in case 'the wind had a message for me from the everlasting hills'. There was no doubt as to its purport: the young Napoleon had a feeling that he 'was not meant to be a mediocrity; the beginning of a determination not to be a mediocrity'.[224]

એ

Draped in a fine Savile Row suit, usually within striking distance of a chauffeur-driven limousine, Lord Reith of Stonehaven was fond of observing that his life had not always been so comfortable. Like his hero John Knox, who claimed to have spent two years as a galley-slave before spearheading the Scottish Reformation, he had undergone his fair share of drudgery. The comparison, however, was perhaps better than Reith intended: for there is as little evidence that he disliked his years of apprenticeship as there is of the great reformer ever handling an oar aboard a slave ship.

The reason was not simply that Reith found the 57-hour weeks and 4.45 a.m. starts invigorating; he was also discovering what it was to be in love. His first romantic stirrings had taken place at few years earlier, while still at Gresham's, when he had flirted naively with the sisters of two of his young companions. These experiences continued in the years after leaving school by means of occasional visits south of the border. On one of these expeditions John Betts asked his sister to run her hands through Reith's hair, as he was known to be partial to this form of petting. Another sisterly friend named Dora Hanmer was likewise invited to satiate the curious Scotsman's thirst for demonstrative affection. In both cases, Reith haltingly asked to give the girls a kiss, which he proceeded to dispense 'very awkwardly', and always on the cheek.[225]

These were by no means the only girls to enliven Reith's dreary solitude. A lifetime later he paid a researcher to track some of them down so that he could discover what they had made of him. One, a former member of his father's congregation, recalled him being 'very autocratic', always speaking of 'how he was going to make his mark in the world'. Dora Hanmer was even more perceptive. She thought him 'very intense, very proud and very sensitive – but determined not to show it'. None of these women, however, dared admit that his real interest was not in them, but in their rosy-cheeked brothers.[226]

For Reith's sexual preferences were by this time decidedly homosexual. Though fond of having 'some pretty girl to keep me company', he had no interest in women beyond that. 'She might have been a boy,' he privately wrote of kissing young Miss Hanmer. 'I was of course as normal as anyone else,' he quickly went on, 'but was as completely repressed as to be almost unconscious of this side of things.'[227]

Life as an apprentice engineer at least kept his mind fully occupied. Owing to the intervention of the family doctor, Reith spent the first two years of his apprenticeship studying the theoretical side of engineering at the Glasgow Mechanical College. This he described as 'something of a nightmare', but he managed in the end to average 90 per cent in his examinations, if only to please his father. Then he started work. For six years he assisted in the manufacture of steam engines in the Hydepark Works of the North British Locomotive Company in the grim east end of the city. His diligence and expertise in carrying out his duties were attested by both the general manager and the foreman at the works, but it is unlikely that the stony-faced youth was much loved by any of the factory hands. In this heartland of the burgeoning Labour move-ment, he was brave enough to 'argue a great deal against socialism'. Reith was accordingly delighted to be told by his bosses that he was 'one of the best apprentices they had ever had through the shops'.[228]

That the young man took himself excessively seriously was by now obvious to all with whom he came into contact. But Reith left ample evidence of his high self-regard in the diary he soon began to keep. The inscription on the cover alone, carefully written in his neat cursive hand, gives the strongest possible indication of the great happenings which he so confidently expected to punctuate his life. 'My Diary', it roundly states, 'being a Chronicle of the Doings both in Public and Private of J. C. W. Reith, Likewise a Survey of his Thoughts Expressed or Otherwise, and a Record of his Transactions with Others'. By the end of his life it would run to nearly five million words; but the tone and tacit assumption of his own importance was consistent throughout.

Easily the most frequent name mentioned in the early volumes of the diary was a Glasgow neighbour eight years Reith's junior by the name of Charlie Bowser. For almost ten years, from the age of twenty-two to thirty-one, Reith made this plucky schoolboy the object of his near-total devotion. The pair had been aware of each other's existence for some years, but they did not have a conversation together until the summer of 1912, when Charlie came for a soft drink in the manse garden. 'Very good looking and awfully pretty eyes', recorded Reith of the fourteen-year-old. They were soon going away on holidays together, carving their names into trees and benches, sharing beds and even hot baths. Their companionship was not approved of by either set of parents, and Reith himself inwardly regretful of the whole business. 'I wish to goodness that I did not like that boy so much,' he wrote in his diary. 'I am frightfully fond of him – it is of course quite ridiculous.'229

What most attracted Reith to Charlie was the complete control which he could exercise over him; not only physically and emotionally, but also in terms of shaping his ideas. Reith had for some time been turning his mind to political problems, and he made a habit of instructing his young friend to note down some of his *bon mots* from time to time. 'Never forget', he observed on one occasion, 'that by birth and education and upbringing you are a gentleman with duties and responsibilities … among them to withstand the democratic trend of modern nations … in order to keep the reins of control in the hands of those most fitted to hold them.' What young Bowser made of these mysterious utterances is unknowable, but his love of Reith was clear. He was flattered to be shown around the Hydepark works by one of its most outstanding apprentices, and he did not mind putting his arms around his much older friend, or even kissing him, in public when their parents were not looking. Reith's disapproving brother Douglas admitted that he

was 'impressed' by this spectacle, though privately found the situation more than slightly odd.[230]

Happily for Reith's sense of decorum he was usually too busy
to spend more than a short amount of time with Bowser. As well
as keeping up the severe hours at the works, he also found time to
parade three evenings a week, summer and winter, as a member
of the Glasgow University company of the 1st Lanarkshire Rifle
Volunteers, soon to be absorbed by Lord Haldane's new Officer
Training Corps. This entailed yet more exams, but Reith again
did extremely well, being among the first three volunteers to be
promoted to the rank of sergeant. 'I was enormously proud of the
resultant gold star over my sergeant's stripes,' he later gloated. 'It
was magnificent,' he needlessly added in emphasis, 'it gave me an
opinion of myself; I had achieved something in the world.' He
received several offers to take up a regular commission, but said
he wanted a higher-status position than that of mere foot-soldier.
Accordingly, in 1912, he was commissioned to a territorial battalion
of the Scottish Rifles, allowing him to remain in full-time civilian employment. Reith, however, remained exceedingly jealous of
the cavalry officers he saw strutting around in their spurs. 'They
clinked,' he later told Malcolm Muggeridge. 'I wanted to clink.'[231]

Reith was not a man to allow a minor impediment such as not
being able to ride a horse stand in the way of this ambition. During
a field exercise shortly after taking his commission, a brigade major
casually enquired if any of the men were able to ride; he needed to
return a horse to the brigadier. 'Reith can,' someone yelled. Most
young officers would have respectfully corrected this misstatement,
but John Reith was never ordinary. At the double he proceeded to

mount the horse 'professionally', being careful to check the stirrup lengths, just as he had seen the cavalry men do. 'To my much relief,' the hero recalled, 'the direction taken by the mare was in accordance with requirements.' But as soon as he was out of sight of his companions the beast resolved to make its way back to the camp, three miles from the rendezvous with the brigadier. Thankfully for Reith nothing more was said of this incident; his reputation as a horseman survived intact. Soon he began taking riding lessons.[232]

It would not be until he was mobilised in 1914, however, that Reith got to wear those clinking spurs. For the meantime he made do with the dress of a regular infantry officer. His wounded pride was in part compensated by an 'unsolicited testimonial' – the first of many such encomiums – he received from his fellow cadets at the end of their training. It would rank among his most prized possessions. 'This is to certify', it ran,

that we, the undersigned, after full and careful consideration and many opportunities of observation, have come to the conclusion that Sergeant John Charles Walsham Reith, a Section Commander of Section Four, A Company, Glasgow University Contingent, Officers' Training Corps, is not only the most efficient Sergeant in the aforesaid Corps, but also the only Sergeant in the Corps with the smallest right to pretensions of honour, manliness or good-fellowship. We furthermore decided to give to him this testimonial of our unqualified respect and esteem. We should go further but our pen is done.[233]

It says much of Reith's exalted view of himself and blindness to criticism that he never suspected that this testimonial was intended as a joke. To those who solemnly handed it to him, however, this only made the game more amusing. As one of them later explained, 'When he told me that before going to the [Glasgow] Academy he'd been sent to Park Preparatory School, a select institution for small girls, I felt I understood him better.' Privately, many of the cadets regarded him as a prima donna and a 'crashing bore'.[234]

Yet no one could deny that by the beginning of 1913 Reith had become a man of substance in Glasgow. He had a good job, a commission in the Scots Rifles and a string of chaste female admirers lining up outside the manse. It shows the strength of his feelings for sixteen-year-old Charlie Bowser that he was willing to throw all this away simply to remain close to him. For in the summer of that year the Bowsers moved to London, and Reith decided that he would relocate to the same city. This news did not go down well with his father. 'You'll be back with your tail between your legs,' he grimly forecast. No one could understand why he should take such a crazy risk with his future for a lad of sixteen.[235]

But Reith never worried about finding a job. With the aid of some friendly letters of introduction, he was soon engaged by one of the largest engineering firms in Britain, Pearsons, for whom he helped oversee an extension to the Royal Albert Dock in Woolwich. He found the work agreeable, but was less happy about his new living arrangements. He lodged for a time in Forest Gate with the chief mechanical engineer at the Dock – 'a very feeble specimen' – whose live-in fiancée gave the young Puritan his first taste of the New Woman. 'I found', he wrote home in disgust, 'that she is not a teetotaller, smokes in public, doesn't go to church, is a rampant suffragette – wishes she were a man, and so on.' 'In about ten words' he explained what he thought of such 'beastly' women and never deigned to speak to her again.[236]

Problems of a more intractable nature were also developing with Charlie. As the child approached the end of his school career, he began to show dangerous signs of independence. He declared that he wished to spend time with other friends, male and female alike. Reith could not disguise his bitter jealousy over this. 'Very unhappy sometimes with C.,' he fumed in his diary. 'Sometimes I even say he was a cad to me.' 'However ridiculous it seems,' he jotted after destroying some other evidence of their friendship five decades later, '… I was obsessed by him.' Even their arguments only led to 'further extravagances about him'.[237]

A photograph Reith had taken of himself for Charlie shows him, aged twenty-four, a powerful, good-looking and well-dressed man about town. Wearing the obligatory frock coat, watch chain and stick-up collar of a Victorian gentleman, he was pleased with himself, and not without good reason. As he happened to be reading John Morley's three-volume biography of William Gladstone about this time, he began to wonder rather hopefully if he might like to fulfil a similar role in his own day. 'We want a Gladstone–Cromwell combination mightily,' he dreamt, with himself clearly in mind. Equally optimistic were his plans to resume his sporting career. Having joined the London Scottish Rugby Club upon arrival in London, he was confident that he would soon be playing fullback for their First XV. 'I see the chance of an international beyond this,' he unblinkingly continued in his diary.[238]

August 1914 obliterated many such fantasies. But as Reith had been forced to resign his commission with the Scottish Rifles when he moved to London, he received the declaration of war with some indifference. While he had no objection to assisting in the war effort in theory, he was planning a holiday in Cornwall with Charlie that summer and did not like to miss it. As the battalion's adjutant had never formally acknowledged his resignation, he wrote again, baldly stating that he was prepared to rejoin his comrades – but only 'if the thing was serious'. Otherwise he was going on his holiday.[239]

No answer came, so Reith did the expected thing by returning to Glasgow. Here he discovered that he was perilously close to being court-martialled for desertion – his mobilisation orders had already been sent, but apparently to the wrong address. There followed a series of unforeseeable developments of permanent significance for Reith's future. First, he was told that he would be assuming command of the battalion's logistical needs. His excitement about this was almost uncontainable: 'the sun shone in an unclouded sky', he remembered. 'The Transport Officer was a somebody; an object of mystification, envy and even respect among his brother officers … a power in the land.' He would, most importantly, be allowed to wear his beloved spurs. But the second unexpected development was not so welcome, at least for most of the troops. Although the 1/5th Scots Rifles was a territorial battalion, the men were going to be deployed at once to France.

'WAR', wrote Reith excitedly in his diary. It was all 'magnificent – like the gold star'.[240]

☙

Reith's high expectations of his role as the battalion transport officer were characteristically overblown. Responsible primarily for ensuring that a 'horse and cart was available at the right moment', he was, contrary to his own opinion, some way down the military pecking order. But he worked his authority into something incredible. By the end of his nine months at the front he was certain enough of his abilities to declare that he would have 'accepted the command of Battalion or Brigade or Division without the least hesitation – and would probably have done very well in it'.[241]

This towering self-confidence did little to endear Reith to his superiors. Almost as soon as he arrived at Armentières, where the battalion were deployed to withstand an expected German advance, he made it his business to make enemies of them. None more so than the battalion's new adjutant, Captain Croft, whose duties included acting as secretary to the commanding officer, Colonel Douglas. Like Reith, Croft was a young man used to having his orders obeyed. Needless to say, they despised one another from the first.

When writing of his war experiences over two decades later, Reith had little to say which did not in some way involve his feud with the adjutant. The man was absurdly central to his war narrative; greater even than the tragedy of the appalling loss of life by which he was surrounded. He epitomised, in Reith's crushing verdict, the 'inefficiency' of the war effort – the 'stupidity, jealousy, [and] managerial incompetence' of the entire operation.[242]

This was doubtless harsh on Captain Croft. Seeing that he ended the war with the honour of a Distinguished Service Order, it may also have been objectively unfair. But Croft certainly failed to manage Reith effectively. It seemed that whenever the young transport officer put a foot wrong, he was lying in wait to make a fool of him.

That was not the way to handle a man like Reith. He could endure any hardship: death, injury, infamy – but never humiliation. It struck too keenly at his pride. 'It always tires me', he complained of another officer, 'to stand looking down at and listening to little men.' What most irritated him about the adjutant was his desire to belittle him in the eyes of the battalion.[243]

A significant part of the problem was Reith's refusal to fraternise with anyone above the rank of sergeant. 'I made no effort to cultivate the Adjutant or my brother officers,' he admitted. While it was customary for lieutenants such as him to eat in the officers' mess and generally make themselves useful, Reith was almost permanently surrounded by an ever-growing band of low-ranking sycophants. Chief among this crowd was lance-corporal Bob Wallace, whose 'clear green-blue eyes' instantly commanded Reith's attention. 'I did not then, as in later years,' recalled Reith, 'take much pride of myself in the article of the judgment of men; but I was drawn to this man in the course of a ten minutes' conversation as I had never been to anyone before.' He made Reith smile, indulged his penchant for long Sunday afternoon walks and generally took his mind off his worries. Incidentally, Wallace was not regarded as a good soldier by the other officers – he was, remarked one, 'a pot-hunter ... I don't think he's any use'.

Reith was eager to make it clear that his liking for the regular troops was in no way a social blemish. The men of the 1/5th Scots Rifles, he later explained, were of a higher social class than 'any regiment in Glasgow'. And there was no question of him 'lowering' himself in any other way. Rather than sharing in the bland leisure-time activities of most non-commissioned officers, Reith sought to give his men a way of life which invited the envy of even the most high-ranking officers in the battalion.

This unorthodox arrangement was symbolised by the grand mansion to which Reith expertly billeted himself on the leafy rue Sadi Carnot. Staffed by three attractive French maids – reported to be the town's last civilian residents – it was said to be the only property in Armentières where a hot bath and a three-course meal could readily be arranged. Reith revelled in his position as lord of this little manor. Surrounded by Wallace and his band of follow-ers, he would pass many an evening bad-mouthing the senior officers, while outlining his grandiose plans for how the battalion should be put into order. Although, like his father, a strict teetotal-ler, Reith procured vast quantities of champagne for this motley gang, which amazed them no less than his ostentatious choice of apparel. Shunning the coarse cotton of regulation army clothing, Reith found a secret supply of expensive yellow shirts, which, combined with his enormous spurs (the largest in the battalion) and sensible rubber boots, made him a legend in appearance as well as reputation.

The posing was by no means limited to the relative safety of the billet. Whenever his duties required him to pay a visit to the trenches some miles away, Reith would amaze the soldiers – and infuriate the officers – by showing a blithe disregard for danger. If a trench was too muddy or overcrowded, he would casually limber up above the parapet and walk along the wire in clear view of the German snipers eighty yards away. 'Weren't you scared?' one

admirer stammered. The silent reply would indicate his answer to
the negative. But in letters to his parents Reith could be even more
Byronic: he told them that he found it 'most thrilling to hear the
shells whistling through the air and to wonder how near they're
going to land'. Religious zealot that he was, he believed himself
to have God's protection, and was fond of making his men read
the Psalms so that they too would come to share this conviction.
Something of the brilliance of his influence is suggested by the fact
that twenty-two of the troops under his command were confirmed
as members of the Free Church while serving in France. His mother
sent each of them a leather-bound Bible, which her son solemnly
inscribed with an apt, though to the recipients completely mean-
ingless, Latin tag.

Covert warfare with Captain Croft began at the outset of January
1915 as a result of a typically petty incident. A pair of dilapidated
sheds had become available, and Reith was eager to claim them
as stables for the battalion ahead of any other transport officer.
Not long after filling them with every horse and wagon in his
possession, Reith received an unexpected message from Colonel
Douglas ordering him to make way for an incoming battalion
of the Leicestershire Rifles. Reith, however, would not budge.
'Has the Colonel had that from Brigade?' he grandly asked the
lackey whose unfortunate task had been to inform him of this development. As no one was sure, the defiant Scot proudly explained to
the senior officer that he would not do anything without an order
from higher up the command chain. 'Amazing cheek,' wrote Reith
of the incident which followed. After declaring that he was going
'to get the General', the enraged infantry captain ordered Reith to

remain where he was so that he would be on hand to move out as soon as he returned. The cheek naturally belonged to Reith.

But it worked. To the amazement even of his own superiors, the officer from the Leicestershire Rifles truly had attempted to 'bluff the Colonel'. Reith's legend accordingly grew – as did his ego. It fell to Croft to knock it back down again. Worthy adversary that he was, the adjutant waited a week and then had an urgent message pushed beneath the door of Reith's famous bathroom at the rue Sadi Carnot property. The note stated that the colonel had been around the transport quarters and had found two horses not groomed; would Reith explain at once? '*Two horses not groomed!*' thundered Reith in disbelief. 'No bath water boiled more vehemently than did my indignation,' he splendidly continued in his memoirs. Soon after emerging from this cauldron he dashed off a 'snorter' to the adjutant, but not without first passing it to Wallace and some of his other cronies for approval. Amazingly, Reith's impertinence was once again rewarded: two days later he learnt that the general had temporarily promoted him to transport officer of the entire brigade.

How Croft's own bath water must have boiled. It was only a matter of time until the pair would literally be at one other's throats. This time the adjutant's criticism of Reith was public and unguarded. It took place late one evening, after heavy German shelling had led the colonel to order the retreat of half the battalion to a safer location. As ever, Reith mobilised his men and gear in impressive time; much faster, he said, even than the infantry companies. Leaving space for these men to fall in on the road ahead, he parked his wagons seventy feet from the agreed rendezvous. After a few minutes of deafening shelling, the adjutant emerged from his villa. 'Where the devil have you been, Reith, and why isn't Transport out?' he barked. Reith was not going to be spoken to like that in front of his men. From the commanding vantage of his saddle, he riposted: 'You've no right to talk to me like that and accuse me of not being on the job at the right time in the middle of a battle.' With a theatrical jab of his spurs, he then swung round 'and shot off down the road in a shower of sparks'.

That could easily have been the end of Reith's tenure as transport officer. But Croft opted to be the bigger man, at least for now. Later that evening he knocked on the door of Reith's stately billet and, after allowing the inevitable crowd of sycophants to 'tiptoe into the kitchen', launched into what Reith gleefully expected to be the best argument of his life. The adjutant's words, however, caught him completely off guard: he had not come to fight, but to apologise. Reith was furious. He later regretted that he had not been wise enough simply to reply: 'Dashed good of you, sir. Won't you sit down and let's have a talk.' Instead he allowed Croft to gain the upper hand. 'I was embarrassed,' he angrily confessed, 'muttered vague thanks and lost control of the situation, which was a new one to me.' Reith disarmed, Croft then proceeded to berate him for his general demeanour – 'said I went hunting around for trouble; putting people's backs up and jumping down their throats'. Following another childish disagreement several months later, Croft succeeded in having Reith 'returned for duty' – sent off to the trenches with the rest of them. For once Reith had been completely outmanoeuvred.

Shortly before the war, Reith had lain in wait with a large spanner for a milkman whose cart had accidently collided with his father.

Croft now unleashed that inner monster. For the next three months, Reith made it his mission to have Croft killed by an enemy sniper – 'I should have been nicely avenged thus', he thought. Yet despite forcing the adjutant into some unusually dangerous positions, including an exposed listening station, no harm came to him. Before long, Reith felt it sensible to volunteer to leave the battalion. A transfer was arranged to the Royal Engineers, and Reith spent his last few weeks at the front overseeing the construction of trenches at Noyelles, soon to become a central location in the notorious Battle of the Loos.

Reith's war was now almost over. He did, however, have the satisfaction of finding, at last, a commanding officer who took him at his own valuation. Whether this owed more to this man's comparative inexperience or Reith's genuine proficiency as a subordinate cannot readily be assessed, but he was undoubtedly impressed. He later described Reith as 'an exceedingly good officer and one who in a short time had inspired great confidence in the men'. No objections were made to his methods or his morals; even occasional visits to his old friends in the Scots Rifles, some fifty miles away, were gladly permitted. Fate, however, soon intervened. Inspecting a damaged section of the trench one morning, Reith was hit by a sniper's bullet in the side of his face. His entire cheekbone was shattered, and the resultant damage suggested that he was almost certain to die. Heroically he called for a slip of paper. On it he scribbled his mother's name and 'I'm all right' – all right with God. Later he signed a note for Charlie: 'Cheer up old boy.' He was going to die, but exactly as he wished.

Reith's reaction to discovering that this magnificent death scene was merely the prelude to a lengthy period in hospital was one of extreme indignation. 'Crossing tonight,' he wrote bad-temperedly to his mother. 'Doing well but very angry, John.' His doctors diagnosed acute delirium, though this only made the young man more furious. 'I've ruined my best uniform,' he kept repeating. The morphine dose was duly increased and he passed, at length, into a gentle sleep.

Reith bore the scars of that day for the rest of his life: physically, a vast seam down his left cheek where his face had been sewn back together; mentally, a sense that his life had been spared for some higher purpose. His self-belief was not long in being vindicated. As he lay recuperating on a hospital bed in London, a grand lady appeared at his bedside. He had no idea who she was, but soon discovered her to be Helen Moir, the wife of the managing director of Pearsons – 'like a visit from royalty', wrote Reith of the encounter. Somehow this ungainly and now unsightly young man won her over. She visited him regularly and, when he was well enough, took him out for several restorative drives in the countryside. Before long she introduced him to her powerful husband, who took it upon himself to help the wounded veteran. After briefly sending him up to supervise production at one of his works in Dumfriesshire, he informed Reith that the Ministry of Munitions needed a man to take charge of the inspection of small-arms contracts in America. He was to have a large salary of £500, and half as much again for expenses. Would he be interested?

Reith was exceedingly pleased with this opening. After accepting the position by return telegram, he called upon his friends and family in the guise of a returning prodigal son. His father had often expressed a liking for expensive fur-collared coats: Reith now arranged for one of the finest tailors in Glasgow to deposit a large selection for him to choose from. Charlie, too, was showered with gifts, though Reith expressed disappointment that the boy had not written to him more frequently while he was at the front. Due to forces beyond Charlie's control, the first of his many letters had been some weeks in arriving.

But by far the most notable incident to occur before Reith's departure for America was his unexpected run-in with his former commander, Colonel Douglas. Reith caught sight of this be-medalled gentleman – recently awarded a knighthood – while he stood chatting in the street with his brother Robert. As Reith later boasted in his diary, 'He smiled broadly and changed his course to speak to me.' The young man, however, could not resist this delicious opportunity for making a snub. 'I just stared at him', he exulted, 'and gave no recognition at all. The smile faded from his face and blank bewilderment took its place as he changed his course again and passed.' It was, continued Reith, 'one of the biggest exercises of will I have ever put through'. The young man was almost overcome with self-satisfaction.[244]

Reith maintained this aloofness for the duration of his eighteen months in America – indeed, it stuck with him for the remainder of his life. Charged with overseeing a large rifle factory in Philadelphia, he could now play tyrant with the knowledge that he was acting within the law. The effect on production was startling. At the time of his arrival in February 1916 the plant was manufacturing a paltry fifty rifles per day; by the middle of June the daily loadings into the huge freight carts had risen to over 500. Equally impressive was Reith's success in negotiating with the factory's managers a substantial modification in the design of the rifles without any additional cost to the Ministry – a favour he regarded as 'a tribute' to himself. But Reith learnt more about management from his American hosts than he cared to admit. For it was in Philadelphia that Reith first saw the effectiveness of stamping out socialism with an iron fist. Particularly impressive was the general manager's mobilisation of a large cohort of mounted police to stave off a proposed strike. Inspired by this scene, Reith wandered down to the rifle range a few days later and summarily dismissed two labourers for no particular reason. 'I enjoyed doing it', he wrote afterwards, 'and the factory management were vastly amazed.'[245]

It was not only the factory managers who were amazed. In his time off work Reith rapidly became one of the most famous foreign residents of the city. 'You may have noticed a man in Philadelphia recently', wrote a local journalist, 'who towered head and shoulders above the men beside him and who bore on his left cheek an angry-looking scar that ran almost from cheekbone to chin.' 'Captain Reith', the admirer continued, 'is an example of what the Great War has done as a maker of Men with a capital M.'[246]

Such accolades rapidly drew invitations for Reith to appear as an after-dinner speaker. He began this unlikely new course at a modest gathering of the St Andrew's Society of Philadelphia with a patriotic denunciation of those selfish workmen who were 'holding up the blood of their brothers to ransom' in order to achieve higher wages. Next he blustered for forty-five minutes to the Business Science Association about the need for non-combatants to learn more of what was happening at the front. And in the greatest of all his American orations, he harangued the Pennsylvanian

Scotch-Irish Society on the evils of pacifism with such vehemence that a pro-American observer wished the floor would open and swallow the speaker up. On that occasion Reith claimed to have outshone a future American President, Herbert Hoover, who was there to argue that his country would probably emerge from the war as the world's greatest power. To this claim Reith had the following withering put-down: the statement reminded him 'of Kaiser Wilhelm'. At the end of one of these debates the audience was on its feet cheering and waving table napkins.[247]

All this had the obvious result of going completely to Reith's head. He wrote in a letter to his father that he was consider-ing remaining in America to pursue a political career, but had discovered that foreign-born citizens were not eligible to become President. This was the sort of job to which Reith believed himself to be fitted. 'Seeing big men always' made him 'stir up and ... feel very impatient'. Their incompetence was tantalising. Disappointed with the American constitution, he decided to return home and see who could be dislodged there.[248]

Before doing so, however, Reith had a couple of holiday romances to put on ice. Far from Charlie, he had taken a shine to a new young companion: fourteen-year-old Jimmy Laws, whom Reith fondly described in his diary as being 'more like an English public school-boy than anything I've hitherto met'. There followed the usual rituals typical of Reith's boyish trysts: long walks in the countryside, tours of the works, lectures about politics, earnest prayers and so forth. 'He is certainly very fond of me', observed the 28-year-old, 'and is very sensitive to any sign of my not liking him.' When the boy asked if he could call the older man by his first name, Reith hesitated and then said that he was to call him 'Charlie'. This was how he was introduced to Laws' sister, Jeannette, who soon became as infatuated with Reith as her little brother. Being eighteen and exceedingly attractive, she was perhaps a more suitable companion for the towering arms inspector, but he admitted to finding her 'frightening'. They held hands a few times, and Reith took her to fire off some rounds at the range. That was all.

Young Jeannette was devastated to find that her 'Charlie' had his eye set on another. She was partly relieved, though, to discover that this did not happen to be her brother. For both she and Jimmy had been eclipsed by a girl named Betty Stewart, the sister of another one of Reith's male acquaintances. She was, he wrote, 'ravishingly pretty' and 'quite put Jeannette in the shade'. He taught her to drive his car, bought her a gold bracelet for her birthday and took enough photographs of her to fill an entire page in his scrapbook. 'She is really rather like a fairy princess,' he gushed. Just before leaving for England in September 1917, he took Jeannette to one side and told her of his greater affection for Betty. 'She did not seem to think it as odd as I had expected,' he wrote in his diary.[249]

The odd thing was that Reith's fairy princess was not yet thirteen years old.

❧

The story of how John Reith became the first general manager of the British Broadcasting Company (as it then was) belongs to radio folklore. He had been back in England for five dreary years, kicking his heels as a military engineer and then, for almost three years, in charge of a loss-making factory at Coatbridge, near Glasgow. Never before did Reith feel himself to be so under-employed. 'Here I am,' he wrote in disgust, 'now conscious of abilities which almost overwhelm me, and yet nothing to do.' At the start of October 1922 he embarked again for London in search of grander, more exciting positions.[250]

On his first Sunday back in the capital, Reith made his way to the Presbyterian church in Regent Square for the evening service. The reading was from the twenty-second book of Ezekiel: 'And I sought for a man among them that should make up the hedge, and stand in the gap before me for the land, that I should not destroy it; but I found none.' Was there not, the minister asked, 'a man to stand in the gap now': perhaps there was 'someone in the church that very night'? Reith went home and brooded on this. 'I still believe there is some great work for me to do in the world,' he wrote before going to bed.[251]

Reith spent the next two weeks at the Cavendish Club, Mayfair, scouring the press for job advertisements. One in particular caught his attention. 'The British Broadcasting Company (in forma-tion),' he read in the columns of the *Morning Post*. 'Applications are invited for the following officers: General Manager, Director of Programmes, Chief Engineer, Secretary. Only applicants having first-class qualifications need apply.' This was the sort of thing he had in mind. A hastily written application for the position of general manager was duly placed in the club's letterbox.

It was a fantastic story; and true, so far as it went. But Reith preferred not to mention the important detail that his first contact with the BBC was not prompted so much by Providence as by a visit he had recently made to his old school, Gresham's. This had ostensibly been made to lecture the boys about choosing the right career. The content of his speech, however, betrays that his own political destiny was of paramount importance. 'The majority of men', he thundered down at his audience, 'are only mediocre': the world was 'crying out for men to come and lead'. At the end of the talk, one of the sixth-formers came up and introduced himself as the son of a backbench Conservative MP, Sir William Bull. 'You see,' he said, 'it so happens that my father's a politician, and I know he'd be glad to see you.' In due course Reith became Bull's 'honorary secretary'; a useful platform for finding more permanent employment in the political sphere. As Bull was also a director of the newly formed British Broadcasting Company, it seems more than probable that it was he who alerted the young man to the positions advertised in the *Morning Post*.[252]

Bull was by no means the only acquaintance to be quietly subtracted from the Reith legend. The same fate was to far more spectacularly befall young Charlie Bowser. 'My beloved friend of nearly ten years', wrote Reith just before returning to London, 'fell sick of a grievous poisoning on 26/6/21 and died 3/3/22.' These were the dates of Bowser's engagement and marriage to Maysie Henderson, a Scottish heiress to whom Reith had introduced Charlie in the hope of breathing new life into their friendship. Serious problems had arisen some months prior, when Reith had unexpectedly announced that he wished to marry a young woman whom he had met while working as a military engineer in Sussex. 'Someone else who I didn't particularly like was interested in her,' explained Reith of Muriel Odhams, 'so I thought I would see if I could cut him out.' This rival appears to have been a fellow engineer named Thompson, but it is not unlikely that Reith also had Charlie in mind. To the horror of Miss Odhams's parents, their prospective son-in-law would often appear at their home with this favourite companion in tow. While it was Reith who was in the best position to marry, a far stronger bond was soon forged between the two youngsters. 'I'm awfully pleased,' enthused Reith on discovering that 'Charlieboy' was as much in love with Muriel as was he.[253]

Inevitably the situation soon turned sour. Ten days after Charlie's wedding to Miss Henderson, he sent the new Mrs Reith 'the most amazing document' that her husband had ever seen. This was followed by an 'abominable' letter from Charlie's mother to Reith, explaining in a 'smug self-righteous way' that his connection with her son must now cease. 'Of course,' the recipient consoled himself, 'they are carried away by Jezebel and all her money.' The old friends would, with the exception of three silent encounters in later years, never meet again. Only the snapshots which Reith would periodically cull from his diaries and return to Charlie remained as testament to the happy years before 'Jezebel' intruded. Fearing mental breakdown, Reith made several visits to a Glasgow psychological clinic, but stopped attending when he discovered that he 'knew as much about psychoanalysis' as anyone there.[254]

Reith, whose father had died in 1919, was now almost completely alone. A bitter dispute with his 'scrounging' siblings about where their widowed mother would live precipitated the breakup of the entire family. Like a man drowning in a raging sea, the 33-year-old was thrashing around for something to keep him afloat. He would find it in his new job at the BBC.

Not that Reith was yet aware of this. By the time he heard back from the chairman of the company, Sir William Noble, on 7 December, calling him for an interview, he had already thrown himself wholeheartedly into his new employment. Following the sudden collapse of Lloyd George's coalition government at the Carlton Club on 19 October, Reith had been frantically scheming on behalf of Sir William Bull to resurrect the Liberal–Conservative alliance. His activities involved paying visits to such crestfallen figures as Austen Chamberlain, Lord Birkenhead, and even the Welsh Wizard himself. 'He said several times that I ought to be in Parliament and said he remembered my father's name,' boasted the young aide. These efforts, however, were in vain. On 16 November a new Tory leader, Andrew Bonar Law, led his party to a landslide victory at the polls. Lloyd George and the coalition were buried forever.[255]

Emerging from this failure, Reith arrived in a slightly bewildered state for his interview with the BBC's board of directors at Magnate House, Kingsway. 'They didn't ask me many questions', he wrote of the event, 'and some they did I didn't know the meaning of.' The truth was that he 'hadn't the remotest idea as to what broadcasting was'. None of this, however, mattered. At the end of the interview, Noble gave him a 'broad wink' to signal that all would be well. The next day Reith learnt that he was to be put in charge of the new concern. 'We're leaving it all to you,' he was cheerfully informed. Improving on the original offer by almost a third, Reith demanded and obtained a salary of £2,000 – considerably more than he had ever commanded in any previous employment.[256]

In preparation for his first day at the BBC, Reith did some homework. As well as calling upon a Glasgow acquaintance who enlightened him about the meaning of 'broadcasting', Reith worked his way through a pile of papers sent through by his new employers. The technical aspects of the enterprise were easily understood. Since the invention of wireless telephony in the early 1900s, the British government had declared that no civilian could transmit sounds through the ether without first obtaining a licence from the Post Office. So inept were the early pioneers of this art that few members of the public had been willing to pay the considerable sum required to obtain a radio set. It was this impasse which had led to the formation of a special broadcasting company underwritten by the six largest manufacturers of these devices. In the hope of stimulating the new industry, the government granted the company a monopoly of the airwaves and the right to a portion of a licence fee paid by listeners to the Post Office. The arrangement was intended to last until the end of 1924, when more competition could be expected.

The modesty of this undertaking was matched by the frugalness of Reith's new surroundings. Arriving for his first day on Saturday 30 December 1922, at the headquarters of the General Electric Company, Magnate House, he was greeted by an evidently surprised janitor. Reith quickly set the tone for how business was now to be conducted:

'BBC,' I said deliberately. 'Nobody there yet, sir, but we're expecting them on Monday for the first time'. 'Who is them?' I asked. 'The new Company,' he replied. So I told him that this was it, or part of it, one-quarter approximately. As he bore me upwards I detected a scornful curiosity in his veiled scrutiny. He was very polite. He conducted me to a door already labelled BBC, which he opened for me with some ceremony. I entered. The door shut, and I heard his footsteps echoing along the corridor. A wild thought came to me that I would hail him and bid him loose me again. But I had heard the clang of the iron gate. It was too late.[257]

Inside this cheerless room, Reith found three long tables and a scattering of chairs. In one corner there was a broom cupboard, six foot square, which had been converted into an office with a stool, desk and telephone. 'This', he thought with considerable disappointment, 'is the general manager's office.' But just as Reith was beginning to have further doubts, there was a knock at the door. Into the room there entered a grave-looking gentleman clutching two attaché cases and an assortment of legal books. This was Major Anderson, the Secretary. 'I saw at once that he would never do,' wrote Reith in his diary. His first decision as general manager had already been made: Anderson had to go.[258]

That left only two other members of staff with which to deal: the director of programmes, A. S. Burrows, and his deputy, C. A. Lewis. Since the company's formation earlier that year, these men had operated out of a makeshift studio on the top floor of Marconi House, some 300 yards from Reith's own office. Progressing from the simple but effective technique of reading out stories from the *Strand Magazine*, they had improvised the first radio plays and had even made trials in the unchartered realm of news broadcasting. As if to stamp some moral authority on this mass of heathendom, Reith's first command to Burrows was that the BBC would henceforth 'observe Sundays'. The day after his inauspicious arrival at

Magnate House, he duly summoned Dr Fleming of Pont Street Presbyterian church and had him placed before the microphone. A new era in broadcasting had dawned.

Reith threw himself into his new work with abandon. There were, he soon discovered, innumerable problems of 'overwhelming intensity and complexity' to be settled. 'Copyright and performing rights,' he listed, 'Marconi patents; associations of concert artists, authors, playwrights, composers, music publishers, theatre managers, wireless manufacturers' – all had to be listened to and answered conclusively. In moments of swollen-headed frustration the pioneer wondered 'what sort of reception Caxton had when he set out'.[259]

The most formidable of Reith's early opponents were the lords of Fleet Street. Instinctively suspicious of a medium which threatened to transmit news and entertainment at low cost through the airwaves, they refused to advertise the modest programmes then being transmitted unless the company paid a substantial fee. Enraged by Reith's blank refusal to acquiesce in this scheme, the *Daily Express* began the first of many vociferous campaigns denouncing the BBC's 'monopoly in transmission', calling upon the Postmaster General to allow it to establish a free rival broadcasting service. As if to rub salt in the wound, the same newspaper encouraged its readers to take advantage of a loophole allowing 'experimenters' to avoid paying the full licence fee.[260]

Reith made it instantly clear that he was not going to be pushed around by the creatures of Grub Street. Remembering that one of the BBC's directors had casually mentioned at the time of his appointment that he would soon know 'everyone worth knowing in the country', Reith demanded a meeting with the *Daily Express*'s feared owner, Lord Beaverbrook. 'I was not a bit afraid of him,' he wrote of their meeting. As one son of the manse to another, the Canadian-born tycoon explained that Reith had 'impressed him very much'. The pair came to an understanding that their differences were not insurmountable: if Reith respected the interests of the newspaper industry, Beaverbrook would allow him to do as he pleased with broadcasting. The lifting of the advertising ban came about more unexpectedly when the owner of Selfridges took out a series of special advertisements in the *Pall Mall Gazette* complete with the BBC's meagre listings.[261]

Trickier was the issue of the licence fee. At the time of the company's formation, the directors had been promised the assistance of the police in enforcing payment. But it rapidly became clear that no one at the Post Office had the least interest in concerning themselves with this problem. Once again, it fell to Reith to bash heads together. Within two months of his appointment, he journeyed up to Birmingham to lecture the Postmaster General, Neville Chamberlain, on the matter. He could not believe what he heard in response: the minister 'scoffed at it being worthwhile to enforce licences'. Within a few years Reith would scoff back with righteous satisfaction that 'when Chancellor of the Exchequer with 8 million licences in force, he thought differently'.[262]

Of even greater importance for the future of the organisation was Reith's victory over Chamberlain's successor, Sir William Joynson-Hicks. Bumping into this dapper minister in the street one morning, Reith was staggered to hear that he was considering reducing the licence fee for cheap crystal sets, and was also planning to open up the market to the 4,000 firms 'clamouring' for a share of the airwaves. Once again Reith refused to be cowed. Scarcely had the minister arrived home that evening than he received from Reith a lengthy screed. The 'Norwich Letter', as the official historian of the BBC calls this document, 'has something of the qualities of an encyclical'. 'The manufacturers who came together by invitation of the Post Office', it sharply began, 'and eventually succeeded in laying the plans for the formation of our British Broadcasting Company, are responsible for the popularity of wireless today.' Any attempt to unilaterally open the airwaves to all-comers would not only be a breach of contract, it would also allow huge profits to be amassed by freebooters whose interest in broadcasting 'six months ago' Reith thought 'doubtful'. Those who complained that programmes were not yet of particularly high quality, the letter ended, need look no further than the Post Office's failure to enforce the payment of licences.[263]

This was not the way to go about winning the support of a man like Jix. But the minister at least accepted that Reith's position was legally sound. In a rare concession, he proposed to establish a parliamentary committee to consider not merely the matter of licences but 'the whole question of broadcasting'. As a personal favour to Reith, whose 'firmness and courtesy beyond praise' he acknowledged, the Postmaster General invited the BBC's general manager to sit on the panel.

This was the first of many lucky breaks which would help free Reith from the tentacles both of the Post Office and his own paymasters, the wireless manufacturers. At the first meeting of the Skyes Committee, as the panel of inquiry was called, he put out an idea which was to become fundamental to the entire conception of the BBC. 'I gave a personal opinion', wrote Reith in his memoirs, that 'broadcasting should be conducted as a public service and under public corporation constitution.'[264]

It would take a further three years of lobbying and another parliamentary inquiry to effect that altruistic ideal. For now, Reith contented himself with the cordial nature of the committee's final report; a document he had naturally co-written. It upheld the right of the BBC to exercise mastery of the airwaves, but proposed that retailers should now be permitted to sell devices free from any royalty obligation to the company. In compensation for this loss, the proportion of the licence fee rendered to the BBC by the Post Office was to be significantly increased, and there was to be an end to the contentious 'experimenter's licence'. Almost overnight the financial position of the company was salvaged. A mere ten days after the report's publication the number of licence holders had bulged from 180,000 to 414,000.

Reith was now in control of a 'going concern'. Turning his attentions to expanding the organisation, he launched a ferocious recruitment drive, increasing the modest staff of the early days to a team which would touch four thousand by the time of his resignation. In the first stages of this staggering growth, Reith made a point of interviewing applicants personally. Survivors of this ordeal remembered it with a shudder. He would invariably begin in a standing position, with his back to the interviewee, while he spoke – or pretended to speak – on the telephone. After a few minutes of 'acute discomfort', he would swing round and 'look quickly at the intruder, sizing him up in one brief but all-absorbing glance'. Then came a volley of questions. What did they think of the 'licence question'? Did they have any 'personal disabilities of character, any weakness that [they] knew of"? How did they pronounce the words 'fire', 'gold' and 'soot' (regional accents were not permitted 'on air')? Did they 'accept the fundamental teachings of Jesus Christ'? And so the inquisition went on until the visitor was abruptly told to depart. 'If he had been playing the part of an ogre', recalled one such hopeful, 'I think the *Children's Hour* producer would have told him to tone it down a bit.'[265]

Of equal importance to the team of engineers and producers he was rapidly amassing, Reith paid particular attention to his choice of secretary. Only the most boyish and adoring applicants were to be considered. His first and most long-suffering of these was Isobel Shields, who had been recommended to him by no less a personage than Lloyd George. A graduate of Girton College, Cambridge, she was the prototype of the intelligent, horsey young woman to whom Reith liked to unburden his heart. It was typical of these bizarre relationships that Reith took it upon himself to rebuke Miss Shields for going to the cinema on Sunday afternoons – 'the only time I could go', she later grimaced. Another female acolyte showed more perception in telling Reith, after sitting attentively though a lengthy after-dinner speech, that he was 'a future Prime Minister'. That was the sort of thing the general manager liked to hear from his staff.[266]

It was not long until the BBC required a more commodious headquarters. Capitalising on the advances promised by the Sykes Committee, Reith decided to move the organisation into larger premises on Savoy Hill, overlooking the Thames. This was to be the home of the BBC throughout its most crucial years. Gradually expanding the hours of daily broadcasting from a paltry one to up to fourteen, Reith made it his work to ensure that the length and quality of programmes increased in tandem. As well as serious lectures by leading public figures such as G. K. Chesterton, George Bernard Shaw and H. G. Wells, he encouraged his producers to broadcast live music – though seldom 'hot jazz', which he regarded (along with abstract art) as 'a filthy product of modernity'. In April 1924 the company achieved 'the biggest thing we have done yet' by broadcasting the voice of King George V as he opened the popular British Empire Exhibition at Wembley.[267]

With the growth of the BBC there was inevitably a corresponding enlargement of the ego of John Reith. 'Wants an honour!' scrawled the BBC's new chairman, Lord Gainford, on a plaintive letter he soon received from his general manager. Before long, however, people in high office were forced to take Reith more seriously. Embarrassing scenes such as when someone insensitively tried to place him in an overflow room at the Lord Mayor's banquet were not to be repeated. Among his first major personal breakthroughs was the acceptance by the Archbishop of Canterbury, Randall Davidson, and his wife, of an invitation to dine with the Reiths at their new home in Queen Anne Mansions, Victoria. Complaining of backache, Reith 'arranged to be engaged on the telephone' at the time of the Primate's arrival, forcing his wife to go downstairs and greet their distinguished visitors alone. This was characteristically grand; but the regal reception was only just beginning. As the party gathered in the drawing room, Reith stealthily flicked the switch on his large mahogany sideboard radio. Music burst into the room; the guests were 'utterly amazed' – 'thunderstruck indeed'. Never content to leave a job half done, Reith then telephoned the station and ordered that a record suggested by Lady Davidson be placed beneath the microphone. In a few moments the gathering were enjoying a crackling rendition of Schubert's *Marche Militaire*.[268]

This was only the first of many such displays of Reith's muscle. About the same time, he found himself within earshot of the Prime Minister, Stanley Baldwin. The premier was explaining that during a recent traffic jam the police had created a diversion along Piccadilly so that he could get to a ceremony more quickly. This, he joked, was the awesome extent of his power. When the polite laughter had died down, the taciturn young Scot at the far end of the table interposed that if he so wished he could pick up his telephone and speak to several million people at any time of the day or night. 'He agreed that that was more impressive than his car exploit,' he smugly wrote afterwards.[269]

Power had come to Reith at last. The question was: how was he going to use it?

 ❧

At the end of his first year at the BBC, the Board of Directors insisted that Reith take a holiday. They declared themselves to be highly impressed by his 'consummate ability and tact' – one director reported that he 'could not find words to express his admiration'. Reith hardly needed reminding of his prowess by these characters, whose opinions on broadcasting he privately regarded as 'humbug'. But their gesture of advancing him an extra ten guineas for his trip, coupled with an instruction that he was to spend more time with his wife, was welcome so far as his marriage was concerned. Although Reith often complained that Muriel was 'no suitable consort for me', the unhappy family soon grew to four with the births of Christopher and Marista.

It was fitting that Reith's first holiday at the BBC was to the city of Rome, the cradle of civilisation. 'As we conceive it,' he wrote rather infallibly the following year, 'our responsibility is to carry into the greatest possible number of homes everything that is best in every department of human knowledge, endeavour and achievement, and to avoid the things which are, or may be, hurtful.' This was the ethos which Reith wished to stamp on his fledgling organisation.[270]

The difficulty was that Reith still had to walk a tightrope between Fleet Street and the Post Office. Too much 'popular' coverage (news in particular) and the former complained that the BBC was abusing its privileges; too much 'controversial' political matter and the latter came out in protest. It took a crisis to break this deadlock: in May 1926 Reith was gifted one in the form of the General Strike.

Reith lived for occasions such as this. Ever ready to substitute himself for one of his team of professional announcers, he gladly interrupted some light dance music on the evening of Friday 30 April, to announce that a coal strike would shortly be underway. During the course of the ensuing nine-day emergency he was rarely far from the microphone, dismissing the more experienced broadcasters as too 'panicky' for the situation. With no newspapers available owing to the disruption, he had to invent what was to become known as 'rolling news' on the hoof – one night he quaintly excused himself from the microphone to answer the telephone. Primitive though this undoubtedly was, Reith succeeded in making the BBC's news coverage an indispensable commodity to millions of people nationwide.

The result was that for the first time Reith became a person of national importance. 'Are you Mr Reith?' snapped an angry Winston Churchill on their first encounter. The Chancellor of the Exchequer was furious at the apparent neutrality of the BBC's coverage of the strike, demanding that more be done to counter the miners' propaganda. 'He was really very stupid,' opined Reith. It was the beginning of yet another feud; one which would ultimately eclipse all others.[271]

The first round in this forty-year rivalry undoubtedly went to the Scotsman. Unsupported by his Cabinet colleagues in his wish to commandeer the BBC, Churchill had to make do with the editorship of the aggressively pro-government *British Gazette*. But Reith's impressive victory owed more than he admitted to a tacit understanding between himself and Baldwin that the BBC would back up the government in any case. Going beyond the call of duty, Reith even took it upon himself to perform personal favours for the Prime Minister, such as standing in Baldwin's place to reject a plea from Archbishop Davidson to address the nation over the airwaves. 'A nice position for me,' he privately gloated, 'to be in between Premier and Primate ... at thirty-six years of age.'[272]

Reith was not unrewarded for these efforts. In the New Year's Honours list of 1927, he found himself the possessor of a knighthood. Strangely, however, he thought this prize insufficient. 'I am not keen on titles,' he untruthfully wrote, before adding that the Order of the Garter 'would not have been too much for what I have done'. 'An ordinary knighthood', he went on, 'is almost an insult.'

After three weeks of silent brooding, Baldwin's secretary was forced to urge Reith to respond to his letter. On 23 December, he replied, 'accepting the wretched knighthood'. [273]

There was less to grumble about with regard to the major developments which shortly followed for the company. In order to deal with the remaining constitutional issues involving broadcasting, a new parliamentary committee had been convened in July 1925 to suggest a way of freeing the BBC from its existing constraints – without, however, giving it an unfair advantage over the newspaper industry. This was where Reith's brilliant ploy of 'public service broadcasting' came into its own. Although he regretted not being once again empanelled ('I cannot control this sort of thing from the outside'), not even the Almighty could have selected a more biased chairman to arbitrate between his needs and those of the press lords. At the time of writing his report, David Lindsay, 27th Earl of Crawford, admitted that he would 'shed no tears' if Reith's creation spelt the end to Fleet Street – a trade which he believed to 'batten and fatten upon all the most unsavoury episodes of the law courts'. [274]

The new corporation was born on 1 January 1927. Reith, as though the head of a civil service department, became Director General. He was to remain at the BBC for a further eleven years, but his major work there was done. He had, he later complained, 'organised and developed myself out of a job'. He was referring to the corporation's innovative structure, which gave executive control to a series of committees and layers of management whose 'controllers' ultimately reported to him. Like his father as moderator of the Free Church, his day-to-day work hereafter took the form of approving decisions made by other people; even ones he inwardly contested. Yet those beneath him were wise to placate his vanity. In recognition of his considerable achievements to date, one of the new governors, an ex-headmaster of Winchester, insisted that a laudatory Latin inscription be placed in the entrance hall of the corporation's new premises at Broadcasting House, Portland Place. 'To Almighty God', it still reads. 'This Temple is dedicated to the Arts and Muses by the first governors of broadcasting in the year 1931, Sir John Reith being Director General.'[275]

This flattering tribute became the source of many jokes among the increasingly independent staff. 'It informed those classically educated', wrote one cattishly, 'that its foundation was due to God and Sir John Reith: the coupling of the two names matching the majesty of the one with the modesty of the other.' Many complained that Reith now seemed to care more about lunching at his club than dealing with mundane affairs at the office. 'We saw and heard less of him', recalled another staff member, '…and it was common talk that he had had enough of broadcasting.' But every so often Reith would re-emerge from Pall Mall, slam open doors and demand to know who people were and what they were doing in the organisation. One of his favourite methods of keeping the staff on their toes was to implement the same kind of draconian managerial tactics that he had learnt in America. As well as ruling that no member of the corporation could belong to a trade union, he believed that the abrupt dismissal of senior employees from time to time was good for morale. This was particularly resented when accompanied by protestations of godliness, as when Reith used a divorce trial as the pretext for removing his overmighty chief engineer, Captain Peter Eckersley. 'My son,' he reportedly told him, 'you have strayed from the paths of righteousness. Our ways must part forever. You are dismissed.' At least one Postmaster General believed that the sultan of Broadcasting House 'would end up in a lunatic asylum'.[276]

This was an impression which Reith almost seemed to cultivate with his new board of governors. As a personal favour to Reith, the Earl of Crawford had agreed only to appoint 'nonentities' to this body, but the arrangement proved to be less congenial than Reith had envisaged. Two governors in particular invited his ire: his first chairman, the well-mannered but unremarkable George Villiers, sixth Earl of Clarendon; and Ethel Snowden, a veteran of the suffragette movement and the wife of a prominent Labour MP. Lady Snowden (as she became in 1931) was by far the most despised of these adversaries. She symbolised everything that Reith hated and feared about women. She was to appear in his diary, at various points in their feud, as the 'Red Woman', the 'Scarlet Woman', the 'Whore of Babylon' and the 'Mother of Harlots and Abominations': 'a truly terrible creature, ignorant, stupid and horrid'. These ungallant scribblings could not even be said to involve matters of high importance to the corporation. Reith's most rankling gripe with the board involved their reluctance to increase his salary by £750 each year despite a vague promise from the chairman that this would be implemented. When a more pliant chairman later agreed to raise the Director General's gross income to the handsome figure of £7,500, Reith sulked that he 'might not accept the increase'. 'The board', he continued, 'had lost a great chance of making me feel happy with them.'[277]

The problem was that few of the governors shared Reith's magnified sense of his own greatness. 'It is impossible', protested Lady Snowden in a letter to Lord Clarendon, 'either to be happy or to contribute one's best if one is to be delivered over bound to the tender mercies of a man whose overwhelming egoism is as distasteful as his character and ability are overestimated.' In the hope of curbing his worst excesses, the board took to meeting informally without Reith's knowledge, either at the Savoy Grill or the chairman's grand London residence. This arrangement, however, came to an unexpected end when Reith's loyal deputies took to breaking up their meetings. Several governors saw no explanation for this alarming development except the employment by Reith of a team of private detectives. 'Come away from the windows,' implored Lady Snowden at the outset of one conference, 'we are always watched by spies'.[278]

Reith may have been telling the truth when he denied these accusations, but he certainly deserved Lady Snowden's testy put-down about his ego. 'What a curse it is', he complained in the midst of their little battles, 'to have outstanding comprehensive ability and intelligence, combined with a desire to use them to maximum purpose.' It was not long until he was speaking quite openly of leaving the BBC to pursue a career elsewhere. As early as 1928 he approached Baldwin for advice in this matter. The premier counselled against a purely commercial role, but made no intimation of the official position for which he was so clearly angling. A little later Reith took his search into clubland, discussing with novelist John Buchan and *The Times* editor Geoffrey Dawson the possibility of becoming either the British ambassador in Washington or the governor of Bombay. 'I said the chief difficulty in that [latter] job', he boorishly explained, '… was that there was a viceroy over the governor.' As if in compromise Reith resolved instead to head for the Cape: 'I really think', the diarist fantasised, 'I would like to be Governor-General of South Africa – not what I would choose, but what else is there?'[279]

Better jobs there certainly were. After reading Churchill's epic account of the First World War, *The World Crisis*, Reith sighed that there was 'no doubt' that he had been 'built for times like that'. With the European situation once again deteriorating in the mid-1930s, this megalomaniac tendency took the form of fantasising about becoming a dictator. 'I really admire the way Hitler has cleaned up what looked like an incipient revolt against him,' he wrote after the gruesome Night of the Long Knives in June 1934. But his longings for absolute power were tempered by a saving love of goodness and awareness of his own staggering inadequacies. 'I do not wish to be a dictator,' he conceded after thinking hard over the matter, 'but I should appreciate this chance of magnifying Christ, and father and mother would be there to help me.' In a telling though rare moment of humility he added: 'but of course I am not fit for this'.[280]

Being a non-party man, it is hard to determine what exactly Reith wished to do with powers of this nature. Human rights and civil liberties were certainly not high on his agenda, nor did he see any point in antagonising rival empires by pursuing a meddlesome foreign policy. What he wanted to see was a return to the Britain of his youth. In a lecture to the Royal Institution in May 1932 he laid down, in the most coherent fashion possible to him, some of the issues he wished to see addressed:

What of the spoliation of the countryside, desecration stalking unchecked on road and meadow, the old character and amenities destroyed? … There is no point in saying that this or that must stop. We have said so long enough. We need more central authority and central determination. How is it that we have become so tolerant, even of monstrous wrong? Is it laziness or timidity, or is it just another instance of the mediocrity which comes from a misunderstanding of real democracy?[281]

This was the spirit which guided Reith through his last years at the BBC. No matter how low the moral standards of the day might fall, he and his corporation were there to remind his countrymen of all that was best about Britain and her Empire. Even in the depths of the abdication crisis, when Reith personally and disdainfully led the ex-king to the microphone to make his historic announcement, the indefatigable Director General looked hopefully to the future. 'Thank God he and his ways have passed,' he recorded in his diary. 'It seemed as if the old England was back.'[282]

A yearning to be admitted to this hallowed enclosure was now becoming an obsession for Reith. To the consternation of his faraway siblings, he began speaking with an acquired Oxbridge accent and even asked the Archbishop of Canterbury to baptise his children into the Church of England. A desire to send his son to Eton, however, led to difficulties when he discovered that the preparatory school to which Christopher had been sent for this purpose had also been patronised by the hated Bowsers. The revelation promoted another one of Reith's famous 'snorters'. 'Dear Mr Bowser,' it began. 'We didn't know children of yours were at Sandroyd until after we had decided (on various recommendations) to send our son there. If any of us chance to meet there (or anywhere for that matter) can't it be as strangers.' The letter went on to correct a litany of misstatements Reith had recently discovered in a secret correspondence which had existed between Charlie and his late mother: 'She wrote', he huffed, 'that I still (i) had photographs of you in evidence (ii) felt friendly towards you (iii) regretted the termination of an acquaintance (iv) desired its resumption.' 'All nonsense,' he bitterly concluded. When a courteous one-line reply came back from Bowser, the recipient delivered his final judgement upon this 'ungrateful little cad': 'He can't write even a formal letter without awkward phrasing.'[283]

Other aspects of Reith's personal and family life were equally unharmonious. According to the evidence of Reith's daughter Marista, it seems that Reith's wife shared many of Lady Snowden's doubts about her husband's genius. On one occasion she was heard to enquire if 'Daddy' really could know quite so many important people. 'You don't think I've been making it up?' he snappishly replied. 'Oh, dear, no,' she recovered. 'Oh no!' 'Well, I can tell you', he continued, 'the new American ambassador, Joe Kennedy, made it known that he wanted to meet me, and so, newly arrived in this country, had me to lunch yesterday … Over an hour and a half's questioning, I was able to tell him all he wanted to know. Most grateful, he was. He appreciated my advice, he said.' A painful silence ensued. 'Is there anything wrong in that?' He swung round to confront his wife. 'Oh no – oh dear me, no,' she repented. 'Of course not.' And there the conversation ended.[284]

Since March 1930 the family had been living in a large Buckinghamshire mansion, Harrias House, which Reith eccentrically had guarded by a pair of retired police constables. In the family circle he existed as a kind of God. Mealtimes were an agony for all concerned, as the man of the house kept up an unceasing commentary on matters as various as 'the weeds in the path or the bones in the fish pie'. His contempt for 'non-eminent' guests was well indicated by his departure at the outset of one modest dinner party to 'red up' (clear out) the coal cellar. But there were also times when he betrayed his immature streak. A favourite game was to try to lie down while he rested a glass of water on his forehead. Other times he might be overheard humming the tune of his favourite gospel ballad, 'Hallelujah', or imploring his children to frolic with him in the open air. 'Saturday,' he once bemoaned in his diary, 'and no one to play with in the garden.'[285]

Reith showed the same tendency towards littleness in his on-going search for new employment. When he was offered the major position of Vice-President of the London, Midland and Scottish Railway Company, he rejected it for the most predictable of reasons: 'The biggest snag', he wrote in his diary, 'is that I should be junior Vice-President.' Had the offer been 'senior Vice-President and if the pay were more' he would have accepted. Similarly, Reith passed over various other lucrative but insufficiently grandiose commercial positions, including the chairmanship of such well-known companies as HMV and Cable and Wireless. What Reith really wanted, it soon became clear, was a part-time civil service job allowing him to continue drawing his £10,000 per annum from the BBC. This ambition was betrayed by his incredible offer in March 1938 to the Minister of War, Leslie Hore-Belisha, to the effect that he was prepared to reorganise the entire War Office in his spare time.

'I could go to the BBC for an hour or so daily', he wrote expectantly, 'and work at the War Office all the rest of the day, and most of the night if required.' Unsurprisingly the offer was not seized upon.[286]

Years later, when Reith was far from pleased with the state of British broadcasting, he complained that he had been forced out of the BBC by a government conspiracy. The evidence, however, points strongly to the more likely explanation that his friends in Westminster merely resolved to offer him an escape. Only six months before his voluntary removal to Imperial Airways in June 1938, Reith had personally overseen the birth of the BBC's Foreign Service – probably the most significant and government-pleasing single innovation of his entire period as Director General. There was little political will to have him displaced. Nor could it be said that most BBC staff shared the view of one critic that the corporation had 'outgrown the original autocrat'.[287]

Reith's first mention of Imperial Airways in his diary makes it plain that this large commercial entity was not some backwater into which he was to be tossed by his foes. 'Imperial Airways is getting bigger and bigger', he wrote of the pioneering aviation firm in March 1937, 'and must be an interesting show to run.' It so happened that its current managing director was an old Glasgow acquaintance, G. E. Woods-Humphrey, who had long ago asked Reith to be the best man at his wedding. They lunched together on several occasions, and word soon began to spread that this was an enterprise of interest to the weary Director General. When a government report was issued in March 1938 severely criticising Humphrey's management of the company, the Prime Minister recommended that the position be put at Reith's disposal. It was to be a full-time job with a magnificent salary equal to his pay at the BBC; Reith was asked if he would be willing to start right away.[288]

Although Reith had for a long time belonged to the Whitehall establishment, he was not a civil servant, and was accordingly under no obligation to accept the offer. What made Imperial Airways attractive to him, besides the salary, was the opportunity he would have of repeating the triumph of converting a private company into a powerful public corporation. No one was better qualified to undertake such a task than he. Yet Reith still wriggled. He told Chamberlain's secretary that if the Prime Minister really wanted him at Imperial Airways he would have to ask him personally. Reith's record of the ensuing conversation – all three and a half minutes of it – reveals the absurdity of the situation. 'I asked if he was instructing me to go,' he minuted. Chamberlain replied that 'he wasn't using that word'. So Reith inquired 'if he wanted me to go'. At this point the Prime Minister threw up his hands, saying 'again that was maybe too strong but that if I went he would be very glad'. It was something of a repeat of the shock Reith had received a few months earlier, when his deputy and protégé Rear Admiral C. D. Carpendale affirmed that the BBC would be able to survive without him. 'Not the reply I was expecting,' harrumphed Reith. Reluctantly, the Director General returned from Downing Street and informed his latest chairman, Ronald Norman, that he would shortly be moving on.[289]

Reith did not quite realise what he had done until his wife came to collect him from his office a few days later. Like his parting from Charlie Bowser all those years ago, the combination of anger, frustration and sadness was too much. Reith broke down and 'cried like anything'. After composing himself he managed to exchange courtesies with the lift operator and one or two bewildered members of staff before striding out of the main entrance, again in tears. The next day he made arrangements for all his personal television sets and radios to be collected from his home. He further mandated that no BBC publications were any longer to be forwarded to his address and forbade his staff from marking his departure in any way. That evening he drove his final BBC secretary, Jo Stanley, up to the high-powered transmitter at Droitwich and personally shut down the large oil engines. The on-looking engineers were as amazed by this spectacle as they were by the ghostly entry he left in their visitors' book – 'J. C. W. Reith, late BBC'.[290]

That should have been the end of Reith's sixteen-year involvement with the organisation. But there still remained one or two small matters to be put right with the governors. The first concerned an enquiry Reith had made as to whether he was entitled to a year's pay in severance. A cursory reading of the relevant documents by the BBC's legal department revealed that the outgoing Director General was not entitled to this bonus, but the chairman stuck his neck out by declaring that this 'didn't now matter' – Reith could have it anyway. The gesture, however, betrayed a misunderstanding of Reith's often contradictory public service ethos. 'It mattered a lot,' he fumed in his diary. 'Damn them!'[291]

Reith's final goodbye to the governors was even more emphatic. A week later he was asked by the chairman if he would put his resignation into writing for the sake of tidiness. Reith was only too happy to oblige. 'Now then,' he wrote, 'just for tidyness' sake':

I resign.

I shall resign.

I have resigned.

There it is – in all three tenses…

Is that sufficient? Or should there be another sentence renouncing all and every claim on the body and absolving it from liability of every sort?[292]

Reith packed up his belongings and left Broadcasting House just short of his fiftieth birthday. He lived a further thirty-three years, but he had already walked out of history.

ⵌ

Reith's biographer Ian McIntyre devotes over 120 pages to his subject's life after leaving the BBC. He examines in minute detail Reith's considerable achievements at a variety of public and private enterprises, including his brief spell as a government minister from 1940 to 1942. His account does not, however, surpass Reith's own pithy summary of these melancholy years: 'Oh, so lonely, so jealous and so unhappy.'[293]

The trouble began on his first day at Imperial Airways. 'I was brought to the door of an old furniture depository behind Victoria station,' recalled Reith. 'Inside were some counters, luggage on the floor, a few people standing about – a booking office evidently.' 'From Broadcasting House to this,' he groaned. Up a dark and narrow staircase he found his new office, in which he was soon confronted by his first urgent memo: would he authorise the expenditure of £238 on a new passenger lavatory at Croydon Airport? 'It seemed', he continued, 'I was to work in very low gear.' He doubted his capacity to withstand this 'unexpected strain on my mechanism'. [294]

But Reith had no intention of remaining long at Imperial Airways. While ostensibly working towards the firm's anticipated merger with British Airways, the inveterate schemer was certain that a government job would shortly be coming his way. He regally approved of Chamberlain's decision to meet Hitler personally at Berchtesgaden ('just what I have been thinking all along'), but was soon complaining in his diary that not enough was being done to prevent another war. 'It is all annoying to me,' he wrote impatiently, 'as I have so much more ability than these PMs ... I ought of course to have been dictator.' [295]

Reith's disappointment on receiving no summons from Downing Street at the outbreak of hostilities the following year was indescribable. 'No message from anyone; I was not required,' he sulked. But he was not without friends in high places, and in January 1940 he at last received the expected call. In their first meeting since the awkward conversation about Imperial Airways two years previously, Chamberlain told Reith that he was to replace the aged Lord Macmillan as Minister of Information. There followed another one of those blunt rejoinders which so often scuppered Reith's chances of advancement: did the job carry War Cabinet rank and membership of the Privy Council? 'No' was the short answer to both these queries. Reith then sighed that he supposed he would have to be elected to Parliament. This, however, elicited the more agreeable news that he would not face any opposition. A few days later Reith was duly returned as MP for Southampton, professing himself to be a 'Gladstonian Liberal, as my father had been'.[296]

The new minister's first task was to aggrandise his department. Disgusted by his lack of control over such integral matters as censorship and overseas propaganda – 'What would Dr Goebbels have made of it all?' he wondered – Reith made a number of tempestuous visits to rival ministries. Predictably, he began with Churchill at the Admiralty. For several minutes the veterans of the General Strike discussed old sores such as why Reith had so rarely allowed Churchill to take to the airwaves. 'A good deal might have been said on that subject,' thought Reith, 'but that was not the moment.' The meeting ended civilly though hardly amicably when Churchill declared that most MPs were 'frightened' of Reith and some were 'laying for' him. [297]

It took Reith two painful months of lobbying to get Chamberlain's support to annex the powers he so coveted for his department. But just as Reith was on the verge of another triumph the Chamberlain government unexpectedly fell following the bitter Norway Debate of 8 May 1940. Upon the subsequent formation of a war coalition under Churchill, a circular went round Whitehall announcing new Cabinet positions. 'Minister of Information', it baldly stated, 'Duff Cooper'. 'Things had run true to form to the very end,' lamented Reith. 'The Minister of Information was late with his final bit of information.' Within ten minutes he was out on the street plotting revenge. 'How filthy this treatment', he blustered in his diary, 'and what a *rotten* government.'[298]

Churchill was wise enough not to let 'that Wuthering Height' (as he soon dubbed Reith) brood for long. Only two days after releasing the crushing circular the new Prime Minister invited Reith back to Downing Street to offer him a 'difficult and important job'. With some show of putting on his glasses and looking down at a long list, he announced: 'Transport ... how does that appeal to you?' Reith made no reply. Unlike being made a transport officer in the previous war, becoming the Minister of Transport did not strike him as sufficiently prestigious. Churchill was forced to repeat the offer 'with some concern'. At length, Reith ungraciously responded that he would 'feel differently if he had been offering me a more important job – such as a service ministry'. Churchill huffed that the war was bound to last a long time. A few moments later Reith emerged from the Cabinet room, 'Minister of Transport and very unhappy'. [299]

His envy was debilitating. Content to leave his ministerial duties in the hands of the civil service, the junior minister stormed off to Buckinghamshire almost immediately. The retreat was ill-timed: it occurred just as the collapse of France forced thousands of British soldiers onto the dunes and beaches of Dunkirk. Unable to find Reith at his office, Sir Harold Hartley of the London, Midland and Scottish Railway rushed down to Harrias House to see what could be done to help bring the stranded troops home. He was amazed to find the nation's transport minister stalking about his library 'like a caged tiger'. He did not seem to comprehend the magnitude of the crisis. When he finally spoke, his words were unnerving: 'There's nothing I can do,' he said. 'Nothing – just nothing.'[300]

But there were times when Reith's jealousy only made him ridiculous, rather than reckless. After reading the contents of Churchill's immortal 'we'll fight them on the beaches' speech in the columns of a newspaper, the reluctant parliamentarian revisited a favourite theme: 'I wish I had had to make [that] sort of speech ... I *could* speak.' In his poisoned state of mind, Reith even imagined that his own oracular efforts would have made those of the war leader seem damp squibs. 'If Churchill had any inspiration or imagination', he continued in his diary, 'or spiritual vision in him, he could make an immortal utterance about Hitler and Mussolini. It's utterly beyond him ... I would do it on the lines of an additional canto to Dante's *Inferno*.'[301]

Despite these bitter private outpourings, Reith's relationship with Churchill appeared to improve in the coming months. But just as with Reith's experiences at the Ministry of Information, these advances proved illusory. Days after securing the premier's backing to incorporate bomb disposal into his department, Reith was summoned again to the big room. This time Churchill came straight to the point: he wanted Reith to vacate both his office and his seat in the Commons. As if to soften this blow – which Reith likened to the sniper's bullet of 1915 – he was to be elevated to the House of Lords and given responsibility for the relatively insignificant Ministry of Works. Again Reith bridled. He complained that he had been hoping for promotion to the Admiralty or War Office, and besides had political aspirations for after the war. Churchill patiently repeated that the war was far from being over; but his willingness to placate his ungrateful colleague expired when Reith speculated on the real cause of his demotion: 'Of course,' he moped, 'I fully appreciate that you don't like me.'[302]

Churchill now launched into a long-overdue offensive. In a few blistering sentences, he firmly placed Reith in his place: how dare he say such a thing; could he not learn to 'temper his dissatisfaction with forbearance'? Yet Reith could not resist picking at the wound. 'I rose,' he imperiously explained, 'said I was not happy about either the job or the Lords but supposed I ought to take both as an order.' That suited the incredulous premier. 'Yes,' he said while ushering the junior minister from the room, 'I command you.' For the third time in his life, Reith felt himself to be spiritually dead.

Reith passed out the remainder of the war as a relative nonentity. When even his modest foothold in the government slipped in February 1942, he amazed friend and foe alike by joining the Navy as a junior administrator. But the nobility of this action was completely undermined by the string of wounded letters he continued to fire at his former colleagues, especially Churchill. Showing how little he understood of politics, he demanded that he be reinstated to the Cabinet at the same time as requesting financial compensation for leaving Imperial Airways. Even after Britain's eventual triumph in 1945, Reith did not let up. In a letter of 1946 he wrote to Churchill as one 'whom you broke and whose life you ruined':

> You could have used me in a way and to an extent you never realised. Instead of that there has been the sterility, humiliation and distress of all these years – 'eyeless in Gaza' – without even the consolation Samson had in knowing it was his own fault. And that is how and where I still am.[303]

Not even Churchill's kindly reply that he had wished to use Reith more but 'always encountered considerable opposition ... on the ground that you were difficult to work with' ended the feud. For the next twenty years Reith would only refer to the celebrated war leader as an 'impostor', a 'menace' or simply 'that shit, Churchill'. Even at the time of Churchill's death, his discontentment raged. During the solemn lying-in-state in 1965, Reith, who was no longer teetotal, took a young friend for a whisky in the House of Lords bar. 'It will be a hundred years at least', he declared, 'before Britain gets over the malign influence of that unscrupulous man.' An eavesdropping bishop cast him a disapproving look, but Reith merely 'glared across, almost daring the prelate to indicate dissent'. Later he told his wife that they would not be attending the memorial service at St Paul's on the grounds that Reith did not like the company of 'eminent people ... when I feel I am or ought to be as eminent myself'.[304]

By this time Reith was a depressingly marginal figure in public life. Old and tired-looking, he passed out the remainder of his career in a variety of dull but important-sounding directorships: the Hemel Hempstead Corporation, the National Film Finance Corporation, the Colonial Development Corporation, British Oxygen and several others. 'Well-remunerated idleness' was Reith's own verdict on these activities. With envious eyes he looked on as the 'mini men' – as he dubbed the politicians of the new era – monopolised public offices; figures who made it their business to revolutionise Britain and dismantle the Empire from within. Reith regarded their handiwork as a personal slight. 'What upset me far more than their decision to evacuate in 1948', he wrote of the Raj, 'was that the playboy Mountbatten had been made viceroy.' 'So that', he wallowed, 'is the job I most wanted on earth gone for good.'[305]

His opinion of his successors at Broadcasting House tended to be equally disdainful. 'I wonder what I would do if Bailey, the new sole Director-General of the BBC, made an approach to me,' he wrote of William *Haley* in 1944. His contempt turned to indignation, however, when he learnt only two years later that the new 'DG' had been given a greater honour than he had ever been offered. 'Haley in the BBC is a KCMG', he wrote incredulously – 'simply shocking'. But Haley was no fool: he responded to Reith's bitter admonitions in the manner of a contrite son. 'If only you could ever realise', he protested, 'what a towering legend you are.' Reith's friendship, he went on, 'is a gift, and those lesser mortals, like myself, who come into contact with it, and feel its radiance, can only praise God that it exists…'[306]

Each of Sir William Haley's brave successors had to go through the same humiliating ordeal until Reith's death in 1971. But as Lord Reith made a point of neither watching television nor listening to the radio, there was little that these exchanges could achieve. 'There is nothing left in broadcasting of what I put there and cared mightily about, is there?' he casually enquired of Haley's replacement, Sir Ian Jacob. When he heard from a friend in 1958 that the corporation was now broadcasting betting prices, he grumbled in the same vein, 'That is about the last trace of my management gone.' Four years later he was yet again complaining that the BBC had 'utterly discarded everything I did, and the vulgarity of the *Radio Times* week by week makes me sorry I ever started it'. His last comment on an individual programme – *Juke Box Jury* – was that it was 'evil'.[307]

Although he was rarely seen in the House of Lords during these years, Reith was occasionally minded to contribute to telecommunications debates. When the matter of commercial broadcasting was raised in 1962, he arose from the shadows to defend the old monopoly system 'using', commented *The Times*, 'a bulldozer rather than a shovel'. For almost an hour he fumed that allowing competition onto the airwaves would be 'an action comparable to the introduction into England of bubonic plague and the Black Death'. The minister responsible refused to answer this 'torrent of vulgar abuse', but asked what Reith meant about the government 'selling the BBC down river' – was there a suggestion of financial impropriety? 'This is usually the point', continued the *Times* sketch-writer, 'at which peers swiftly jump up to disclaim any such implication.' Not so Lord Reith: '"If the cap fits, my Lords, let him wear it," he said dourly, and the silence in the House became almost palpable.'[308]

It was an impressive performance. But Reith had changed his tune by the time commercial television became a reality. Over lunch with the BBC's latest chairman, Lord Cadogan, he blithely explained that the corporation 'no longer deserved its monopoly'. Not satisfied merely to switch sides privately, he also approached the directors of ITV in the hope of delivering their inaugural broadcast. Unfortunately, however, his proposed fee of £5,000 was deemed 'a shade too commercial' even for the BBC's new rivals.[309]

The decline of Reith's prestige within the BBC was matched by his increasingly dysfunctional relationship with members of his family. With his two children now fiercely independent young adults, and his wife unwilling to continue living with him on a permanent basis, Reith felt more useless than ever. 'God Almighty,' he cried out like Job, 'what a crime committed that I should ever have married, or had children.' When his daughter became engaged to an unworldly young cleric named Murray Leishman, Reith declared that he had lost a daughter. Incredulous acquaintances would hear him boorishly explain that he had added 'the man Leishman' to his 'black list' of enemies. Marista, whose unusual name derived from her father's misreading of the old Scots word 'Mariota', was solemnly struck out from the family Bible.[310]

As if further to abandon his past, Reith became a tenant of the Archbishop of Canterbury, Dr Geoffrey Fisher, by renting a small flat in the Lollards Tower, Lambeth Palace. Unable to fend for himself, he survived here on a diet of biscuits, bananas and marmalade for long stretches of the year, always hoping that some new job would be offered to keep him occupied. Even as late as his seventieth year, he envisaged that he might be recalled to Broadcasting House to sweep the ungodly squatters from his temple. But the invitation never came. Instead he passed day after day 'awaiting the hearse'. A single diary entry from these tortured years gives a pathetic glimpse of the man Reith had become: 'A large daddy-long-legs was walking and flying about,' he wrote. 'It seemed as if it were lonely and came to me, and stayed near me for company. I felt I was getting some company from it.'[311]

There were, however, several women to whom Reith could turn for comfort and consolation. These were his so-called 'goddaughters': a collection of sprightly young women ranging from thirteen to thirty-one whom Reith picked up during the course of his official work and holidays. The pattern of the relationships was nearly always the same. To begin with Reith would overwhelm them with work – late nights at the office, 'redding up' his paperwork, reorganising his diaries, slaving to keep his biscuit tin and whisky cabinet adequately stocked. Then Reith would impress them with a meal at the Ivy, a day at Ascot or an overseas trip, hobnobbing with greyed colonial governors. For the most favoured girls, presents soon followed – jewellery in particular. In the end, however, Reith would invariably cut them dead over an imagined slight. The gifts would be confiscated, and the woman's name surgically excised from the diary, usually by the next victim. One such henchwoman never forgot the sight of Reith storming into his office one evening and casting several handfuls of these trinkets across his desk.[312]

It was always a source of intense speculation whether or not these relationships were sexual. A request to have a friend released from the typing pool at the War Office prompted an internal memo from the Minister of War himself: Sir James Grigg was not going to have his staff 'shunted about to suit the convenience of John Reith, who somewhat late in life has discovered the art of fucking'. But this dignitary's cynicism was almost certainly misplaced. Asked point blank about the matter, one of Reith's chief goddaughters, Dawn Mackay, was explicit: 'No,' she laughed – 'good gracious, no. Nothing could be further from the truth, or less likely, frankly.' 'At his best,' she continued, 'he was a very good companion. He could be very funny and very amusing – he did have a great sense of humour when you could dredge it up to the surface … I learnt a lot from him … [but] I don't think I was altogether real.'[313]

That was about the fairest thing anyone ever said about John Reith. For despite the perpetual misery of the man, there was, as has been written of another eminent malcontent, 'a kind heart beneath the iron breastplate'. His careful planning of his own earthly demise demonstrates beyond any doubt that he was not a man of ordinary stamp. Forbidding any mention of his death to be made on the BBC, or eulogy delivered at his Spartan funeral service, the first Director General took himself up to Scotland, where he hoped to die atop a mountain. He had to settle in the event for an officer's nursing home in Edinburgh, but Reith did not let this practicality spoil his plan. Recalling an epitaph he had once admired – 'lost in the hills she loved' – he requested that his ashes be placed in a ruined Highland churchyard among those immortal hills where only the wind could listen.

ᥱᖯ

At the height of his powers at the BBC, someone told John Reith that it would take twenty or thirty years for his achievements to be adequately recognised. Reith sighed to himself. 'No,' he thought, 'nor then.' Over eight decades later it cannot be said that this gloomy prognosis has been proved correct. His name has become iconic: along with Macintosh and Spooner it has entered the English language. 'Reithian,' says the *Oxford English Dictionary*, 'Of, pertaining to, or characteristic of Reith or his principals, especially relating to the responsibility of broadcasting to enlighten and educate public taste.' Yet for all his posthumous fame, it cannot be denied that practically everything Reith lived for has died.

The annual Reith Lectures, delivered in his honour since 1948, provides just one instance of the debasement of his legacy. Originally intended to defend the BBC's improving credentials in an era of mass entertainment, the talks have often strayed into the waters of commercialism and superficiality. One wonders if it was cruelty or ignorance which led the 2013 Reith lecturer, Grayson Perry, to adopt *Playing to the Gallery* as the title for his series. But it was perhaps a fair reflection upon a corporation which has often failed to live up to its founding father's exacting standards. 'He who prides himself on giving what he thinks the public wants', he once boomed, 'is often creating a fictitious demand for lower standards which he will then satisfy.' In an era of audience targets and ratings, no conscientious producer could really afford to do otherwise.[314]

Reith would have lamented this not merely for culture's sake. He was, after all, a man singularly lacking in that commodity. This hardly mattered. Like his avowed love of morality, his interest in promoting the 'best' in the arts was primarily selfish: he knew that it was the foundation of the BBC's enormous power. As soon as the corporation stooped to laying on entertainments for the masses, or failed to present itself as a bastion of virtue and righteousness, the edifice would crumble. In the wake of a series of modern-day scandals at the corporation, his unbending doctrines have been vindicated – but possibly too late.

For all that, Reith did not exist in a vacuum. His ideals took root because they chimed with the views of millions of people across the country. Even his uncompromising approach to matters as diverse as management and religion were commonplace until relatively recent times. The tragedy for him was that as the twentieth century rumbled on, those sharing his views ceased to be archbishops, prime ministers and university professors. They were instead lonely eccentrics with personal characteristics worryingly like his own. It was this realisation which slowly rotted him from within, driving him almost to the point of madness.

If it cannot be said that Lord Reith had a happy life, neither could it be claimed that he would have wished it to have been. For, like Samson and so many other great men, he was 'deeply indebted to those who tried to destroy him'.[315]

Sir John Reith

© Press Association

CHAPTER 4

THIS ENGLAND: THE ISLAND STORY
OF SIR ARTHUR BRYANT

For all that I have yet seen, give me old England.

– Edward Hyde, Earl of Clarendon

On a July evening in 1939 a tall, elegantly dressed Englishman gazed down upon the sports field of the Olympic Stadium at Berlin. He had not come to watch any athletic contest. No; he was there to admire the most physically impressive representation of Hitler's New Order – an order for which he had a sneaking sympathy. As he cast his eyes around the vista of swastikas and heroic statuary below, he reluctantly gave in to the same feeling of exaltation which overcame the protagonist of one of the most significant novels of the late Victorian age, *Confessions of a Young Man* by George Moore. The visitor would later quote a passage from this book with a mixture of disapproval and self-loathing:

'Hail, to the thrice glorious virtue injustice! What care I that some millions of wretched Israelites died under Pharaoh's lash or Egypt's sun? It was well that they died that I might have the pyramids to look on, or to fill a musing hour with wonderment.'[316]

For the esteemed patriot and ultra-conservative historian Arthur Bryant – later to be publicly honoured by Labour Prime Minister Harold Wilson and feted by every other British premier from Stanley Baldwin to Margaret Thatcher – was just now flirting dangerously with Nazism. Disillusioned by what he took to be the economic and moral collapse of his own beloved country, he regretfully wondered if the armies of the 'newer Pharaoh' might not, like the barbarian hordes of old, regenerate the 'too highly civilised' nations of the West with a welcome dose of Spartan courage and manly self-sacrifice.

It was a disquieting reflection. But it was revealing of the inner conflict at the heart of this self-professing 'very late Victorian'. Although steadfast in his dislike of tyranny and political chicanery, Bryant's engrained suspicion of intellectual subversion and revolutionary socialism often brought him worryingly close to doctrines he inwardly abhorred.

Born on the royal estate at Sandringham on 18 February 1899, Bryant boasted of being a Victorian both by the date of his birth and the manner of his upbringing. The son of an official in the secretariat of the future Edward VII, he inherited 'the beliefs, ideals, prejudices and tastes' of that era from some of its most distinguished figures: indirectly, at least, from the eponymous monarch herself. This would serve Bryant well in his long career as a twentieth-century Jeremiah. 'It often amuses me,' he told readers of his weekly newspaper column in 1954, 'living in a seemingly different world – the world of the atom-bomb, the aeroplane, television parlour-games, boogie-woogie and the strip cartoon – to find … that I believe in very much the same things as Queen Victoria and Lord Tennyson and Mr Gladstone.'[317]

His father, Francis Morgan Bryant, 'a small, upright figure dressed in the regulation top hat and frock coat of his calling', had been brought up in rural Suffolk before, unusually, completing his education at the German university of Clausthal. From there he was, in the 1870s, recruited into the royal household. Over a century later, his famous son would regale fellow diners at the Beefsteak Club and other establishment venues with a story that his father's position was 'rather like being head of a civil service department where the Private Secretary corresponds with the Cabinet Minister'; but this was something of a filial exaggeration. The diligent courtier's own description of his duties was altogether less heady: 'I am going to give you a rough idea of what I have to do,' the chief clerk wrote to his future wife from Sandringham in 1897.

> First there are lying at least 40 letters of various descriptions – some important and urgent – then there are all the salary, wages and various cheques (about 120) to be written, and forwarding letters to be sent with the various cheques. Then there is all the Estate Office work, and last but far more urgent, I have to issue 330 tickets for the Entertainment this evening and to arrange the seats, taking due care that the proper allowance of what is made for the Royal Party, the Country People, the Tenancy, and the many, many grades of Servants ... Never mind, I am very, very happy, having plenty to occupy my thoughts, so God Save the Queen![318]

Within four years of writing this letter, Queen Victoria was dead, and Francis Bryant, now married to May Edmunds, the granddaughter of a prominent Birmingham merchant, moved into a small house adjoining the wall of Buckingham Palace gardens. From Sandringham they brought with them their first son, Arthur, who was soon joined by a younger brother, Philip. The boys lived in a sheltered world – 'a monastery', as Bryant later described it – forbidden to venture unaccompanied beyond a wicket gate at the top of a narrow staircase. When they were allowed to do so, it was invariably to benefit from their father's stern advice about etiquette and self-improvement while he took his morning constitutional through Green Park. 'Don't forget to maintain a smart and clean appearance,' he wrote to his fully grown son almost twenty years later. 'When you become an Air Field Marshal or a Cabinet Minister, it will not matter at all about what appearance you keep up, but there is no question that until a man has made his position, neglect of the above mentioned matters tells heavily against him.'[319]

The contrast between Bryant's sombre, taciturn father and his warm, emotional, 'wise poet' mother was enormous. Artistic and somewhat scatterbrained, May was also two decades younger than the middle-aged man to whom she had been wed in her mid-twenties. In some respects she was the only woman Bryant ever loved – or who loved him. 'What I was when I first held you in my arms,' she wrote adoringly to him at the time of his first marriage, 'so it will be through all your life – and beyond.' But owing to the strict protocol of Victorian parentage, rigorously enforced by her punctilious husband, it was a sturdy Hampshire farmer's daughter, curiously known to Bryant as 'Other Nan', who saw to most of his childhood needs. Her dismissal soon after the birth of Philip would be recalled in later years by the eminent historian with much rancour and regret.[320]

Other Nan's successor did not take so kindly to Arthur. Her domineering, rather selfish charge was prone to take his dissatisfaction out on his weaker, more saintly brother. A particular hobby for the future court historian was to decapitate Philip's 'model royal family' made from the figurines of their railway set. It was clear that the child badly needed contact with other boys, but when Bryant was finally sent to a suitable London day school, Francis Holland in Chelsea, at the age of six, he was already too old to make friends naturally. It was a skill he would have to acquire, like so many others, as an adult. Susceptible to embarrassing emotional outbursts, Bryant fast became the bane of his teachers, who saw no way of silencing his crying on one occasion than to lock him up in a large cupboard in the assembly hall. Bryant would never forget the day that he was hauled from this makeshift prison – with unmistakably sodden trousers – in front of all his peers, unhappily joined that day by a visiting canon of St Paul's Cathedral, Dr Henry Scott Holland. The gathering was left in no doubt that the tormented child had 'upset himself'.[321]

After further misery and lack of academic distinction at a variety of preparatory schools in both London and Kent, Bryant was sent away at thirteen to board at Harrow. This was the making of the man. His housemaster, C. H. P. Mayo – a kindly pedagogue of the old school who had once attempted to teach elementary mathematics to a young Winston Churchill – made it his mission to reform him. Being a good Victorian, he began by addressing the boy's scruffy appearance. 'Arthur is getting on *so* well now', his wife enthused to Mrs Bryant at the end of the boy's first term, 'and is the model of cleanliness.' But Bryant's schoolmates remained unimpressed. Aside from his unkempt get-up and much-ridiculed habit of kissing his mother in public, they were repelled by his instinctively haughty demeanour. Complaints soon reached home of his 'bullying propensities', and a string of boys refused to go on sharing a room with him: 'Arthur sweeps the carpet with Benis's hair and clothes brush', lamented Mr Mayo in another letter home, 'and when remonstrated with promises Benis a "jolly hot time", which he seems to have done.' More alarmingly, Bryant became 'fond of flourishing a cake knife', spitting indoors and, on one occasion, preventing his roommate from dressing in the morning. In the end a defeated Mayo resolved to give the boy a room of his own.[322]

Bryant found no sympathy from his father throughout these travails. This was not through want of conveying his unhappiness to his parents. So miserable was the child that at the end of one school holiday he actually made his way home after saying farewell to his father at the railway station. When the latter returned to the house that evening he was astonished to find 'the Boy' (as he always called his eldest son) ensconced in his library. In the ensuing argument the fifteen-year-old begged to be allowed to leave school and enter a 'Bank or some other office'. But his father would not hear of it. 'He cried a good deal but gave no reason for not wanting to return to School,' fumed the angry parent in his diary. 'I told him he must be mad – that he was absolutely unfitted for a post as a clerk and that I would not hear any more nonsense and that he must catch the next train to Harrow.' Only with great reluctance did Arthur admit the real source of his problems – that 'all the boys bullied him'. This, however, simply worsened matters. 'I pitched into him', continued the diarist, 'and told him I was ashamed of him and hoped he would stand up to the next boy who bullied him and try to knock him down.' Still crying, young Bryant was clapped into a cab and sent back to his housemaster.[323]

The transformation of this ugly duckling into one of the school's most cherished old boys – later to serve for three years as

President of the Harrow Association – began almost immediately. Recognising that all boys aged between twelve and sixteen were 'cruel little beasts', he learnt that they would never tease 'anyone, however objectionable, if there's no fun to be got of it'. To this end he befriended several of the boys in his house and set about making himself an upstanding member of the school community. Although not good at sports, Bryant won the respect of his peers and masters through taking a prominent part in worthy but understated activities such as the 'Harrow Mission'; a charitable organisation providing entertainment and amenities to the residents of the slum district of Notting Dale. The experience would instil in Bryant a strong interest in the poor and an idealistic desire to improve their lot.

Bryant's teachers up to this point had recognised none of his latent abilities. Deemed too intellectually weak to pass through the prestigious 'Classical Side' of the school, he progressed slowly through the 'Modern Side', focusing on allegedly more manageable subjects such as History, French and Geography. His distinction in the field in which he was later to earn so much fame had hitherto been underwhelming. But he had, even before arriving at Harrow, demonstrated something more important than mere fact-learning – enthusiasm. While at his prep school on the south coast he had carefully read through such classics as Robert Louis Stevenson's *The Black Arrow*, Charles Kingsley's *Hereward the Wake: 'The Last of the English'*, Sir Walter Scott's *Ivanhoe*, and – by no means least – several of the historical plays of Shakespeare. At Harrow, Bryant built upon these impressive early encounters with plodding devotion to Sir Archibald Alison's massive and influential *History of Europe* (1833–42). So inspired was the lonely dreamer by the picturesque battle scenes in this work that he soon took to commanding an imaginary battalion around the games pitches. 'Long before Hitler turned his attention to war', he rather inappropriately joked in later years, 'and while he was still sentimentalising over architecture in Vienna or splashing paint on window-frames in Munich, my plans for global conquest were complete.'[324]

The outbreak of the First World War at the end of Bryant's second year at Harrow had little impact on his schooling. He had already expressed an interest in becoming a soldier: war merely brought home to him what exactly this would entail. Taught by his Victorian elders to regard the British Empire as 'the greatest Empire under heaven', he and his peers relished the prospect of laying down their lives in defence of its much-vaunted ideals. Over seven hundred Old Harrovians were to do so by the time of the Armistice four years later.[325]

Being slightly younger than the worst-affected of the war generation, Bryant was able to complete his studies at Harrow before joining in the war effort. This would have a great bearing on his development as a historian. The reason was his entering, in his penultimate year, the essay class of one of the most famous teachers in the school, George Townsend Warner. Tall and strik-ing in appearance, Warner had swept the boards at Cambridge before, for over thirty years, reigning supreme as head of History at Harrow. Among his first intake of pupils had been George Macaulay Trevelyan, who, as well as being an acclaimed historical writer in his own right, was also the great-nephew of the most celebrated historian of the nineteenth century, Lord Macaulay. Bryant would later rival Trevelyan's status as the public's favourite chronicler of the nation's 'island story', becoming, in the process, a close friend and admirer of the distinguished author of *England Under Queen Anne* (1930–34) and *English Social History* (1942). Such heights, however, were unimaginable in 1912. The first time that Bryant met Warner it was only to be dismissed by the older man as the 'grubbiest little boy I have ever seen'. Now, as the same pupil, increasingly self-assured and better-groomed, approached his seventeenth year, a more cordial relationship blossomed between the pair. Warner became the first of several important father figures.[326]

Warner's approach to history has been passed down to generations of schoolchildren through his mantra 'Who, What, Where, When, How, Why?' But beneath this tear-soaked formula there was a historian of great sensitivity and literary ability. His little book *On the Writing of English* remains one of the best short introductions to the subject ever written. (A section 'On Succulent Bivalves' – 'what the Bad Journalist called the Oyster' – is unsurpassed). Bryant imbibed Warner's style and discovered, to their mutual satisfaction, that he had a natural flair for writing. While some boys mocked the self-conscious intellectualism of the Warner group – poetry was much read and discussed – it was not owing to the pretentiousness of the man at its centre. Warner's chief objective was to encourage his students to avoid the long-winded clichés which marred so many pages of modern scholarship. If a boy employed a hackneyed phrase such as 'when one surveys the course of history', he was invited to the front to draw himself engaged in this activity on the blackboard. And anyone fool enough to try 'as Macaulay wisely says' was reminded that the master of English prose did not require a 'pat on the back' from a schoolboy. Purple passages in Bryant's essays were accordingly scored through with 'bosh', 'pom-pom' and other favourite admonitions of the veteran stylist.[327]

All seemed to be going well for Bryant as he reached the pinnacle of his Harrow career. But on his first day back in the autumn term of 1916 he learnt that 'G. T. W.' had died from a massive heart attack – induced, jibed a few knowing cynics, by his discovery that his teenage daughter Sylvia had been engaged in a long-running affair with his counterpart in the music department. Bryant was devastated. With a view to gaining entry to Warner's old university, he put off his plan to join the Army Class and devoted himself to the study of history. So as to avoid this delaying his entry into the war, he resolved to join the newly formed Royal Flying Corps, exempting him from the mandatory year at Sandhurst required for a regular Army commission. The plan worked brilliantly. Lieutenant Bryant emerged from Harrow in the summer of 1917 with an Exhibition to Pembroke College awaiting him. The young man was on his way.

❧

The First World War affected Bryant to a degree comparable to his near contemporaries Siegfried Sassoon and Robert Graves. Like them, he would continually cast his mind back to the lost world of 1914 – the sandy country lanes, the magnificent and overfilling parish churches, the 'boa-ed and highly upholstered ladies', and the bustling, confident conurbations of pre-war England. 'It is difficult to believe', he wrote with characteristic hyperbole towards the end

of his life, 'that there can ever have existed on earth a lovelier countryside than that of this island sixty or seventy years ago.' Never
were the fields so green, the ties of community so strong or the
people so happy.[328]

It was a familiar refrain. But Bryant departed from his more
famous literary contemporaries in that he did not hold his parents'
or grandparents' generation responsible for the catastrophic world
war which had put an end to this pleasant idyll. They had, he
protested, no choice but to fight the leaders of pre-1914 Germany
'to the death' or to see the destruction of 'every standard of honour
and decency that our religion and history had taught us to believe
in'. So pronounced were Bryant's counter-revisionist views that he
even defended the reviled Field Marshal Douglas Haig, architect
of the Somme campaign, as a great commander unfairly maligned
by ignorant and complacent civilian critics. Bryant's only sustained
grievance about the running of the war was that the politicians of
the day had allowed it to go on for too long.[329]

These distinctly unfashionable views owed something to the fact
that Bryant, as a pilot, never served in the trenches. What little
fighting he did see was from an elevated, if not necessarily safe,
altitude. After his first flight he tellingly wrote to his mother that
he found it incredible to think that anyone 'could love or hate or
have any feelings at all towards such absurd little creatures' as the
ones he espied through his cockpit window. To him and his brother
'knights of the air' the goings-on of the infantrymen below were
distinctly 'vulgar'. While the latter waited hopelessly in muddy, rat-
infested trenches they soared to glory and popular acclaim. Several
of them became household names.[330]

This was all the more remarkable for the fact that aviation was barely a decade old. It had only been quite recently that Bryant had stood on the cliffs near Dover in his shirt-sleeves and school cap to witness Louis Blériot become the first man to cross the Channel in an aircraft. In the eight years since that historic occasion the British military authorities had shifted from a position of strong disapproval to warm embrace of the new invention, increasing the air fleet from just 150 machines in August 1914 to over 22,000 by November 1918. War in the air had become a reality.

Selection for the fledgling Flying Corps was not exactly scientific. Hopefuls such as Bryant were asked, after a few preliminary questions about their intentions, 'Do you ride?' The relevance of this was never fully explained or understood, but it indicated clearly enough the elitist propensities of the recruiting officers, as well as the foolhardy mindset of many of the applicants. Novices were quickly handed the controls of their primitive machines, often with fatal results. The first time that Bryant attempted a loop-the-loop in his 'Blériot Experimental' he almost killed himself by forgetting to cut the engine as he completed the first part of the manoeuvre. 'To this day,' the daredevil recalled years later, 'I can remember exactly what my instructor called me when I reached the ground.'[331]

Inefficiency, however, spared Bryant from an even more probable death. While the most talented aviators were rapidly dispatched to France, where life expectancy could be as brief as two weeks, bunglers such as him could remain grounded at British airbases indefinitely. Not that this was at all his intention. In the almost daily correspondence that he kept up with his mother throughout his training, Bryant complained of his lack of fighting opportunities.

So eager was the young man to be sent to France that on one occasion he asked her to lobby his commanding officer on his behalf. This delicate task she wisely delegated to a family friend, who wrote to Bryant's colonel, another Warner, that the feisty young pilot was 'anxious to either go overseas or to be made more use of'. 'I do not know if there is anything in the matter,' he went on, 'but he was at Harrow, and is, I should say, a young sportsman.'[332]

The plea was in vain: Bryant remained stranded for many more months at Farnborough – 'the filthiest hole I ever struck', as he described the training camp. Only his delight in strutting around the base in his uniform, issuing commands to luckless petty officers and mechanics, compensated him for this long period of inactivity. 'By Jove,' wrote the young Blimp in one letter home, 'if I was in command of this camp for a month I'd make things hum.' But when he was finally dispatched to France towards the end of 1918 the war was already drawing to a close. Bryant's vivid and often highly moving impressions of the conflict came second-hand, but were no less haunting for it: 'I was', he recalled, 'a silent witness of a heroism which had been and in which I had had no share.'[333]

On his return to England after the Armistice, Bryant was in no mood to resume civilian life as an undergraduate at Cambridge. With his enthusiasm for history apparently diminished, he spoke seriously of rejoining the forces and remaining in the military for the remainder of his career. But his father talked him out of such an enterprise. His first action on seeing 'the Boy' after his demobilisation was to scold him for keeping hold of an Army blanket, which had been clung to for warmth during a chilly return journey from France. Scrupulous to a fault, the angry official insisted that the stolen item be repaired, washed and returned to the War Office without delay. Half under his breath, young Arthur expressed 'in military parlance' what he hoped they would do with it.[334]

Bryant was clearly straining to become his own master. Deterred by the time and expense of proceeding to Cambridge, he made use of his modest Army pension to enrol instead on a shortened history course at Queen's College, Oxford, where he had briefly stayed during his military training and where several members of his mother's family had also studied. Bryant did not, however, take to the hedonistic atmosphere of post-war Oxford. 'The streets are full of noise ... flashy girls ... and a sordid unreal gaiety,' he complained to his mother. 'And behind it all, in the little grey courts of old Oxford, nothing but an intense loneliness.'[335]

Lack of female companionship was evidently part of the problem. Bryant's only exposure to young women had hitherto taken the form of his 'girl-cousins', whom he was fond of trying to lure unaccompanied into the shrubbery of his maternal aunt's Dorset home. More chastely, Bryant kept up an elevating correspondence with one of these unwilling companions, to whom he regularly suggested 'improving' literature for her edification. His quaint entreaties were mitigated only by saccharine remarks about her looks and intelligence. Earnest though he was, Bryant was not overly successful. 'I am starting to read the list of Eighteenth Century history and literature that you gave me,' she wearily responded to one of his urgent reminders – 'I forgot all about it.' When Bryant declared his love for her a few months later he was gently, but decisively, rebuffed.[336]

The budding sage was little more successful in his efforts to impress his history tutors at Oxford. Although several of them admired his enthusiasm and pluck, they did not take him seriously as an intellectual. Bryant would gladly repay their condescension in later years, claiming to have learnt nothing from them except a discriminating taste in port. He did not care for what he took to be their specialist, 'dry-as-dust' approach to their subject. Fired solely by guns, poetry and battles, Bryant became one of the few post-war residents of the college to focus his attentions on military history. 'My essays were deemed dangerously reactionary,' he wrote shortly after graduating with a Distinction in the summer of 1920. One left-wing tutor felt it necessary to incinerate an early sample of his work.[337]

Towards the end of his time at Oxford, Bryant started to think more seriously about the future. With unemployment at an all-time high, and the country teetering on the edge of bankruptcy, he saw the need to utilise every family connection available to him. 'Does Daddy know anyone at the Foreign Office worth asking?' came one enterprising letter home. A few months later he was thinking instead of journalism. 'If you know any [newspaper editors] I wish you would mention my desire to get a job as a leader-writer,' he tried. But it was no use. Neither Fleet Street nor Whitehall was quite ready for Arthur Bryant. The young man was not consoled by the less impressive offers engineered by his well-intending parents, including the editorship of *Burke's Peerage* and a position as aide-de-camp to a colonial governor.[338]

Bryant felt himself to be destined for greater things than these trifles. Yet he fully realised that to reach the top he would have to begin at the bottom. For this reason his first steps in adult life were distinctly unglamorous. First he joined the Council of the Harrow

Mission, and, shortly afterwards, became a teacher at a poor county council school in Holloway, north London. Oxford friends such as the war poet Edmund Blunden were staggered at his decision to fall so rapidly into poverty and obscurity. His father, too, wondered at his erratic choice of vocation. 'I've got some kind of Bolshevik on my hands,' he confided to King George V upon being knighted in 1921.[339]

But Bryant certainly knew his world. As the 1920s dawned, state education was experiencing growth only dreamt of by his Victorian predecessors. The opportunity for a young Harrow and Oxford man of his ability to make his mark was considerable. Bryant rose to the challenge. In the manner of a latter-day Thomas Arnold, he attempted to take the public school ethos into the newly built schools of the slums, instilling in the boys under his control the values which had forged the British Empire: duty, self-sacrifice and leadership. His methods included allowing his pupils to elect their own prefects, who were then given free rein over their subjugated peers. 'They were given the powers of a Nero', enthused the young master, 'tempered by the humanity of a constitutional monarch.'[340]

Within a year Bryant was given an opportunity to propagate his unusual educational views in a series of articles for a popular liberal newspaper, the *Daily News*. His readers were told that nothing transformed an unruly child more than responsibility: they simply needed to be empowered. 'Under the nine o'clock caps of school-going boys', he wrote, 'there may lurk a Pitt, a Gladstone or a Lloyd George.' Eager to capitalise on this unexpected prominence, the rising educational guru wrote to school governors and administrators all over the country, stating his desire to apply his methods on an even larger scale – as a headmaster. His success in pursuing this typically bold course can be gauged from the unprecedentedly extravagant reference he shortly afterwards received from his old headmaster at Harrow, the Rev. Lionel Ford:

> When Arnold was elected to the Headmastership of Rugby it was largely on the strength of one testimonial, which stated that if elected he would change the face of education all through the Public Schools of England. My belief is that if Arthur Bryant is elected he will prove another Arnold in the Secondary Schools of London.[341]

With such fantastic backing, Bryant did not have to wait long for his chance. At the age of just twenty-four he became the youngest headmaster in England as Principal of the Cambridge School of Arts, Crafts and Technology. 'Dr Arnold' was in charge.

❧

In the year 1858 John Ruskin opened an art school for working men on Sidney Street, Cambridge. To the assembled gathering the famous cultural critic expressed his wish that the school would 'teach the citizens of Cambridge to apply practical skills with a sense of beauty'. Sixty-five years later, the same institution, now relocated to a small building on Collier Road, north-east of the ancient university, had for its headmaster a man steeped in the same values. Idealistic, Tory-leaning and paternalistic, Bryant had much in common with the man who had famously stated his educational ideal to be the propagation of happier carpenters.

Bryant was not alone in seeking to revive these bygone ideals. Just two years before his installation, the destinies of thousands of young residents of Cambridgeshire had been placed in the hands of a no less visionary educationalist by the name of Henry Morris. Self-taught and ambitious, Morris was at the outset of a long career devoted to manning every factory and workshop in the country with self-reliant, intelligent men and women, who might keep a copy of Milton or Thomas Hardy at the ready beside their lathes.

In 1923 this was no utopian fantasy. Under the same legislation which had given Bryant his first teaching experiences at Holloway, the teenage manual workers and shop assistants of Cambridge were entitled to take part-time courses in a variety of vocational and liberal arts disciplines. It was Bryant's task as headmaster to combine the differing branches of the curriculum so as to ensure that neither the arts nor technical side became too dominant. It also fell to him to keep the town's employers and trade union officials satisfied that their interests were being upheld. No less importantly, he had to persuade the all-powerful Educational Committee, presided over by Morris, that he was providing the rate payers of Cambridge with value for money and measurable results in terms of practical education.

It was a tall order for a man of only twenty-four. But Bryant was no ordinary young man. Already possessed of self-confidence well beyond his years, he regarded no challenge as too great. 'Don't be afraid to ask *boldly*,' he wrote in a fatherly letter to his brother. 'You won't get things unless you do, and by *asking* boldly you are sure to get them.' Where audacity failed, continued Bryant in another letter, one should always be ready with more Machiavellian tactics:

'Remember that nearly everyone in this world is a snob,' he wrote. 'Don't despise them for this fault … use it for all you're worth: only be careful not to let them know you're using it.'[342]

So equipped, Bryant set about transforming a school with less than 300 pupils into a thriving centre of learning, attended by nearly 1,500 boys and girls when he resigned two and a half years later. In the opinion of the Educational Committee, the school had 'entered upon a new lease of life … mainly owing to Mr Bryant's personality and the way he centred on the organisation of the school'. Pupils and colleagues alike were won over by his 'infectious enthusiasm' and his passion for subjects as diverse as art, metalwork, motor engineering, book-keeping, printing, plumbing and mothercraft. Bryant even succeeded in introducing a nude model into the art studio, despite strong opposition from a distinguished Nonconformist member of the Committee. Bryant placated this strict Puritan by inviting him to invigilate, which he proceeded to do 'with every appearance of approval'.[343]

Masterly as Bryant proved in managing his meddlesome colleagues, he was scathing of their alleged mediocrity. Within only a few months of his appointment he was complaining of the 'drivelling incompetence' and the 'stupidity, laziness, envy and backbiting' with which he was surrounded. Perhaps he judged his staff too much by his own exacting standard. Regularly compelled to spend over twelve hours a day at Collier Road – in the evenings he lectured to the adult members of the Workers' Educational Association – Bryant was soon demanding a higher salary and greater investment in the school. It was this which ultimately led to the breakdown of his relationship with Morris. By the time of his departure from Cambridge the two men had ceased to fraternise, regarding one another as social interlopers and control freaks. Yet Bryant was not one to hold a grudge. 'I ask for your forgiveness,' he wrote in his final letter to Morris. 'I have felt this [animosity between us] bitterly in the past ... [but] I have now lost any such feeling.' The two men departed as friends.[344]

Whether this was all part of Bryant's master plan to 'storm the workaday world' can only be supposed. Certainly by the end of his first year as a headmaster he was already contemplating embarking on a more public career. In a wide-eyed letter to his mother he described 'an inward nagging at my conscience that one day I am bound for politics and perhaps to play some part in shaping the future'. Secretly the young man dreamt of becoming Prime Minister.[345]

But first he had to marry. To this end Bryant passed the summer of 1923 touring the countryside on his motorcycle, attending parties thrown by the parents of his wealthy school and university friends. 'It was rather like collecting stamps or butterflies,' he later wrote of the great balls of the '20s. Described by the wife of the Archbishop of Canterbury, Lady Davidson, as a 'nice dark young man with ... beautiful brown eyes and [a] jolly face', Bryant was both attractive to women and socially ambitious. What he lacked was the easy manner and wealth of his more eligible competitors. Young ladies whom he approached for a dance were often – in the quaint phraseology of the ballroom – 'missing seven', leaving him to brood angrily in an unobserved corner. Only by chance did he end up proposing to a wallflower named Sylvia Shakerley; mostly, his enemies suspected, on the grounds that she was the daughter of a great country gentle-man, Sir Walter Shakerley of Somerford Park, Cheshire.[346]

Yet all was not as it seemed with the Shakerleys. As Bryant was ungraciously swift to point out to his prospective bride, the match was not likely to bring him any advantage. 'You have very few rich friends,' he complained in an early courtship letter. Painfully he learnt that the Shakerleys, in common with thousands of old landed families, were on the verge of financial ruin. A steep decline in estate revenue combined with rising costs would shortly lead them to call in the notorious 'estate-breaker', selling their every worldly possession down to the last brick. Bryant made no attempt to take this blow stoically. In another early letter to Sylvia he explained that their marriage would 'cause lots of people to shrug their shoulders and say – "well, there goes another clever young man – his chance in life wasted"'. Particularly galling for him was her family's refusal to indulge his desire for a grand London wedding: he had to make do with 'having to drink champagne and eat overcharged cake… with a large number of strangers' at her parents' ill-fated home. The marriage was not destined to be a success.[347]

Any residual hopes that Sylvia would assist Bryant in his upward trajectory were quickly disillusioned. As Bryant's fellow historian A. L. Rowse cruelly reminisced, Sylvia 'had no interest in climbing the social ladder with him'. When the couple left Cambridge and took up residence in a large, unmodernised Elizabethan farmhouse called the White House in the village of East Claydon, Buckinghamshire, she made no attempt to ingratiate him with their titled neighbours. In the absence of her support, it fell to Bryant to assume the role of the vain and ambitious wife depicted in Oliver Goldsmith's novel *The Vicar of Wakefield*, filling their rustic cottage with large works of art and antique furniture – mostly acquired at heavy discount from the Somerford estate sale. Although several local grandees proved friendly towards the Bryants, others spoke ill of the couple. 'Not quite our class, dear,' confided one rich neighbour to a young relative. They were in danger of becoming social pariahs.[348]

From a worldly perspective, this hardly mattered. Bryant had far more serious worries to contend with. 'I understand', he wrote to his mother at the time, 'how the poor devils feel who pinch something worth ten bob from a shop counter because they can't get work and have a hungry family at home.' After prematurely ending his career as a headmaster, he was in the difficult position of having to begin his working life all over again. He did so with caution as well as tenacity. Helped by friends and relatives, he began by becoming a part-time lecturer in local history for the University of Oxford Extension Delegacy, an outreach programme with little to do with the university proper. He also started reading for the Bar, and for several months travelled up to London each morning to sit as a pupil in the chambers of an eminent family friend, Frederick van den Berg, KC. But he was ultimately advised against seeking his fortune as a barrister: the livelihood was too precarious. It also seems that Bryant was not entirely suited to the profession – 'I know absolutely nothing about law,' he confessed after receiving his wig and gown from the Inner Temple. Almost as a last resort, the young man drifted into the new Educational Department of the Conservative Party in the humble capacity of textbook editor, proof reader and general 'ideas man'.[349]

This development, however, would have unexpected results for Bryant. In the space of just eighteen months he transformed himself from a jobbing party hack into a significant Tory backwoodsman

and educational director of the newly founded Conservative training college at Ashridge, a mere ten miles from his home. He owed
his rapid advancement largely to the support of two prominent
Conservative figures, both of whom happened to live in the vicinity:
the novelist John Buchan and the future party chairman J. C. C.
Davidson. Bryant lost no opportunity in impressing his usefulness
upon these eminent men. When he was unceremoniously sacked by
the Educational Department at two days' notice in December 1928,
he called upon them to recompense him in some way. With some
embellishment, he told Buchan that only a 'personal belief in your
judgment and word' had caused him to give up profitable 'other work
and hopes' in favour of working for the party – 'a retrograde step in
my career'. This skilful protest was rewarded when Buchan came
for lunch at the White House to offer Bryant a more important job
as a Tory propagandist. This led directly to Bryant's first published
book, an election pamphlet entitled *The Spirit of Conservatism* (1929)
for which Buchan wrote a short foreword. The famous novelist was
evidently satisfied by his young colleague's epigrammatic defence
of Disraelian 'One Nation' conservatism, which was at the time
coming back into fashion after several decades of neglect.[350]

Soon Buchan was willing to do more for Bryant. When the
Educational Department was wound up shortly after the election,
he and Davidson ensured that he was given oversight of Ashridge,
requiring him to be present at the college for just one day a week in
return for a considerable salary.

This was an important step, but Bryant remained hungry for more.
There were simply not enough outlets for his torrent of energy. At
the same time as organising lecture programmes on citizenship and

politics for the college, and editing the instantly popular *Ashridge Journal*, he began to contemplate undertaking an even larger project: a popular historical biography to match one of Buchan's own forays into the genre. A series of pen portraits in the *Ashridge Journal* on the 'Makers of the English Character', beginning with the lives of Queen Elizabeth and Dr Johnson, give some indication of the broad lines upon which his mind was working; but he had by no means given up the idea of embarking on something more substantial. While still living in Cambridge he had infuriated his wife by spending almost every evening poring over a large collection of family papers dating back to the Middle Ages lent to him by her father. 'As casually I began to turn a few of the papers over,' recalled Bryant of the Shakerley Papers, 'something of their meaning came dimly to me. Here was the actual past, of which I had read unimaginatively in books. I could touch it and peer into it and savour its musty, faint but vivid perfume. Curiosity gripped me.'[351]

It was not long before Bryant was given an opportunity to make something of this unexpected boon. Like everything else in his whirlwind career, it arose from a strange combination of luck, opportunism and dogged hard work. During the course of a weekend visit to East Claydon, an old Harrow friend revealed that the publishing firm Longmans intended to reissue a thirty-year-old biography of Charles II by Osmund Airy. Impulsively, Bryant suggested that he might be able to improve upon this lightweight and censorious account of the 'Merry Monarch'. A sample chapter was boldly promised.

That document would change Bryant's life forever. In a passage which would ultimately begin the book, Bryant took up Charles' story at the close of the disastrous Battle of Worcester. It would, in time, become a sample of vintage Bryant:

'As the last streaks of daylight, 3 September 1651, fell on the Worcestershire landscape, a tall dark fugitive drew in his horse on a lonely heath. About him clustered some sixty lords and officers, whose looks told a tale of peril and defeat.'

In this romantic style, sustained for just under 300 pages, Bryant took the reader on an epic tour through the palaces, streets and fields of seventeenth-century England. From the quaint manner in which the peasants of Devon 'clotted their cream with sugar to crown their apple-pies' to the lavish pageants of Restoration London, Bryant depicted an idealised nation, overflowing with milk and honey: 'how lovely this open, lonely land was, and how rich its people in everything that made life worth living!' he interjected in a typical flourish.

At the centre of this highly impressionistic account of seventeenth-century England stood the king himself. Vilified by generations of democracy-worshiping 'Whig' historians as a tyrant and a perfidious, lazy debauchee, Bryant presented him instead as a great man who had stood imperially above the 'imbroglio of squabbling politicians' and 'that house of talkers' – Parliament. So pronounced were Bryant's revisionist views that even Charles' most notorious act of statecraft, the secret Treaty of Dover linking Britain with the expansionist France of Louis XIV, was hailed as a masterstroke of diplomacy. 'He was quite ready', wrote Bryant in a pregnant passage, 'to allow France liberty to overrun the Netherlands, Spain, or any other country, provided that she yielded him certain safeguards.' It was characteristic of Bryant's version of events that

Charles' parliamentary opponents were contemptuously referred to throughout the book as 'the Faction'.

While academic historians disputed the soundness of Bryant's basic thesis, the public delighted in the book. Reviewers fell over themselves to praise the gripping narrative, the ingenious new interpretations of well-worn facts and the crisp, elegant prose. In the *Sunday Times* the book was said to be 'as entertaining as Hume, Macaulay or Froude', while the reviewer in the *Saturday Review* commended 'the easy and attractive style [with] which he states the case for the defence of Charles'. Within a month of its publication it was taken up as a Book Society 'choice', ensuring it bestseller status; by the summer of 1932 it had been through seven imprints, selling well over 20,000 copies, and in the process making Bryant an extremely wealthy and highly regarded man.[352]

Yet the 31-year-old was only just beginning. He now turned his attentions to becoming something of a Caroline figure himself.

∾

Of all the criticisms made by academics of Bryant's historical works over the years, the most prevalent was that he attempted to draw false parallels between past and modern events. This old-fashioned approach was savagely attacked in the same year as Bryant's *Charles II* in an essay by a young Cambridge don named Herbert Butterfield. Entitled 'The Whig Interpretation of History', this watershed in academic history marked the end of the era of Macaulay and Trevelyan as far as university departments were concerned. 'The study of the past', wrote Butterfield, 'with one eye, so to speak, upon the present is the source of all sins and sophistries in history, starting with the simplest of them, the anachronism.' This applied only too well to Bryant. As the two men became familiar with each other's work in the coming decades, Butterfield would disdainfully bracket his Tory contemporary with the most unfashionable of all the Whig historians – Macaulay. Needless to say, Bryant was delighted by this backhanded compliment.[353]

The same enviable comparison was made with better grace by Trevelyan himself. In a letter to Bryant prompted by a query about his next project – a short biography of his great-uncle – the fellow graduate of Townsend Warner's essay class wrote, 'I was delighted to get your letter because I have greatly enjoyed your *Charles II* and longed to make your acquaintance.' 'You have two great gifts', he wrote a little later – 'the power of biography in the strict sense of the word – and the gift of telling social history the way men used to live ... I see in you the coming historian ... You will hold an important place – you do already – as interpreter of the country's history to the new generation, probably more important than anyone else soon.'[354]

This was praise indeed. From a position of complete obscurity and academic irrelevance, Bryant had not only become a bestselling author, he had also won the admiration of the recognised master of the historical craft – and, incidentally, the doyen of the political establishment. Bryant was not a man to waste such a propitious connection. It was no coincidence that the project about which he had written to the older man concerned his distinguished forebear. This book cemented Bryant's friendship with Trevelyan, who invited him and his wife to stay at his family's Northumberland stately home, Hallington Hall, for a long weekend in September 1932. Here Trevelyan saw firsthand that behind Bryant's easy style was a prodigious amount of labour. '*Do not kill yourself with work,*' he wrote soon after Bryant's departure. 'You must learn to say "NO", to have leisure and health to cultivate your great talents for writing history.'[355]

Unfortunately for Bryant's constitution, marriage and general well-being, he did not heed these wise words. Between 1931 and 1939 he authored or edited a staggering sixteen major works of history, as well as directing a huge naval pageant at Greenwich, admired by over 100,000 spectators and described by a Fellow of the Royal Academy, Philip Connard, as 'one of the most beautiful productions of recent years'. Added to these Herculean tasks, from June 1936 Bryant took over from G. K. Chesterton the oldest weekly column in British journalism, 'Our Note Book' for the *Illustrated London News*, which he kept up until the week of his death in 1985. 'That Arthur Bryant', wrote his secretary and biographer Pamela Street, 'did not kill himself with overwork at a young age always seemed to me, as to many other people, little short of a miracle.' This was no exaggeration.[356]

Running through all Bryant's work in the 1930s was the same disguised commentary on present-day events which had been so criticised by Butterfield. Aghast at the toxic clash between capitalism and socialism – not only in Britain, but on a far deadlier scale in Europe – Bryant used his numerous history books, weekly articles and biographies to celebrate a higher form of politics than that of party and faction. His timing was often too perfect: in the very month that *Charles II* had appeared the electorate of Britain was asked, for the first time in ten years, to vote for a coalition government – the National Government – comprising the less extreme elements of the Conservative and Labour parties. Old feuds were forgotten; ideologues and extremists were banished. A Cabinet of seemingly disinterested patriots had come together to save the country from ruin – just as Bryant had envisaged in the pages of his acclaimed bestseller.

Alongside the Prime Minister, Ramsay MacDonald, the man at the centre of this coalition was the Conservative leader, Stanley Baldwin. A tolerant friend of Labour and a passionate lover of rural England, he became the first of many high-ranking statesmen to take Bryant into his confidence. Along with their fellow Old Harrovian, Trevelyan, Baldwin was quick to praise Bryant for his magnificent literary debut, adding how pleased he was with the work he was doing for the party at Ashridge. Once again, Bryant rose to the occasion. 'The book was only meant as a token', he wrote in reference to a slightly later work, 'of the honour in which I and those who think like me – and there must be millions – hold you: even when we disagree with you, for generally in the end we discover that you were right and we were wrong, and we should still honour you if we didn't.'[357]

Through such flattery, Bryant was quickly embraced by the conservative elite. Even before the success of *Charles II* he had twice been asked to stand for Parliament, but had declined on the grounds that politics was a rich man's profession. 'Legislation', he later explained, 'was as expensive a luxury as polo.' He accordingly focused his attentions on building up a large amount of capital through his literary and journalistic work, keeping his eye open for an opportunity to enter politics in style at a later date. The first part of this plan he executed faultlessly. With the aid of a growing fortune he bought a series of valuable properties in London, culminating with a large mansion in Rutland Gate, where he lived a luxurious though busy life. At one time he was simultaneously directing the Greenwich Naval Pageant, giving a series of talks on the BBC on the 'National Character' and writing the definitive multi-volume biography of Samuel Pepys. The only time in which he had to conduct his correspondence was in the back of a taxi going to and from Euston station.[358]

All this took its toll on Bryant's marriage. Neglected and bored, Sylvia soon found solace in drink. Eager to keep her happy, Bryant suggested at the outset of 1936 that she take a cruise to South America in the hope of finding 'a lover, or someone to love'. But the plan backfired spectacularly when the man she eventually took up with wrote to Bryant complaining of his behaviour towards the 'poor woman'. Although this gallant seducer accepted that Sylvia was 'bad tempered, mean beyond description, abusive, low in [her] language and dissipated', he attributed many of these faults to her husband's cruel neglect. This assessment was probably correct. Only a few weeks after Sylvia's return from the South Atlantic, Bryant callously explained what he had been getting up to in her absence. 'For some time', he wrote, 'I've been regularly unfaithful to you, and to put it bluntly shall go on being so.' Aware that his wife would require proof of these liaisons to secure a divorce from him, Bryant suggested that she make enquires at an address near St James's Square where she 'should be able to get evidence enough of my infidelity'.[359]

There was some irony in this. While his marriage slid further into an abyss of dysfunction and adultery, Bryant was becoming well-known as a champion of 'old-fashioned values' in the columns of the *ILN*. 'The established certainties of the Victorian era have vanished,' he lamented in a typical contribution, 'and the younger generation is groping for new faith and new certainty.' With almost every societal development, from the decline of corporal punishment to the elitist, left-wing bias of the BBC, Bryant signalled his disapproval. 'It is merely symptomatic', he wrote of 'progressive' thought in general, 'of an attitude of mind that is widespread among our ruling classes, and particularly among those who have received a prolonged and expensive education.' But divorce reform remained the one area in which Bryant sided with the progressives. At the time of the Abdication Crisis in 1936, he refused to sanction Trevelyan's high-minded opinion that the king's undoing was a victory 'against the view that sexual license is a natural right of man'. More honestly, Bryant commended the 'dignified and self-sacrificing' actions of the ex-king, reminding his readers that 'the only effective court of judgment in questions of morality is a man's own conscience'. When A. P. Herbert introduced a controversial Divorce Bill the following year, Bryant threw his weight behind the measure; thirty-five years later he surprised many friends by delivering a grateful peroration at his funeral.[360]

After their divorce in 1939 Sylvia went to live in a small cottage near Salisbury Plain, supported by a modest stipend drawn from her ex-husband. Her concerned relatives speculated that this amount was so meagre that she was supplementing her income by offering her services to the local troops in the manner of a latter-day Nell

Gwyn. Although this seems unlikely, Bryant was informed that the bungalow in which she lived with her cherished dog and new husband was frequently overrun with soldiers. Bryant attempted to put the whole matter out of his mind. When Sylvia died from her addiction a few years later he consoled himself with the seemingly bizarre thought that she had at least been loved by 'that beautiful, gentle dog that worshipped and lived for her'. A keen animal lover himself, who would later write a short 'biography' of his rescue dog, Jimmy, the reference was almost certainly not meant ironically.[361]

Bryant's failings as a husband were rarely so calculating: they stemmed almost entirely from his devotion to his career. He could not hold back; he could not spare himself for even a moment. And this was not solely out of a desire for worldly success. Just as in his days as a teacher, he seriously believed that his literary and historical work could affect the destinies of the nation for the better.

From this commendable intention arose the most dangerous passage in Bryant's working life. With the rise of Nazism in Germany, politics in the late 1930s had become increasingly split between those who favoured the establishment of either a communist utopia or a totalitarian dictatorship. Favouring neither, Bryant focused his attentions on attacking the left-wing intellectuals who had gained so much ground in Britain since the last war. 'We want no more Cromwells', he told his *ILN* readers in April 1937, 'to save us against our own will, whether they wear red shirts or black.' In the same article he denounced the new darling of the left-wing press, George Orwell, for failing to recognise in his popular book *The Road to Wigan Pier* that the stark industrial town was not 'Hell' in the eyes of its inhabitants. 'The painter has failed to enter the soul

of his sitter,' he remarked. In voicing such views, Bryant believed
himself to be speaking up for the sensible, silent majority who were
happy with Britain and the manner in which it was governed.[362]

Where Bryant's position became less justifiable was in his
conviction that these intellectuals were wrong in their hysterical
denunciation of the fascist regimes of Europe. Drawing a highly
tendentious and tactless parallel between those dictatorships and
the persecuted Catholics of Restoration England, Bryant called
upon his countrymen to show more 'toleration' towards their continental neighbours. 'A nation,' he wrote in April 1938, 'like a man
or woman, may call itself Fascist or Communist: it still remains a
form of human society composed of human beings ... a subject
... for understanding and sympathy.' Even though this seemingly
blinkered outlook was well beyond the pale in the eyes of a more
belligerent school of liberals, personified by Churchill, it restored
Bryant in the estimation of Trevelyan. 'How good that we should
think so much alike,' he wrote upon reading Bryant's contribution. 'Your *ILN* article states exactly what I feel about two sorts of
"Liberalism". I think I have, taught by the last war and advanced
years, moved out of the one into the other, and met you there!'[363]

The comparison which Bryant frequently drew in these years
between Cromwell and Hitler was one which his enemies were wont
to misrepresent. As he had always made clear in his *ILN* articles and
his lectures at Ashridge, he was anything but a hero-worshipper of the
Puritan regicide. His 'imaginative idealism', he once wrote, 'was alien to
the spirit of England'. What he admired in both Cromwell and Hitler
was their undeniable capacity not only to 'give laws to their peoples',
but also to 'inspire them through some mystic idealism or power of

personality with the desire to obey those laws'. Even in his most flattering and premature assessment of the German dictator – made in 1933 in his capacity as a teacher – his words were underscored by the same tacit qualification. 'Hitler,' he told the students of Ashridge,

> like all the best Germans, is a mystic: and nothing could be further removed from intellectualism and free republicanism of France than the mystic dream of inspired leadership and disciplined unity which is Germany's ... His words, if there is any meaning in words at all, seem as full of this vital and passionate quality as those of our Cromwell.[364]

This was the mindset with which Bryant watched the tragedy of the 1930s slowly unfold. He took the descent of Spain into civil war in 1936 and the brutal murder of tens of thousands of clergy and civilians by republican 'freedom fighters' as further evidence of the destructiveness of the forces against which Hitler and Mussolini were arrayed. As tensions rose, Bryant was dispatched to the Peninsular at the behest of his old ally, J. C. C. Davidson, in order to keep the Prime Minister informed of developments. 'Outside the world of big hotels and international highways', he wrote to Baldwin upon his return, 'there is a general impression that the foundations of civilisation are being undermined.' On the walls of every village he saw 'symbols of the Hammer and Sickles and in the streets the undisguised signs of bitter class hatred, fomented by unceasing agitation by Soviet agents among a poor and cruelly misled peasant and working-class population'. To these vivid impressions Bryant uncritically added statistics gleaned from the pro-Franco Spanish embassy in London, where he became a frequent visitor.[365]

These worrying developments emboldened Bryant in his defence of European fascism. One after the other, he publicly attempted to justify the cut-throat diplomatic manoeuvres of the Hitler regime: the Germans, he contended, were merely redressing past wrongs. The Treaty of Versailles he denounced in the *Manchester Evening News* as a cruel and unpatriotic scourge, a betrayal of 'our traditional good nature, moderation and love of fair play'. Accordingly, he saw no reason why the German government should not extend 'popular political memory' back to the nineteenth century, when German and Italian nationalism had been fashionable among liberal intellectuals, by effecting a bloodless *Anschluss* of Austria. Likewise, he could see no justification for denying the German population of the Sudetenland the right to reunite with their countrymen: it would, he wrote in the columns of the *ILN*, be 'a monstrous thing to impose war, and all its appalling suffering and risk on our own people' in support of such a denial. In a celebratory editorial for the *Ashridge Journal* after the Munich crisis, Bryant duly paid homage to Chamberlain for 'undoing that which had been foolishly done in the war-engendered passions of 1919'.[366]

These contributions helped make Bryant something of a hate figure in the eyes of the left. But when his enemies reached out to him personally, as did H. G. Wells regarding some statistics quoted in one of his articles, Bryant could be the embodiment of charm. 'It has always been a source of sadness to me', replied Bryant,

> that my attitude ... should have earned me the disapproval of many whom I respect. But I hope you won't think me guilty of flattery and insincerity when I say that I feel it was almost worth it to have

drawn an autograph letter from the author of *Tono-Bungay* and *Mr Polly* and one who has given me more pleasure and instruction than I could ever hope to express.[367]

Bryant's habitual courtesy did not, however, prevent him from publicising his view that there were too many left-wing journalists in the British media, especially at the BBC. In a letter to Chamberlain written shortly after the Munich agreement, he railed that the broadcaster's 'attacks' on both the British Prime Minister and the German government were 'doing a great deal of harm' to the delicate international situation. He regarded these onslaughts as a symptom 'of the left-wing campaign that has been going on for years for monopolising all the organs that form public opinion'. With equal concern, Bryant explained to Stanley Baldwin that apart from Dean Inge and himself there was scarcely a single conservative journalist left in the country. 'For many years,' he complained,

> *The Observer* employed Mr Gerald Gould, a strong socialist and 'reader' to Messrs. Gollancz, to review its novels, and the *Daily Telegraph* Mr Day Lewis, a Communist who appeared to judge books not by literary but by political and social standards. In *The Bystander*, Mr A. G. Macdonell, writing as a regular columnist, maintains a spirited war with the Government's foreign policy. Writers like Mr G. D. H. Cole and Professor Harold Laski, who make large incomes out of their advocacy of Left-wing views in press and platform, find no difficulty in obtaining commissions to express their opinions on specialist subjects in Conservative and Capitalist papers.[368]

This rather exaggerated picture was enough to persuade Baldwin to lend his name to a Conservative book club envisaged by Bryant as an antidote to the fashionable Left Book Club founded by Victor Gollancz two years previously. 'The National Book Association', as it was called, became Bryant's chief occupation during the final years of the 1930s. The titles which he released on a monthly basis read like a back catalogue of the doomed Appeasement movement. Its first number was an impassioned tribute to Baldwin penned in just three weeks by Bryant to mark the premier's sudden retirement in May 1937. A few months later he issued a collection of his *ILN* articles, provisionally entitled 'Colonel Blimp Answers Back', but ultimately released as *Humanity in Politics*. Later Bryant issued a collection of Neville Chamberlain's speeches entitled *In Search of Peace*. And in the Association's final instalment, Bryant served up an expurgated translation of *Mein Kampf*, which he described in a brief Preface – as far as the Führer's emphasis on 'national character' was concerned – as 'Disraelian ... pregnant, [and] incisive'.[369]

Yet while Bryant's position seemed ever more extreme, his popularity and reputation had never stood higher. Sir John Reith was so impressed by his work that he invited him to become his private assistant with a view to replacing him as Director General of the BBC. 'It should be', wrote Bryant to Reith shortly after the war, 'what you started to make it: the voice of England's conscience and thought ... like the Church of England used to be.' Similarly the veteran editor of *The Observer*, J. L. Garvin, allowed Bryant to write his Sunday leading articles for three months during the summer of 1937 in the hope that he would one day succeed him as editor. 'No living historian', he wrote to Bryant a few years later, 'equals the lucid glow that you have now ... you are among the very few whose upholding of heroic patriotism will do immeasurable good.' Only Bryant's immense success as an independent author prevented either of these opportunities from coming to fruition.[370]

That Bryant could look askance at such openings illustrates the heights he had reached by 1939. He had achieved fame of which he had scarcely dreamt. His total book sales far exceeded the 100,000 mark; he had the ear of people at the centre of politics, and he had an almost daily outlet for his personal opinions in the press. It was all too good. The bold young Tory was about to overreach himself in a tragic and spectacular fashion.

❧

Five years after Bryant's death in 1985 Andrew Roberts was given access to the late historian's private papers and the corresponding government files held by the National Archives at Kew. What he found appalled him. They showed, he wrote, 'that far from being the patriot he so long and loudly proclaimed himself, Bryant was in fact a Nazi sympathizer and fascist fellow-traveller, who only narrowly escaped internment as a potential traitor in 1940'. In a matter of days, Bryant's reputation was irreparably damaged.[371]

This righteous denunciation of Bryant was understandable. But it savours exactly of the 'Whig Interpretation' for which Bryant was so rightly assailed by his contemporaries. It is the judgement of a man who knows how the story ends. Bryant had no such vantage point, at least as far as his own history was concerned.

Bryant's transformation from armchair pundit of the Hitler regime to a man with dangerous links to its centre is not as surprising as it may seem. Through his ceaseless hobnobbing with Baldwin, Chamberlain and the managers of Central Office, he had by the late 1930s become a useful man to the government: a free agent who could be used, if needed, for special projects. At the same time he was, in the eyes of more reactionary figures, someone who could be employed to lobby ministers in a more extremist direction. What Bryant held in common with both these camps was a belief that European civilisation could not afford another world war; where he went further was his conviction, along with Baldwin, that Britain also needed to rearm – fast.

The result of this seemingly contradictory position was that Bryant gradually fell out of favour with the supporters of appeasement, becoming instead one of the most vocal champions of the British war effort led by Churchill. His delay in taking the offensive against the German government stemmed, more than anything else, from his preference for the isolationist politics championed by Charles II and several of his other historical idols.

Bryant's informal links with the Nazi regime began in the summer of 1938 when one of his writers for the National Book Association, the popular novelist Francis Yates-Brown, put him in touch with the chairman of the Anglo-German Friendship Society, Thomas Chambers. This nineteenth-century organisation had been founded with the idealistic belief that Britain and Germany should always remain allies, no matter how different their political systems might become. Out of this connection, Chambers asked Bryant if he would play host for an afternoon to a delegation of Hitler Youth leaders whom he was entertaining that summer.

There was nothing particularly unusual about this: it was exactly the sort of event which might come to the attention of the educational director of the country's leading Conservative training college. The sinister aspect was certainly lost on Bryant, who shared with his guests nothing more subversive than the third volume of his Pepys biography; expertly judged, though it was, with its defence of authoritarian government over mob rule, to chime with the political situation. It was not until a year later that the incongruous gathering had any significant effect on Bryant's career and reputation.

This occurred when one of the visitors, Dr Kurt Blohm, asked Chambers to arrange a second meeting between himself and the famous British publicist. Blohm was prompted to do so by Hitler's chief adviser on English affairs, Walther Hewel, who planned to use the Anglo-German Friendship Society as a means of gauging public opinion across the Channel.

Bryant was more than happy to assist. During the course of a 'very frank talk' with Blohm, he voiced the opinion that the British government would not countenance Hitler forcing a 'settlement' of the thorny 'Danzig question' – whether it would follow northern Czechoslovakia into the Nazi empire. Armed intervention in Danzig, or anywhere else in Poland, warned Bryant, would 'inevitably provoke war'. There could be no second Munich.

It is clear that this was not merely Bryant's private opinion. He had evidently discussed the matter with Chamberlain, whom he was scrupulous in keeping abreast of his activities. When he heard that Chambers had had a second meeting with Blohm, at which it was intimated for the first time that Hitler would find a way of annexing Danzig peacefully, Bryant immediately passed on this information to Chamberlain, adding in a note to the Prime Minister exactly what he had told Chambers: that 'the best service he could do England was to let all his influential German friends know without any shadow of doubt that, whatever his own wishes in the matter might be, war was inevitable if any incident should occur'.[372]

No one could have given a plainer warning to the German government that the British would honour the guarantee made to Poland after the Munich summit. Chamberlain was highly satisfied, and responded warmly when Bryant informed him shortly afterwards that Hewel had invited him to Salzburg to discuss these matters in more detail. As part of a wide-scale initiative overseen by Chamberlain to establish informal, non-political connections between London and Berlin, Bryant was the perfect man to act as bridge-builder.

Before his departure from Croydon Airport on 9 July, Bryant sent Chamberlain a secret memorandum explaining his plan of action. Keen to appear judicious and impartial to his German hosts, Bryant proposed to meet his own expenses, preferring to present himself as an ex-serviceman with no official connections whatsoever. Bryant knew that this deception could do great damage to his 'professional career and livelihood', but was willing to go through with the charade for the sake of preventing war. 'If by any miracle', he rather grandly explained to the Prime Minister, 'I succeed, I should be doing a far greater service than millions of others [who] may be called upon … at far greater sacrifices' should mobilisation commence. Aware that Chamberlain might be surprised by this large claim, Bryant stressed that he would be taken seriously by his hosts on account of his 'sympathetic understanding of the German historical background', and for the fact that he was 'no pacifist', being 'known to have taken a national line' in his writings at a time when it was 'still very unfashionable in intellectual circles to believe in one's own country'.[373]

In order to further the illusion that he was in Germany merely in a private capacity, Bryant spent several days as a tourist in Berlin, visiting the Olympic Stadium and several other major landmarks. His report on what he saw reveals, however, that his keen historical eye was plainly wanting when it turned to the contemporary scene. He informed Chamberlain that there was 'no obvious militarism' and later admitted in print that he had been taken in by the cheerful swagger of Hitler's Germany. 'For it was a land', he wrote, 'which, for all the miseries of the minorities tucked out of sight and hearing, seemed at unity with itself and in which the common man felt himself part of a great nation moving, as he supposed, proudly and gladly towards a happier and assured goal.' He did not yet fully comprehend 'that the goal was the crucifixion of Europe'.[374]

Bryant's indifference to the 'minorities tucked out of sight' can be easily explained: the domestic situation was not part of his brief. But his outlook was undoubtedly tinged by the commonplace anti-Semitism which pervaded the higher echelons of British society. At Harrow he had grown up in an environment in which persecution of Jewish pupils had been routine. As his near contemporary, the future Indian president Jawaharlal Nehru, remembered, 'there was always a background of anti-Semitic feeling' at the school. 'They were "damned Jews", and soon, almost unconsciously, I began to think that it was the proper thing to have this feeling.' Added to this unwholesome background was Bryant's increasingly friendly connection with the lords and ladies of high society, whose racism could be even more overt. When the Conservative politician Duff Cooper met the Duke of Westminster outside the Savoy in September 1939 he was amazed to hear him 'abusing the Jewish race and rejoicing that we were not yet at war'. Compared to these flagrant outbursts, Bryant's willingness to draw a sympathetic veil over the Nazi regime's discriminatory treatment of the Jewish population seems restrained, if not excusable.[375]

The high point of Bryant's German tour was his meeting with Hewel in Salzburg on 11 July. Just as with his discussions with Dr Blohm in London, Bryant emphasised that Chamberlain intended to stand by his guarantee to Poland. If Bryant was eager to charm and impress his host, he certainly did not hide from him the seriousness of the situation. 'Though I was not at first attracted by his personality', he reported to Chamberlain, '...I felt I was talking to a man of the world and a gentleman.' In the course of a halting conversation, he reiterated that military action against Poland would lead to a war with Britain which 'would end by destroying everything we both valued in the world and leave the Communists the only gainers'. With equal tact and skill, Bryant later told Hewel that he would regret this not only from the perspective of his own country, but also on the grounds that it would plunge Germany back into the doldrums. Contrasting the 'amazing creative activity and widespread social well-being' he had recently seen in Berlin with 'the miserable and broken Germany' he had seen during a brief visit in 1923, he implored his host to inform his master to tread carefully.[376]

After their meeting, Hewel paid a visit to Hitler at Berchtesgaden to report Bryant's stern warning. But when the official returned to the conference room the following day he 'could bring me back no other answer but that of a closed mind'. Defeated and exhausted, Bryant returned to England with a 'dying, desperate hope' that war could still be averted. To further this end, he submitted to Chamberlain another lengthy memorandum, this time detailing the nature of his conversations with Hewel. The document was duly passed on to the Foreign Secretary, Lord Halifax, who gave it his attention. Although the Prime Minister privately believed the dialogue to have an 'air of frankness and even naiveté', he wrote to Bryant that he was 'deeply obliged' for his services and volunteered to reimburse his travel expenses from the intelligence fund.[377]

Two days after Bryant's return, he made his usual appearance at Lords for the annual Eton v. Harrow cricket match. Having discharged his official duties, he was looking forward to getting on with his neglected historical work 'and to watch a little cricket at the same time if I am not wanted elsewhere'. But the presence of the former Prime Minister Stanley Baldwin prevented him from pursuing this course. Throughout the match, Bryant kept up an almost ceaseless commentary with the veteran statesman about his recent diplomatic mission. His interlocutor, however, was not particularly interested. 'Baldwin looked grave,' recalled Bryant.

He kept nodding, though keeping his eye on the cricket all the while. I remember Harrow were doing rather badly at that moment. Once, when he started to say, 'The trouble is', I thought he was going to make some comment on my cheerless reports, but he simply continued, 'our bowlers just aren't good enough for them.' Almost immediately, two Eton wickets fell and the match moved forward again to a long-awaited Harrow victory.[378]

If Bryant's informal lobbying displayed too much eagerness to prevent war from commencing, he showed no such lack of spine in his weekly *ILN* column. At the same time as giving his sympathetic reports on Germany to Baldwin and Chamberlain, he proclaimed to his readers that the nation was prepared to meet Germany's 'lust for power' with force. By contrast to the jackbooted patriotism of the Nazis, he marvelled at the British people's superior 'good humour, humanity, and … invincible spirits'. Should the 'cruel necessity' of a war arrive, he wrote a little later, he had no doubt that British resolve would triumph over the material greatness of the Third Reich.[379]

Bryant stood by these comments when German tanks rolled into Poland in October 1939. Ahead of his fellow appeasers, he instantly wrote to *The Times* denouncing this 'barbarous act'. But he asked his countrymen to resist the clamour to avenge it by commencing a war to the death with the most powerful country on continental Europe. Instead he called for a limited military campaign, designed to check 'Hitler's fatal method of conducting foreign affairs, and not the right of the German people to choose their own governors'. Echoing his warning to Hewel, he concluded by stating that an 'angry and bloody victory' over the entire nation would not be in Britain's interests. It would leave Europe 'exhausted and ruined … an anarchical desert'.[380]

While it is true that this letter secured Bryant the support of many of the most notorious Nazi-sympathisers in the country, it did little harm to his reputation in government circles. The day after the letter appeared, Bryant was contacted by the Labour MP Richard Crossman, who invited him to join the Home Publicity Division at the Ministry of Information. Bryant was too large-minded to be put off by Crossman's previous lack of sympathy with his political views. 'After the inspiring and truly Christian example', he replied, 'set us by Hitler and Stalin, our own ideological differences of the past seem trifling!'[381]

In addition to his collaboration with Crossman, Bryant prepared for the deputy Foreign Secretary, R. A. Butler, two more secret memoranda setting out the kind of peace terms he believed to be acceptable to the Nazi regime. These proposals enlarged significantly on his *Times* letter in suggesting that Britain come to terms with a 'new international order' in which the world would be divided into 'a few great self-sufficing regions each with an economy controlled in accordance with the needs and desires of the people who inhabit them'. This plan, as Bryant adeptly pointed out, was the same imperial vision of Britain which had been championed forty years previously by the Prime Minister's venerable father, Joseph Chamberlain. In his desire to bring about this late Victorian scheme, Bryant was even willing to suggest that Britain accept the cession of Poland and Czechoslovakia to Nazi hegemony after all. It seemed unlikely, in his view, that the Versailles status of those countries could 'ever be restored any more than that of Latvia, Estonia and Lithuania'; though he added, in an afterthought, that 'they no doubt can and must be given some measure of independence'.[382]

Such views increasingly brought Bryant into the orbit of those who regarded Nazi Germany not merely as a political reality to be accommodated, but a force for good in the world. As long ago as June 1937 the pro-German writer who had put him in touch with the Hitler Youth delegation, Yates-Brown, had written to Bryant that 'many of us [with Nazi sympathies] look to you in these days'; later the likes of Rudolf Pomaroli, who signed his letters 'Heil Hitler', commended his public defence of a compromise with Hitler as a 'momentary beam of sunshine in the blackness in which Europe again finds herself'. Even his own brother, Philip, expressed his sympathy for the Nazi regime, while the pro-Nazi Lord Brocket expressed relief that 'all the people in England are not yet mad!'[383]

These multifarious characters had their own ideas as to how the peace of Europe could be secured: not, as in Bryant's case, by lobbying the government and public opinion directly, but by reaching out to senior Nazi officials personally – an action which would have been plainly treasonous. The scepticism with which many of these would-be allies regarded Bryant is clear from a complaint made by the richest and most important member of the group, the former Tory MP Henry Drummond Wolff. In a letter to the Cabinet minister Leo Amery – whose son John would later be executed for defecting to the Nazis – Drummond Wolff described Bryant as 'a brilliant and resourceful writer', but warned that he needed to be 'fairly strictly supervised and controlled'. 'He suffers from an emotional complex', he wrote, 'which has manifested itself in a hatred of that dying element, wealth, accompanied by an inconsistent form of socialism.' Unimpressed by Bryant's recent championing of 'Federal Union' in the *ILN*, the former Tory MP

pronounced that his 'judgement is not sound, he is somewhat inac-
curate and not always faithful to clearly defined principles'. When
Bryant later marshalled Drummond Wolff's muddled and Nazi-
accommodating economic ideas into book form under the title
Britain Awake!, those at the extreme end of the appeasement group
dismissed the publication as 'very boring' and 'very poor stuff'.[384]

But Bryant was sufficiently valued by the likes of the Lords Brocket
and Rushcliffe to be asked, on one occasion, to pass a message to
the Foreign Secretary from one of their Nazi contacts. This agent,
Bengt Berg, had been assigned by Hermann Göring to bring about
a rapid peace treaty with Britain in anticipation of the conquest
of Russia. Bryant's reluctance to act as a conduit for what Halifax
fairly described as 'this sewer' is demonstrated by his explanation to
the Foreign Secretary that he had only done so on the grounds that
his noble friends were temporarily indisposed. 'With the greatest
reluctance,' explained Bryant, 'for it was no concern of mine, I rang
up your secretary at the Foreign Office and asked for orders.'[385]

Bryant was equally well-meaning, but ultimately wrong, in his
attempt to promote a better understanding between the British
and German publics when, in August 1939, he put the finishing
touches on his latest book, *Unfinished Victory*. Originally commissioned by the British Council to appear in the German press under
the byline of the newspaper proprietor Lord Kemsley, the book
provided a convincing explanation of how Nazism had grown out
of the wasteland created by Versailles. In the first chapter, 'Famine
Over Europe', Bryant drew on contemporary accounts to paint a
disquieting picture of life under the British blockade two decades
previously. Appalling stories of hollow-cheeked parents feeding

their babies with paste made from black bread and lard; gangly youths collapsing in the street from starvation, and queues of homeless veterans awaiting their dinner from soup kitchens provided a sombre backdrop.

It was his sympathy for these real sufferings which fatally led Bryant – in his search for objectivity – to offer some explanation for the German people's growing hostility against the Jews. The root cause, he judged, was the hyperinflation years, during which anyone 'able to command foreign currency or credit' had been able to buy up 'the assets of a nation at "knock-out" prices'. 'It was the Jews,' he continued, 'with their international affiliations and their hereditary flair for finance who were the best able to seize such opportunities.' Although he showed sympathy for those Jews who were 'long domiciled in Germany [and] had learnt to live and think as Germans', he felt that many of their co-religionists had been 'arrogant ... vulgar ... [and] vicious' in their display of new-found wealth. Moreover, Bryant felt that although as many gentiles as Jews had engaged in disreputable profiteering, especially from the sale of backstreet pornography, 'it was the Jews rather than the Christians among the promoters of this trade who were remembered in after years'.[386]

Even were these views to have been published in August 1939, it is unlikely that Bryant would have been afforded much public acclaim. The fact that delays led to the book not being released until January 1940 ensured that he was fiercely denounced. Criticism came from sources as unlikely as his fellow conservative Ernest Barker, Master of Peterhouse College, Cambridge, who declared himself 'puzzled, and on the whole, saddened' by the book. Of particular offence to

Barker were passages in which Bryant compared Hitler to figures such as Cromwell, General Booth and 'that which Dr Johnson loved – a good hater'. But Bryant never pretended that his admiration for Hitler was absolute. 'His racial theory may be repulsive gibberish,' he told his readers, 'his ambitions barbarous and ridiculous, his motives cruel and sadistic, but only a man deliberately shutting his eyes to realities can deny his astonishing genius for leadership.'[387]

Not all of Bryant's friends expressed their disapproval of the book. Edmund Blunden described it as 'clear and humane', while G. M. Trevelyan expressed his 'agreement ... in essentials if not every detail'. Added to this gentle chorus of support came encouragement from the book's publisher, the Conservative MP Harold Macmillan – no advocate of appeasement – who wrote to Bryant shortly afterwards: 'I do not at all regret the publication of *Unfinished Victory*. As you say, the disappointment is the fault of Hitler, not of us.'[388]

Reviewers were less understanding. In the *New Statesman*, Richard Crossman reverted to his original view of Bryant by savaging the book. He alleged that the author was 'so eager to confess our betrayal of Germany' that he had neglected to take account of the 'traitors within, who exploited the desperation of the masses for their own designs'. A leading article in the *Jewish Chronicle* even went so far as to suggest that the author should be interned as a potential traitor.[389]

By the spring of 1940 such a humiliation was undoubtedly a possibility. No fewer than fifteen prominent public figures, including several of Bryant's former associates, were imprisoned under emergency wartime legislation. Evidently concerned about his own position, Bryant called on his official contacts, offering whatever services they required of him – he even offered to go and work in a munitions factory. But it was agreed that the greatest service he could do his country would be to commence a series of patriotic works which would galvanise the public against Hitler. As the Oxford historian Hugh Trevor-Roper, at the time an intelligence officer at Bletchley Park, cattishly recalled: it was decided that Bryant 'could be "turned" to become a lucid propagandist for the Allied cause'.[390]

Bryant did not disappoint. Throwing over a series of highly lucrative contracts to write biographies of Disraeli, Rupert Brooke and the final instalment of his *Pepys*, the discredited historian launched into his most effective paean of national history to date: *English Saga*. Written in the shadow of an anticipated Nazi invasion, Bryant rediscovered his voice in an almost biblical account of his country's triumph over adversity in the hundred years leading up to the war. In a rousing climax, Bryant concluded:

> An island fortress, England is fighting a war of redemption not only for Europe but for her own soul. Facing dangers greater than any in her history she has fallen back on the rock of her national character. Her future and that of the world depend not only on her victory but on her ability to restate in new form the ancient law of her own moral purpose and unity. By so doing she may discover a common denominator for human reconstruction more glorious than anything in her long past.

In those lines, Bryant spoke for the nation, and the book was a runaway success. According to Harold Wilson, the entire Cabinet secretariat read it in the air-raid shelter beneath Downing Street, while the late commander of the British Army Lord Gort declared it to be the only book besides the Bible which he took with him overseas. Later during the war, Bryant continued with his morale-boosting histories with an epic three-volume retelling of the Napoleonic Wars, beginning with *The Years of Endurance* (1942) and *The Years of Victory* (1944), which complemented his stirring articles in the *ILN* extolling the superiority of British leaders such as Pitt and Wellington over Napoleon and other would-be world dictators.

So impressed was the military establishment with these efforts that Bryant not only became required reading for cadets at Sandhurst, he was also invited to lecture to troops all over the theatre of war: his wartime travels took him as far afield as Orkney, Baghdad and Cairo. Few guest speakers received such a warm welcome from the troops as Bryant, whom even a critic described as a 'winning lecturer'. One left-wing serviceman was so enthused by his evocations of Britain's martial past that he proposed to found an 'Arthur Bryant Club' to help make his books even more available. In grateful recognition for these services, Field Marshal Montgomery himself lobbied the government after the war to have Bryant publicly honoured, first as an OBE, then, in 1954, as a Knight, and finally, in 1967, as a member of the Companionship of Honour. 'To Arthur Bryant,' inscribed the victor of El Alamein in a copy of his own speeches, 'who, in rendering great service to his country as an historian, has also rendered unique service to the British Army.'[391]

But not everyone was convinced. Among his many critics, remindful of his former position as court historian of the Baldwin–Chamberlain era, was his own brother Philip, now the chaplain at Harrow. 'You and your entourage made me believe that the things which you now describe as "evil and destroying violence" was pure and cleansing, noble and devoted and that the forces of Barbarism was Communism and corrupt Jews and financiers against which it contended,' he wrote with as much exaggeration as inelegance. 'If you were wrong then,' he went on, '…you owe it to your disciples to say so, and to give the reasons which led you into your mistake then and the reasons which led you into your disillusionment now.' Bryant's reply to this letter is not preserved among either brother's papers, but it is clear that the two men barely kept in touch until Philip's death in 1960.[392]

For A. L. Rowse – who gladly accepted Bryant's dedication of *Years of Endurance* – the reason for Bryant's 'reinvention' was no more elevated than a desire to cash in on Britain's growing resolve to defeat Hitler. This, however, was not the case. Not even in his darkest hour of appeasement did Bryant propound the view that Nazism was morally superior to the constitutional democracy of Britain. He simply wanted to pursue the best interests of his country, whether by means of peace or war. Years later he would defend himself with candour from an unsuccessful attempt by the historian David Irving to publicise details of his pre-war activities. 'Where, like many other people, I was undoubtedly wrong', he confessed in a private letter to the editor of the *Sunday Express*, John Junor, was in supposing that it was possible to avert the appalling tragedy of a second world war by reaching an agreement with Germany when its leaders, relying on our weakness and that of our allies, were resolved to precipitate that tragedy by imposing their will by force … Whether I was right or wrong in still believing [that the British public did not want a war with Germany] so as late as August 1939 is hard to determine.[393]

If Bryant had been blind, foolish and misguided in his well-intended diplomacy, he had betrayed neither his country nor the principles upon which his entire life and career were founded.

༄

Although Bryant was only in his mid-forties when the war ended, he was already a veteran. No longer interested in embarking on a parliamentary career himself, he reluctantly severed his remaining links with the Conservative Party, preferring instead to criticise its leaders from the outside. 'After twenty years of disillusionment,' he wrote to a military correspondent shortly after VE Day, 'I am too old to crusade any more for Tory ideals only to find that one is being a smoke screen for stupidity, inertia and greed.' For the remaining forty years of his long life he would exist as a lingering relic of a bygone age: a prophet in the wilderness, vainly warning his fellow countrymen of the inglorious decline awaiting their once-proud nation. 'Over the great houses', he wrote as early as 1949, 'I can still see, caught in the gleam of the pallid winter afternoon's sunrays, the sinister inscription: "Mene, mene, tekel, upharsin." "God hath numbered the kingdom and finished it. Thou art weighed in the balances and found wanting. Thy kingdom is divided, and given to the Medes and Persians."'[394]

The 'Medes and Persians' were, for Bryant, the ministers of the socialist government of Clement Attlee. Despite initially hailing the shock Labour victory of July 1945 as a boon for post-war Britain, Bryant soon became convinced that the heavy taxation, state benefits, trade unionism and excessive bureaucracy which that government introduced and encouraged would undermine the national character. In countless post-war articles and works of history he reminded his readers with increasing resignation that Britain's wealth had arisen from a fundamentally different set of values. As the euphoria of VE Day dissolved into the gloom of Austerity Britain, Bryant railed that the great stock of patriotism and grit achieved in wartime was being squandered in an attempt to perfect human nature by legislation alone.

An increasingly isolated figure, Bryant's public life became somewhat uneventful. Walled up in his large house in Rutland Gate, he passed his days composing histories with his lucky mascot – a wooden totem named 'Bear' – looking down on him from his ink stand. In the evenings he would regularly venture into Pall Mall to dine at one of the six clubs to which he belonged. Dressed in an elegant three-piece suit and his old school tie, he would often be seen reading a large book in the smoking room or exchanging compliments with distinguished members at one of the convivial dining tables. While many of these individuals retained fond memories of him being 'extremely courteous', some felt that he was 'too ingratiating' and 'eager to be liked'. There was, wrote Sir

Roy Strong, 'something about him which made me draw back'. A man 'loath[ing] gossip' and with 'absolutely no small talk', Bryant was certainly an odd, but not unlikable clubman.[395]

Behind this mask of formality, however, Bryant's private life remained as colourful as ever. In 1941 he married Anne Brooke, niece of the last 'White Rajah' of Sarawak, Charles Vyner Brooke. She was an attractive woman, considerably younger than himself, but without a great deal of interest in his historical work. 'I have known for some years', wrote her brother in a letter to Bryant, 'that Anne would never marry anyone but what the French call an "*homme serieux*", and as she is sprung from illiterate stock, and doesn't know many, I doubted that she would ever marry at all!' Just as with his first marriage, Bryant's devotion to Anne took the unusual form of interesting himself in her family's history. When Sarawak was ceded to the British Empire in July 1946 – Britain's final colonial addition – he launched a forlorn crusade to preserve its status as a privately governed kingdom. Letters to the Lord Chancellor and an assortment of other worthies led to a parliamentary debate on the matter in which Churchill himself lent his support. But these efforts were no more successful in sparing Sarawak from annexation than they were in breathing life into Bryant's marriage. 'Madly jealous' about her husband's insatiable 'womanising' and 'philandering', Anne spent their years together sulking in her bedroom or wallowing at their vast Dorset country house, Smedmore. By the time that her brother Anthony lost his legal battle to be restored as Rajah in 1951 the marriage was in ruins, and the couple parted shortly thereafter.[396]

Like all the other women in Bryant's life, Anne appears as little more than a shadow in his mass of correspondence and journalism.

But she was perceptive in recognising one of the most important sources of her husband's personal defects: 'there wasn't anybody else to stand up to him'. Lionised by his mother ('He is a genius'), newspaper proprietors, politicians, booksellers and publishers, he became overly conscious of his status as a 'national treasure'. This eminence was confirmed in the summer of 1953 when Buckingham Palace asked him to write an essay for the official coronation programme of Queen Elizabeth II. His contribution, 'The Queen's Majesty', celebrated the monarchy as 'a more wonderful miracle than the greatest achievement of science'. His connection with the young queen was strengthened a few years later when he defended her from the anti-establishment peer, Lord Altrincham – like the former Viscount Stansgate (Tony Benn) preferring to be known by his ordinary name, John Grigg – who had penned a scurrilous article describing the sovereign as 'a priggish schoolgirl, captain of the hockey team, a prefect and a recent candidate for Confirmation'. In recognition of these services, as well as his late father's long connection with the House of Windsor, Bryant was asked in 1977 to give a peroration in Westminster Abbey on the occasion of the Queen's Silver Jubilee.[397]

To some, all this confirmed Bryant's longstanding reputation as an establishment toady and lickspittle. But he remained capable of infuriating even the most reactionary of his followers. The greatest of all his post-war heresies was his desire to erase the 'false legend' that Churchill, with the help of American finance and military assistance, was alone responsible for the Allied victory against the Nazis. He did so with great effect in his two most successful post-war books, *The Turn of the Tide* (1957) and *The Triumph of the*

West (1959), based on the war diaries of the Commander of the Imperial General Staff, Lord Alanbrooke. These acclaimed works of history suggested the war leader to have been an incompetent drunk and military ignoramus, who had only dimly recognised how close Britain had come to defeat. In a much criticised passage reproduced by Bryant, Alanbrooke described how Churchill had called him in for a meeting shortly after emerging from his bath 'looking rather like "Humpty-Dumpty" with a large body and small thin legs'. The scandal caused by these revelations led to a huge backlash against Bryant, not least by the still-living war leader, who was reported to be 'very angry indeed' about the publications. But even Churchill retained his admiration for Bryant as a historian. Although he vetoed a plan for him to write the Queen's coronation broadcast (a task he reserved for himself), he told Clement Attlee that Bryant was the living historian he most admired – an opinion surprisingly shared by the Labour leader.[398]

As the 1950s gave way to the permissive era of the 1960s and 1970s, Bryant saw his popularity wane. Britain had moved on: 'The age of giants has gone forever,' he wrote at the time of Churchill's death in 1965. Contemptuous of the smug complacency and unscrupulousness of modern political life, he gradually began to lose faith in the ruling elite. Nothing seemed to confirm his fears about the decline in standards more than the discovery in the summer of 1963 that the Minister for War, John Profumo, had lied to Parliament regarding his affair with a London showgirl named Christine Keeler. Yet Bryant was never one to succumb to the vice of self-righteousness. 'If anyone is to be judged and condemned', he wrote in his *ILN* column, '...that condemnation must comprise ourselves and the whole standard of outlook and conduct which now pass for "progressive", "fashionable" and "contemporary".' The demoralising effects of these developments on the rest of society were only too plain in his eyes: teenagers without 'constructive outlets for [their] youthful vitality and creativeness' were resorting to pop music and drug-taking; businessmen, unconcerned by morality or a sense of responsibility, had become mere 'computers' looking out for the 'bottom line', and daily journalism had degenerated into an unedifying cauldron of putrid sensationalism and malicious satire. 'If that testy old sage', wrote Bryant of Thomas Carlyle, 'were alive today and could read the "Daily This" or the "Daily That" I suspect that, if any powers of speech remained to him after the experience, his comment would be that anyone could see that a cad had written it.'[399]

Despite his generous treatment of individual malefactors, there was undoubtedly a note of hypocrisy in this catalogue of grievances. Not only was Bryant a working – and highly remunerated – journalist, his own moral behaviour often left much to be desired. As late as his eighty-second year he was still receiving wounded letters from former lovers – 'wretched discards', as one aptly described them – thrown over in his unseemly desire to involve himself romantically with a member of the aristocracy. Like his sometime friend and admirer Barbara Cartland, who admitted to 'cribb[ing]' from his histories, Bryant saw this as a just reward for his hard-won successes as an author. When Cartland introduced him to the 65-year-old Dowager Duchess of Marlborough at a Foyles literary lunch in the spring of 1980, he audaciously proposed. An announcement of their forthcoming nuptials duly appeared in *The*

Times, but Lady Marlborough decided not to go through with it. 'All coy Laura will permit herself', sneered the gossip columnist William Hickey, 'is "Nothing to say". Bride's nerves perhaps? Or is the whole thing OFF? One thing's for sure: time is running out.'[400]

Where Bryant continued to have an impact on the outside world was in his championing of reactionary causes. His manifold activities, ranging from opposing the building of a new international airport in the Buckinghamshire village of Cublington to spearheading the movement to protect Britain's historic buildings, were impressive and often highly successful. But by far the greatest of all Bryant's later-life campaigns was his involvement in opposing Britain's application to join the European Economic Community in 1962. Although in retrospect a natural progression of his conservative outlook, the post-war consensus favoured Britain's involvement in the nascent European project. At the Conservative Party conference of 1961, the Prime Minister, Harold Macmillan, had been confident enough to observe that only 'thirty or forty [delegates] voted against [entry to the EEC] in a huge assembly of four thousand or more'.[401]

This would not do for Bryant. In a series of punchy articles in the *ILN*, collected and republished at the behest of Lord Beaverbrook under the title *A Choice for Destiny*, Bryant made a strong historical argument against Britain's entry into Europe. Drawing on the constitutional history that he had been familiarising himself with for his latest project – a seven-volume history of Britain entitled *The Story of England* – Bryant declared that the Treaty of Rome threatened to destroy 'six or seven hundred years' of tradition by binding future parliaments and relinquishing sovereignty outside

the realm. So impressed was the octogenarian newspaper proprietor with these arguments that he invited Bryant to join his stable
of journalists at the *Sunday Express*. Beaverbrook's faith in Bryant
was all the more remarkable for the fact that the historian had
successfully sued him less than five years previously over a libellous
article by one of his journalists, Robert Pitman, who had falsely
accused Bryant of not obtaining official permission to publish the
Alanbrooke diaries. Reciprocating his new employer's magnanimity, Bryant not only came to be a great admirer of Beaverbrook,
he also became friendly with the journalist who had maligned
him. When Pitman unexpectedly died in 1969, Bryant dedicated
a collection of his journalism to him and made arrangements for a
substantial portion of his *Sunday Express* retainer to be made over
to his widow.[402]

Bryant's determination to prevent Britain's entry to the Common
Market won him some unlikely allies and admirers. For years ridi-
culed by his fellow popular historian A. J. P. Taylor as a 'scissors and
paste' man, Bryant now entered into friendly relations with his near
contemporary, who also wrote under the *Sunday Express* masthead.
In a letter congratulating Taylor for an article on Europe, Bryant
wrote that although the younger man had 'sometimes in the past
criticised my writing', he hoped that he would not 'on that account
resent a fellow historian writing ... to say how much he admired
your article'. Taylor would later reciprocate by congratulating 'dear
Arthur' for the final book published in his lifetime, *Set in a Silver
Sea*, with uncharacteristic warmth: 'Your latest book is the most
astonishing of all your achievements,' he wrote. 'I read it with
a mixture of wonder and admiration.' Even more gratifying for

Bryant was the respect which his stance on Europe won him from many senior members of the Labour Party, who broadly shared his scepticism over Brussels. It was from his bestselling pamphlet that the party's leader Hugh Gaitskell drew inspiration for his famous attack on the Treaty of Rome as an affront to 'one thousand years of history'. After Gaitskell's sudden death in January 1963, his successor Harold Wilson continued to champion Bryant, telling journalists that he had a collection of all his books in the Chequers library and that he admired *English Saga* above all works in the English language.[403]

Underlying Bryant's dislike of the European project was his sadness at the dismemberment of the British Empire. By entering a trading zone which would automatically exclude the former colonies which had done so much to maintain Britain during the war, the country would be discriminating against 'our kinsmen nations' in favour of those of 'different race, language and allegiance who, to put it in the mildest form, have no such claim on our gratitude'. Defending the British Empire against the charge that it had merely been a cloak for exploitation, racial chauvinism and subjugation, Bryant reminded his readers that, for all its 'humbug', imperial rule had also protected private property and the rights of every subject, irrespective of race or creed. 'There is nothing like saying', he wrote in 1969, 'over and over again, in the face of all evidence to the contrary, that no men shall we deny or sell justice, that all men are equal, that liberty is the birthright of every subject, to make a society in which these improbables begin to approach reality.' When Westminster later attempted to impose democracy on Britain's former colonies, Bryant became one of the few public figures to argue that this would result in financial collapse and the overthrow of law and order. Focusing particularly on the fate of post-colonial Rhodesia, he defended the country's maverick Prime Minister, Ian Smith, who attempted to prevent the extension of the franchise to the native population by unilaterally declaring independence. Bryant lived long enough to see Smith's worst fears realised under the murderous regime of the British government's favoured candidate in the country's first democratic election, Robert Mugabe.[404]

While many sharing these views were openly racist, Bryant showed no scintilla of prejudice against the denizens of Britain's former colonies. A strong admirer of Nelson Mandela, he wrote in 1964 that black Africans 'should be admitted, as heirs of our common humanity, to the free man's right to say and control his own affairs as soon as he is able to exercise it with fairness and tolerance towards others'. His primary opposition to the mass immigration which began to gather pace in subsequent years was that it was a betrayal of the liberal imperialism of Cecil Rhodes, whose goal had been to make countries such as Rhodesia desirable places in which to live – not poor, war-torn wastelands from which the most ambitious would emigrate. Of equal importance, however, was Bryant's conviction that a multiracial Britain would create a new rift in British politics, defined by race, which had been unknown since the time of the Normal Conquest. These views led him to write bold articles in favour of Enoch Powell in the years after his infamous 'Rivers of Blood' speech in 1968. Bryant regarded him as 'an Ishmael in his own country' and hoped that he would one day return as the leader of his party.[405]

Bryant's increasing ostracism from mainstream politics was matched by his isolation in the field of historical writing. While he continued in his attempt to woo a poor and uneducated readership with old-fashioned narrative histories such as *The Age of Chivalry* (1963), *Protestant Island* (1967) and a characteristically blimpish regimental history, *The Jackets of Green* (1972), a more dynamic kind of popular historian was emerging. Personified by talented Marxist historians such as Eric Hobsbawm and E. P. Thompson, they catered for an aggressively anti-establishment market which always eluded Bryant. By the end of Bryant's life, few university libraries continued to place orders for his publications.

Yet there were still many who kept the faith, especially among his ageing hinterland of readers. 'Thank you for the things that roll back the years,' wrote a reader from Toronto, 'the clip-clop of bus horses, and almost motor-less days.' 'Oh my,' wrote a more prominent admirer, Lord Reith, 'how magnificently you are to be envied in what you have done, and in what you will leave behind.' Equally lavish in his praise was the exiled novelist P. G. Wodehouse, who wrote from his home on Long Island that he was one of Bryant's 'greatest fans'. 'I have devoured everything you have written', he enthused, 'and am a regular reader of your *ILN* page,' which he admitted to applying for as long ago as 1905 – 'What a nerve I had!' Among Bryant's small circle of admirers in the academic world was the aged Regis Professor of Modern History at Oxford, Sir Vivian Galbraith, who wrote after the publication of *Makers of the Realm* (1953), 'No brother historian will but envy the beauty and simplicity of the writing. You have achieved your avowed purpose more completely than any other book of its kind that I can remember.'[406]

Occasionally, Bryant would invite one of these prominent admirers for dinner at his home. Notable guests included the Lord Chief Justice, Lord Goddard, and the Poet Laureate, Sir John Betjeman. Bryant would always go to great pains to make his visitors feel welcome. 'I felt them to be evenings not altogether of the present day,' wrote a regular companion at 18 Rutland Gate. 'They seemed to belong to another era, Edwardian perhaps. The conversation, the candlelight and the courtesy of the host as he poured the wine, seemed to set them apart.' After one such dinner party, Betjeman wrote in thanks, 'The memory of that burgundy lingers yet, so deeply satisfying in the mysterious half-light of your stately Victorian mansion. I enjoyed every minute of it.'[407]

Living on his own throughout these years, Bryant came to rely heavily on his new assistant, Pamela Street, to provide for his domestic needs. She later recalled her employer as 'bewildering, unreasonable, irrational, inconsiderate and sometimes extremely bad-tempered' – but 'underlying these temporary lapses there was an unfailing quality of … lovableness'. 'In a single unexpected gesture he could redeem a whole unfortunate harassing situation,' she remembered. Something between a nanny and a mother to the older man, she was constantly worrying about his habits, from chewing his pencils excessively to staying up all night composing his masterworks. In time, though, she was to become his Boswell. 'What is needed in this country', he once announced to her over the top of his morning newspaper, 'is for everyone to work harder, look forward and stop belly-aching.' A habitual user of public transport, he would keep up a 'delightful commentary' on the new-fangled advertisements of 'ladies in various stages of dress and undress' – 'What would my mother have said?' When on foot, he would complain to her of speeding drivers. 'If a fairy were to grant me one wish,' he once interjected, 'I should ask for a little gun to point at the worst offenders and render them immobile forever.' On the rare occasions that they travelled together by taxi, he was known to slide open the glass partition and take charge. Suggestions such as 'I think it might be better to turn off here', or, 'Better turn round altogether and go back the way we came' were riposted with such classic examples of cockney wit as, 'It's a one-way street, sir', or, 'Well, sir, if I was driving this cab, I think that's the way I'd go, too!'[408]

But what most struck Pamela Street about her elderly friend was his underlying melancholia. '*So long…*' he murmured the day they visited his childhood home, 'I've lived so *long.*' Unable to take time off even when illness confined him to his bed, let alone for the sake of a holiday, he complained of deriving absolutely no benefit from the expensive world of social security which his taxes helped fund. Although 'never a bore about income tax', his secretary felt that, 'income tax spoilt the end of his life'. Only his publisher, William Collins, seemed to gain more from their joint enterprise than the taxman: 'All at the Dorchester, I suppose,' he thundered upon finding the entire staff out to lunch one day, 'eating quails eggs at the expense of their hard-working authors.' Although he had saved up a considerable fortune over the years, it was close to the bone when he wrote towards the end of his life that there were 'a dozen authors who a little while ago were, and in some cases still are, household words, who, after contributing for years the bulk of their earnings to the State and having thereby earned as good a right of retirement as any man, are today having to go on scribbling as they did when they were young hacks at the outset of their careers'. This, it sometimes seemed to Bryant, was the level to which he had been reduced.[409]

A few years after Miss Street began working for Bryant in 1971 he sold his London home – one of the last private residences in the square – and moved to a comfortable house in the shadow of Salisbury Cathedral. Surrounded by books and antique furniture, he passed his final few years working on an ambitious three-volume History of the British People; a project he regarded as the culmination of his life's work. But the magic had gone. Partly released after his death, *Set in a Silver Sea* (1984), *Freedom's Own Island* (1986) and *The Search for Justice* (1990) lacked the vitality of his earlier works. Overly mannered, forbiddingly lengthy and sterile in their feigned impartiality, the books did little to enhance Bryant's faded reputation as a historian. Yet there were some who remained inspired by his defiant brand of Victorianism. In one of his last articles for the *ILN*, Bryant reproduced a letter from a twenty-year-old student at the London School of Economics who had chanced upon his writings for the first time. 'You have opened up for me', the stranger wrote, 'the history of the country I live in and love in a marvellous, almost poetic way. I assure you that your book will be read more by the young than anyone, for our "radical" elders seem to care nothing about it.'[410]

The apotheosis of Bryant's career as a historian took place on the occasion of his eightieth birthday, when friends and admirers hosted a large dinner in his honour at the Vintners' Hall in the City. The guest list alone stood as testament to his national status: it included the Labour Prime Minister, James Callaghan; the former Conservative premier, Sir Harold Macmillan; the Archbishop of

Canterbury, Dr Donald Coggan; the Regis Professor of Modern History at Oxford, Hugh Trevor-Roper; the Poet Laureate, Sir John Betjeman; the editor of *The Times*, Sir William Rees-Mogg, and several of the rising stars of the new generation of popular historian, including Lady Antonia Fraser and Philip Ziegler. In a speech on behalf of his 'entire generation', the veteran chairman of The Times Newspapers, Sir Denis Hamilton, told Bryant, 'You gave us inspiration, a love of country ... You gave us understanding of the need for moral purpose.' Afterwards Macmillan rose to say, 'You have chronicled greatness, those times in history when the English people have played their special, unique role ... You have, like Macaulay, not written a single book that was not also a fine piece of literature.' Touching lightly upon the years of appeasement and *Unfinished Victory*, he went on:

> It is not now the time to speak of 1936, '37, '38, when all our concen-
> tration was then too upon internal dispute ... The British people
> will respond to the demands made upon them; they need only the
> leadership that has the inspiration of the cause of country, and
> the cause of the world.[411]

After years of denigration and ridicule, the values which Bryant had for so long championed were coming back into fashion. For this he owed a great deal to the final Prime Minister to pay homage to his talents: Margaret Thatcher. Singled out by Bryant as early as 1975 as a future leader of the party, she wrote to Bryant on the eve of her 1979 election victory briefly thanking him for his encourage-ment and support. His faith in her leadership was reaffirmed by her decision to defend the Falkland Islands from Argentine invasion in 1982, which he regarded as the most creditable act in the Royal Navy's 'long, glorious and sacrificial history'. Although unsatisfied by some of Thatcher's social and economic policies – the cause, he said, of 'other people's monetarist theories' – it seems likely that had he lived a few years longer, the Prime Minister would have asked the Queen to admit him to the coveted Order of Merit.[412]

Bryant died after a brief illness at New Hall Hospital, Salisbury, on 22 January 1985, shortly after completing his final piece for the *ILN* – the last instalment of the longest-running series by a single contributor in the history of British journalism. His life was commemorated two months later at a memorial service at Westminster Abbey attended by the usual eclectic group of supporters. Having no living family with whom he had any contact, the event had the solemnity of the kind of state occasion which he had so relished. The Queen Mother, unable to attend, was represented by Lieutenant Colonel Sir Martin Gilliat; the Prime Minister, likewise indisposed, was deputised by her husband, Sir Denis Thatcher; from the legal world came the veteran Master of the Rolls, Lord Denning; among politicians were numbered such unlikely companions as the Labour leader Michael Foot and John Profumo; stalwarts of the *ancien régime* included the Dowager Viscountess Davidson, the Lord Chancellor, Lord Hailsham, and Churchill's former secretary, Sir John Colville. A learned panegyric was delivered by the Tory peer and historian Lord Blake of Braydeston, recalling Bryant as a 'writer whose works gave more pleasure to more people than those of any other historian past or present'.

Yet it was the simple words of Bryant's neighbour at the Close in Salisbury, the Rev. Ian Dunlop, Chancellor of Salisbury Cathedral, which best captured the spirit of the day: 'As we remember his intense patriotism, let us pray for this land and its great institutions.'[413]

◈

A decade after Bryant's death, his old friend and intermittent critic A. L. Rowse asked: 'How much of his work then remains – of all that mountain?' Aside from the biography of Samuel Pepys and a few collections of essays, the inveterate curmudgeon did not see much hope of a revival. Although once a Book Club favourite and one of the most well-remunerated writers of his generation, by the end of the twentieth century his name was all but forgotten. Such is the transience of literary fame.

But Bryant's irrelevance was not enough for a more hostile revisionist cohort. Led by the Tory historian Andrew Roberts, they attempted to demolish Bryant's hard-earned reputation as the 'national historian' *par excellence*. With the assistance of stale clubland gossip and a selective reading of the documents bequeathed by Bryant to the military archives at King's College, London, they portrayed this unlikely hate figure as not only a 'Nazi sympathiser and a fascist fellow-traveller', but also 'a supreme toady, fraudulent scholar and humbug'. Scarcely less brutally, Ludovic Kennedy – a former colleague of Bryant's at Ashridge – paired up with Peter Cook to resurrect the recently deceased historian in a BBC miniseries aptly entitled *A Life in Pieces*. Over the course of twelve Christmas episodes, viewers were treated to the rambling reflections of 'Sir Arthur Streeb-Greebling' – a pompous, stupid, bigoted, drunken old bore.[414]

Nor was this drubbing sufficient. Eleven years later, the release of a new edition of Lord Alanbrooke's diaries gave the intellectual elite a fresh chance to drag Bryant's name through the muck. *The Times* gave an entire page to the respected military historian M. D. R. Foot to denounce the Field Marshal's first editor for 'suppress[ing]' key sections of the diary and 'bowdleris[ing]' the rest 'barbarously badly'. Omitting to mention that Bryant had been castigated at the time for revealing so *much* sensational material from the diaries, and that he had worked scrupulously with both Alanbrooke and the relevant government authorities throughout, Foot rebuked his predecessor for not going further. A point of especial contention was that Bryant had not included an entry in which Alanbrooke questioned Churchill's sanity ('I often doubt whether I am going mad or whether he is really sane') and another in which he berated General Montgomery for his 'lack of tact' and 'egotistical outlook'.[415]

Where were Bryant's 'friends' to defend him from these nonsense charges? Not one of those who had so lately toasted his health on the occasion of his eightieth birthday at the Vintners' Hall, or had sung his praises in the Abbey, or had exchanged self-congratulatory letters with the eminent old man, were willing to weigh in. Their voices had dried up. It had become fashionable to disown him.

Ironically, Bryant's only posthumous champions have come from within the academic establishment which so maligned him during his lifetime. In the most detailed account of his career yet published, Dr Julia Stapleton of Durham University has conclusively disproved the accusations of intellectual dishonesty and pro-Nazism made by Bryant's critics. As well as setting his wartime activities in their proper context, she has demonstrated that his success as a historian was as merited as it was phenomenal. 'His prominence', she has written, 'was due to an uncommon ability to both engage the minds of ordinary readers – by whom he set enormous cultural store – and network relentlessly across the British establishment.' 'He was a master of obsequiousness,' she fairly concedes, 'but he pursued his own agenda, and many of those whose attention he sought recognised his talent as a writer as much as a flatterer.'[416]

Even Bryant's belief in appeasement has been favourably reassessed. Emphasising the enormous sacrifices made by Britain in launching a successful war against Hitler's Germany, historians such as Maurice Cowling and John Charmley have lamented the 'lost peace' of 1939–40. Had the olive branch offered by Chamberlain been accepted by Hitler, they have suggested, Britain might have retained her position as the world's policeman, while the wealth of Germany and Russia would likely have been dissipated by protracted warfare. Such an outcome would almost certainly have prevented the decline of the British Empire and the rise of America as the dominant superpower – realities which Bryant felt to be detrimental to the stability of the world.

Whether these scholars will succeed in righting the academic wrongs of the past seems doubtful. Even were it not for his thankless work for the Chamberlain government, criticism of Bryant's literary approach would still remain. As the great Herbert Butterfield explained in a dismissive review of the final volume of the Napoleonic trilogy, *The Age of Elegance* (1950), Bryant 'carried the tendencies of his [Victorian] predecessors to the point of caricature'. 'At times the tapestry is rich,' he sniffed. 'The camera has been poked into every nook and cranny of the country and the scenes have been packed together so that they tumble after one another with the speed of a cinematographic film.' The picture lacked balance. Having little sensitivity for 'both light and shade', and wilfully confusing typical and exceptional occurrences, Bryant often seemed to care more about literary effect than historical accuracy. If a future historian were to apply these methods to Bryant's own times, joked Butterfield, the flaws would be instantly recognisable:

> Those were the days when a youth of 18 might murder a shopkeeper to get £50 and on the park wall at dead of night men would paint: 'The people say, Hands off Korea'. At an undergraduate 'rag' a man could throw a hand-grenade to damage the Senate House of his university. Even the BBC allowed itself to be used as an instrument for the propagation of unbelief.

Except this *was* how Bryant viewed the modern world. The skill of his narrative histories lay in his ability to write of past events as though he were himself a bystander. Such a talent is more than merely academic: it goes to the root of what makes great literature. He never pretended that his goal was to provide his readers with a mass of dry statistics or complex theories. An unapologetic amateur and enthusiast, he merely wished to inspire them with a deep love of their country. The success with which he did this for so many years is testament to his many fine qualities both as a man and as an author.

As long as there is an interest in history as a branch of literature there will always be writers like Bryant. They will not, however, always be of his exceptional quality. In the absence of anything better, the void will only be filled by whatever Hollywood and its imitators pass off as fact. By comparison to these productions, Bryant's work seems uplifting and heavyweight. For despite his supposed failings of intellect – so patronisingly detected by his academic critics – Bryant had both an ability to tell a good story and the integrity to remain faithful to his sources. His error was to overcommit himself, ensuring that the brilliance of his earlier works was gradually smothered beneath the weight of his later commercial offerings.

Like his predecessor at the *ILN*, G. K. Chesterton, Bryant saw the modern world through the eyes of the old. He did not set himself up as a debunker or a wiseacre: 'He was miles away from the Bloomsbury intellectuals,' wrote Rowse, 'at the opposite pole to Lytton Strachey'. This was the key to his character. He was both a Victorian and a modernist; a Tory and a radical, a dreamer and a man of action. Though he began his career with a very un-Victorian biography of Charles II, he never mocked either the 'eminent Victorians' or derided the old queen herself. 'He was wise in that,' wrote the historian Asa Briggs, 'for he has lived long enough to see the Victorians taken seriously again.'[417]

This was as much Bryant's doing as anyone's. Throughout years of adversity and neglect, he had stuck to his beliefs, much to the amazement of the fainthearted: 'How *could* he go on with the old record', sighed Rowse, 'when it was all over?' It may yet be some time before this proud Jacobite is adequately restored in the eyes of posterity. As his final *ILN* editor, James Bishop, wrote shortly before his death: '[He is] a man who has often been much misunderstood, and often out of fashion, but who will, I think, be better understood by future generations than he has perhaps been by his own.'[418]

© Sayle Literary Agency/The Estate of Ronald Searle

ACKNOWLEDGEMENTS

My debts in writing this book have been considerable. First and foremost, I would like to thank the fourth Viscount Brentford of Newick, Crispin Joynson-Hicks, for allowing me to quote from his distinguished forebear's personal papers, and also for providing me with some excellent anecdotes and photographs for use in this book. Likewise, I am grateful to Viscount Brentford's cousin, Peter Joynson, for his many kindnesses, most notably temporarily removing an entire page from a family album for my perusal.

For permission to quote from the diaries of W. R. Inge and A. C. Benson, I am grateful to the Master and Fellows of Magdalene College, Cambridge, as well as to the staff at the Pepys and Old Libraries for making my numerous visits to the college both possible and highly rewarding. I am also pleased to extend the same gratitude to the trustees and staff of the Liddell Hart Centre for Military Archives, where I passed many productive summer days working on the papers of Arthur Bryant. Elsewhere, visits to Lambeth Palace Library; the BBC Written Archives, Cavendish; the East Sussex Record Office; Durham Cathedral library; the National Archives, Kew; the London Metropolitan Archives; the Churchill Archives Centre, Churchill College, Cambridge; the Harrow School Archives; and the Manuscripts Department of the Cambridge University library have been made a pleasure by the helpfulness, expertise and diligence of their respective staffs.

Among modern authorities on the Victorians and their successors, I would like to record my especial gratitude for the works of Lord Briggs, the Rev. Professor W. Owen Chadwick, Professor Sir Richard J. Evans, Professor Sir David Cannadine, Professor W. D. Rubinstein, Professor Samuel Hynes, the late Professor Walter E. Houghton, Professor Peter Mandler, Professor Susan G. Pedersen, Professor Antony Lentin, Professor Richard Aldous, Dr Tristram Hunt, Dr John Gardiner, Matthew Sweet, A. N. Wilson and Simon Heffer. Among the Victorian survivors and iconoclasts themselves, I am thankful (if sometimes a little reluctantly) to Lytton Strachey, Hugh Kingsmill, Esmé Cecil Wingfield-Stratford, G. M. Young, E. F. Benson, Harold Begbie, and A. G. Gardiner, whose works first kindled my interest in the post-Victorian world.

As with my biography of W. T. Stead, I have benefited immeasurably from a wealth of scholarship covering similar ground to my own. These publications can be found cited frequently in the endnotes, but I cannot emphasise enough my particular debt to the work of Dr Huw F. Clayton, Jonathon M. Hopkins, Ronald Blythe, Anne Perkins and Diana Souhami for the chapter on William Joynson-Hicks; Professor Arthur Burns and the late Canon Adam Fox for that on W. R. Inge; Lord Briggs and the late Ian McIntyre for that on John Reith, and Professor Richard Griffiths, Dr Julia Stapleton and Andrew Roberts for that on Arthur Bryant. Even where my conclusions have differed from these authorities – sometimes markedly so – they have always provided me with a guide and an example which I have attempted to follow.

For generously sharing their memories and opinions of the subjects of this book, I am especially grateful to the late Lord Rees-Mogg, the late Kenneth Rose CBE, Lady Antonia Fraser, Lord David Hacking, Sir Roy Strong, Sir Ronald Harwood, Paul Johnson, Robert Low, Andy Todd, Ben Patterson, Sabina Bryant, Dr R. G. Davies, John Saberton (on behalf of the parish of Berkswich) and several of my former colleagues at the BBC.

I would also like to thank Professor Sir Richard J. Evans and the Fellows of Wolfson College, Cambridge, for electing me a Research Associate and providing me with such congenial surroundings to work on this book. To friends and family members who commented on the manuscript, I would especially like to thank (while, as usual, absolving them of responsibility for errors) Professor Antony Lentin, Fletcher Robinson, Sarah Treanor, Maurice Bourcier, Dr David Adams, Tara O'Leary, Neville Bass, Caislin Boyle and Sara Holm. I extend the same thanks to my publisher, Jeremy Robson, and editor, Olivia Beattie, who have each been, as always, both meticulous and encouraging.

My last acknowledgement is more personal. Not many biographers discover in the course of their research that they are distantly related to one of their subjects. While it is curious to be almost brought into the story of *The Last Victorians* in this way, I will only say, in the interests of preserving my own sense of impartiality, that this discovery took place long after the first draft was completed.

W. Sydney Robinson
Cambridge, 10 May 2014

ENDNOTES

1   *The Times*, 20 May 1898; V. Woolf, 'Mr Bennett and Mrs Brown' (1923), reproduced in *The Common Reader: Virginia Woolf* (London, 1953), p. 180; N. Annan, *Our Age* (London, 1990), pp. 59–60.

2   *Daily Mail*, 13 July 1978.

3   M. V. Brett and O. S. B. Brett (eds), *Journals and Letters of Reginald Brett, Viscount Esher* (London, 1934–38), IV, p. 258; C. L. Mowat, *Britain Between the Wars, 1918–1940* (London, 1955), p. 142.

4   H. A. Taylor, *Jix, Viscount Brentford: being the authoritative and official biography of the Rt Hon. William Joynson-Hicks, First Viscount Brentford of Newick* (London 1933), p. 13; W. Joynson-Hicks, 'Princess Elizabeth'. Brentford Papers (East Sussex Record Office).

5   W. Joynson-Hicks to the Rev. B. Jones, 21 January 1931. Brentford Papers. For following see Taylor, *Jix*, pp. 13–28.

6   W. Joynson-Hicks, 'Early Manhood and Early Ambitions'. Brentford Papers.

7   C. Brentford to W. S. Robinson, 11 January 2013.

8   Joynson-Hicks, 'Early Manhood'.

9   W. Joynson-Hicks, 'The Beginnings of my Legal Career'. Brentford Papers.

10 Joynson-Hicks, 'Beginnings of my Legal Career'.

11 Taylor, *Jix*, p. 28.

12 Joynson-Hicks, 'Beginnings of my Legal Career'.

13 For following see Taylor, *Jix*, pp. 34–162; J. M. Hopkins, 'Paradoxes Personified: Sir William Joynson-Hicks (Viscount Brentford) and the conflict between change and stability in British society in the 1920s', University of Westminster MPhil thesis (1996), pp. 17–33; W. Joynson-Hicks, 'Early Parliamentary Career'. Brentford Papers.

14 Joynson-Hicks, 'Early Parliamentary Career'.

15 Taylor, *Jix*, p. 88.

16 Taylor, *Jix*, p. 86.

17 *Daily Telegraph*, 25 April 1908.

18 Taylor, *Jix*, p. 101.

19 K. Middlemas and J. Barnes, *Baldwin: a biography* (London, 1969), p. 283.

20 Joynson-Hicks, 'Early Parliamentary Career'.

21 A. Lentin, *The Last Political Law Lord: Lord Sumner* (Newcastle, 2008), p. 111.

22 *Parliamentary Debates* (Fifth Series), vol. 131, col. 1765.

23 Taylor, *Jix*, p. 127.

24 *The Times*, 16 and 17 December 1920; ibid., 6 April 1922. For following

see M. Cowling, *The Impact of Labour, 1920–1924: the beginning of modern British politics* (Cambridge, 1971), pp. 185–7.

25 J. Ramsden, *The Age of Balfour and Baldwin, 1902–1940* (London, 1978), p. 180.

26 *Morning Post*, 3 and 11 December 1923.

27 *The Times*, 28 February 1924; ibid., 12 April 1924.

28 *The Times*, 27 October 1924.

29 *The Times*, 27 October 1924; Ramsden, *The Age of Balfour*, pp. 200–206.

30 Hopkins, 'Paradoxes Personified', p. 40; M. Aitken, *The Decline and Fall of Lloyd George* (London, 1963), p. 21.

31 Middlemas, *Baldwin*, p. 283; Taylor, *Jix*, p. 175.

32 *The Times*, 27 January 1925. For following see H. F. Clayton, '"A Frisky, Tiresome Colt?" Sir William Joynson-Hicks, the Home Office and the "Roaring Twenties", 1924–1929', University of Aberystwyth PhD thesis (2008), pp. 190–205.

33 Clayton, 'Joynson-Hicks', p. 191.

34 G. Lang, *Mr Justice Avory* (London, 1935), p. 293.

35 Clayton, 'Joynson-Hicks', p. 205.

36 *Parliamentary Debates* (Fifth Series), vol. 180, col. 1261; ibid., vol. 210, cols. 2040–41.

37 *Parliamentary Debates* (Fifth Series), vol. 222, col. 1729.

38 W. Joynson-Hicks to Victor Perosino, 28 December 1928. Brentford Papers.

39 Clayton, 'Joynson-Hicks', p. 209.

40 For following see Clayton, 'Joynson-Hicks', pp. 249–72.

41 *Evening Standard*, 14 May 1928.

42 For following see D. Souhami, *The Trials of Radclyffe Hall* (London, 1998), pp. 176–212; Clayton, 'Joynson-Hicks', pp. 123–52.

43 Souhami, *Radclyffe Hall*, pp. 176–8.

44 Souhami, *Radclyffe Hall*, p. 179.

45 Clayton, 'Joynson-Hicks', p. 136.

46 E. Waugh, *Vile Bodies* (London, 2000 [1930]), pp. 19–20.

47 Clayton, 'Joynson-Hicks', p. 125.

48 W. S. Churchill, 'The Truth about Jix', *Sunday Pictorial*, 9 August 1931.

49 Souhami, *Radclyffe Hall*, p. 189.

50 Ibid., p. 183.

51 Ibid., p. 194.

52 R. Kipling to W. Joynson-Hicks, 11 and 25 October 1928. Brentford Papers.

53 Souhami, *Radclyffe Hall*, p. 202.

54 Ibid., pp. 190, 214.

55 J. T. Boulton et al. (eds), *The Letters of D. H. Lawrence*, 8 vols (Cambridge, 1979–2000), VII, p. 227.

56 D. H. Lawrence, *Pornography and Obscenity* (London, 1929), pp. 12, 14–15.

57 Ibid., p. 12.

58 W. Joynson-Hicks, *Do We Need a Censor?* (London, 1929), p. 24.

59 Hopkins, 'Paradoxes Personified', p. 94.

60 *The Times*, 26 November 1925.

61 W. Joynson-Hicks, 'The General Strike'. Brentford Papers.
62 Middlemas, *Baldwin*, pp. 390–91. For following see A. Perkins, *A Very British Strike* (London, 2006), pp. 104–72; Taylor, *Jix*, pp. 192–202 and Joynson-Hicks, 'The General Strike'.
63 *New Statesman*, 22 May 1926.
64 R. S. Churchill and M. Gilbert, *Winston S. Churchill*, 8 vols (1966–88), IV, p. 163.
65 Perkins, *British Strike*, p. 104.
66 Joynson-Hicks, 'The General Strike'.
67 Perkins, *British Strike*, pp. 152, 160.
68 Gilbert, *Churchill*, IV, p. 162; R. R. James (ed.), *Memoirs of a Conservative: J. C. C. Davidson's memoirs and papers* (London, 1969), p. 243; Joynson-Hicks, 'The General Strike'.
69 Perkins, *British Strike*, p. 232.
70 Taylor, *Jix*, pp. 200–201.
71 Lentin, *Sumner*, pp. 184–5.
72 R. Jenkins, *Baldwin* (London, 1987), p. 85; L. Knowles, *Court of Drama* (London, 1966), pp. 74–91; F. Bresler, *Reprieve: a study of a system* (London, 1965), p. 105.
73 British Library Sound Archives.
74 J. Campbell, *F. E. Smith, First Earl of Birkenhead* (London, 1983), p. 787; Taylor, *Jix*, p. 227.
75 Taylor, *Jix*, pp. 222, 231; Interview with P. Joynson, 30 January 2014.
76 W. Joynson-Hicks to H. Hicks, 26 June 1925. Brentford Papers.
77 Hopkins, 'Paradoxes Personified', pp. 48–9.
78 W. Joynson-Hicks, 'The King and Queen'. Brentford Papers.
79 G. K. A. Bell, *Randall Davidson, Archbishop of Canterbury* (Oxford, 1952[1935]), p. 1337.
80 Bell, *Davidson*, p. 1338.
81 O. Chadwick, *Hensley Henson: a study in the friction between Church and state* (Oxford, 1983), p. 193.
82 *Daily Express*, 16 December 1927; *Parliamentary Debates* (Fifth Series), vol. 211, col. 2537.
83 *Parliamentary Debates* (Fifth Series), vol. 211, col. 2550.
84 *Daily Express*, 16 December 1927.
85 *The Spectator*, 24 December 1928; Churchill, 'The Truth about Jix'.
86 Taylor, *Jix*, p. 259.
87 Hopkins, 'Paradoxes Personified', pp. 115–16.
88 *The Times*, 18 May 1928.
89 Taylor, *Jix*, p. 261.
90 *Evening Standard*, 13 July 1929.
91 Hopkins, 'Paradoxes Personified', p. 57.
92 Ibid., p. 122.
93 Ibid., p. 117.
94 British Library Sound Archives.

95   D. Cesarani, 'Joynson-Hicks and the Radical Right in England after the First World War' in Tony Kushner and Kenneth Lunn (eds), *Traditions of Intolerance: Historical Perspectives on Fascism and Race Discourse in Britain* (Manchester, 1989) , p. 134; W. D. Rubinstein, *A History of the Jews in the English-Speaking World: Great Britain* (London, 1996), p. 272.

96   Jenkins, *Baldwin*, p. 85.

97   Churchill, 'The Truth about Jix'.

98   MagColl:F/WRI/33, 4 December 1933.

99   W. R. Inge, *Vale* (London, 1934), p. 8.

100 S. Inge to W. Inge, 27 March 1865. Inge Papers.

101 *Evening Standard*, 24 October 1923; MagColl:F/WRI/36, 5 March 1939; Inge, *Vale*, p. 29.

102 MagColl:F/ACB/130, 17 April 1912; MagColl:F/WRI/15, 13 December 1902; A. Fox, *Dean Inge* (London, 1960), pp. 8–10.

103 D. Newsome, *On the Edge of Paradise, A. C. Benson: the diarist* (London, 1980), p. 29.

104 R. Davenport-Hines, 'Oscar Browning (1837–1923)' in *Oxford Dictionary of National Biography*, 60 vols (2001–04).

105 Newsome, *Benson*, p. 29; Fox, *Dean Inge*, p. 18.

106 MagColl:F/WRI/6, 20 February 1893.

107 *The Nation*, 5 November 1919; Fox, *Dean Inge*, p. 26.

108 Fox, *Dean Inge*, p. 40.

109 Inge, *Vale*, pp. 31–2.

110 MagColl:F/WRI/2, 3 March 1904, 2 April 1889.

111 MagColl:F/WRI/3, 6 June 1890; Fox, *Dean Inge*, p. 50.

112 MagColl:F/WRI/9, 12 May 1896.

113 MagColl:F/WRI/7, 31 December 1894.

114 MagColl:F/WRI/4, 31 December 1891; MagColl:F/WRI/7, 1 January 1894; ibid., 26 February 1894; Fox, *Dean Inge*, p. 60.

115 MagColl:F/WRI/5, 5 October 1892; W. R. Inge, *The Things that Remain* (London, 1958), p. 120.

116 W. R. Inge, *Diary of a Dean: St Paul's 1911–1934* (London, 1949), p. 34.

117 MagColl:F/WRI/16, 23 May 1903; MagColl:F/WRI/9, 1 January 1896.

118 Fox, *Dean Inge*, pp. 74–5.

119 G. B. Shaw, *Too True to be Good* (London, 1934), p. 85; Fox, *Dean Inge*, p. 74; MagColl:F/WRI/20, 21 November 1907.

120 Fox, *Dean Inge*, pp. 73–4.

121 MagColl:F/WRI/17, 30 December 1904.

122 MagColl:F/ACB/123, 3 May 1905.

123 R. S. Cowan, 'Sir Francis Galton (1822–1911)', in *Oxford Dictionary of National Biography*; *Eugenics Review*, 2 July 1954.

124 Fox, *Dean Inge*, p. 81.

125 Fox, *Dean Inge*, pp. 79, 82.

126 W. R. Inge to R. Davidson, 21 April 1911. Davidson Papers (Lambeth Palace Library); Fox, *Dean Inge*, pp. 95–7.

127 MagColl:F/WRI/21, 1 January 1908.

128 *The Times*, 19 May 1908; MagColl:F/WRI/22, 20 May 1908.

129 *The Times*, 8 February 1910.

130 Fox, *Dean Inge*, p. 99.

131 MagColl:F/WRI/3, 31 December 1890.

132 MagColl:F/WRI/23, 8 May 1910.

133 Fox, *Dean Inge*, p. 115.

134 Fox, *Dean Inge*, p. 103.

135 Fox, *Dean Inge*, p. 105; R. Davidson to W. R. Inge, 21 April 1911. Davidson Papers.

136 MagColl:F/WRI/23, 19 April 1911.

137 *The Observer*, 14 January 1930.

138 Fox, *Dean Inge*, p. 113.

139 Inge, *Diary of a Dean*, p. 11.

140 J. L. Collins, *Faith Under Fire* (London, 1966), pp. 148–9.

141 Fox, *Dean Inge*, p. 115.

142 Ibid., p. 115.

143 Inge, *Diary of a Dean*, p. 18; M. de Wolfe Howe (ed.), *Holmes-Laski Letters: the correspondence of Mr Justice Holmes and Harold J. Laski, 1916–1935* (Oxford, 1953), II, p. 454; *Church of England Newspaper*, 5 March 1954; R. Dataller, *A Pitman at Oxford* (London, 1933), p. 81; B. Hillier, *John Betjeman: new fame, new love* (London, 2002), p. 61.

144 S. Dark, *Five Deans* (London, 1923), p. 212; Inge, *Diary of a Dean*, pp. 153–4.

145 Inge, *Diary of a Dean*, p. 7.

146 MagColl:F/WRI/24, 25 November 1913; *The Times*, 22 and 26 November 1913.

147 MagColl:F/WRI/24, 7 December 1913.

148 W. R. Inge, *The Church and the Age* (London, 1912), p. 15; W. R. Inge, *More Lay Thoughts of a Dean* (London, 1931), p. 127; *Evening Standard*, 12 December 1923.

149 Inge, *Church and the Age*, p. 19.

150 MagColl:F/WRI/22, 15 October 1908; MagColl:F/WRI/23, 11 November 1911.

151 MagColl:F/WRI/27, 14 December 1917.

152 Inge, *Diary of a Dean*, p. 42.

153 B. Russell, *History of Western Philosophy* (London, 1961), p. 291.

154 Inge, *Diary of a Dean*, pp. 43, 52–3.

155 W. R. Inge, *Outspoken Essays* (London, 1919), pp. 9, 10, 26, 30, 92.

156 *Everyman*, 22 November 1919.

157 MagColl:F/WRI/28, 1 January 1920.

158 *Isis*, 29 November 1922.

159 *Evening Standard*, 15 May 1924; ibid., 29 March 1921.

160 *Evening Standard*, 9 February 1921.

161 Fox, *Dean Inge*, pp. 201–3; *Evening Standard*, 10 February 1921.

162 Reproduced in *The Tablet*, 27 June 1925.

163 'Dean Inge and Lord Hugh Cecil', unpublished chapter from G. K. A. Bell, *Randall Davidson, Archbishop of Canterbury* (London, 1935). Davidson Papers.

164 *Evening Standard*, 7 May 1924; W. R. Inge, 'The Victorian Age', reproduced in *Outspoken Essays*, 2nd series (London, 1922), pp. 184–208.

165 *Isis*, 7 December 1922.

166 W. R. Inge, *Lay thoughts of a Dean* (London, 1926), pp. 211, 231.

167 Fox, *Dean Inge*, pp. 123, 185.

168 Ibid., p. 184.

169 Inge, *Diary of a Dean*, pp. 102–3.

170 Ibid., pp. 100–104.

171 S. J. D. Green, *The Passing of Protestant England: secularisation and social change, c. 1920–1960* (Cambridge, 2011), p. 112.

172 Keene et al. (eds), *St Paul's*, p. 96

173 Inge, *Diary of a Dean*, p. 104.

174 J. Vincent, *The Crawford Papers, the journals of David Lindsay, twenty-seventh Earl of Crawford and tenth Earl of Balcarres, 1872–1940, during the year 1892 to 1940* (Manchester, 1984), p. 551.

175 D. Keene, *St Paul's: the cathedral church of London, 604–2004* (Yale, 2004), p. 96.

176 Chadwick, *Hensley Henson*, pp. 217–18.

177 *Church Times*, 21 October 1927.

178 J. Barnes, *Ahead of his Age: Bishop Barnes of Birmingham* (London, 1979), p. 195.

179 *Evening Standard*, 26 October 1927.

180 *Evening News*, 17 June 1930; Barnes, *Ahead of his Age*, p. 204.

181 *Evening Standard*, 18 January 1928; ibid., 15 April 1928; *The Observer*, 23 September 1934; *The Listener*, 9 December 1931.

182 W. R. Inge to M. R. James, [n. d.]. Cambridge University Library Special Collections, MSS Add 7481/I; MagColl:F/WRI/34, 31 December 1934.

183 Inge, *Diary of a Dean*, pp. 168, 174.

184 Ibid., p. 180.

185 Ibid., p. 55.

186 Fox, *Dean Inge*, p. 261.

187 D. H. Laurence (ed.), *Bernard Shaw: Collected Letters 1926–1950* (London, 1988), pp. 273, 488.

188 Fox, *Dean Inge*, pp. 161, 196; *Evening Standard*, 22 May 1935.

189 Henson Diaries, 5 November 1936. Henson Papers (Durham Cathedral Library); MagColl:F/WRI/36, 17 January 1939.

190 *Evening Standard*, 3 July 1935; MagColl:F/WRI/33, 22 May 1933.

191 Inge, *Diary of a Dean*, pp. 31–2, 72.

192 Rubinstein, *A History of the Jews*, p. 299.

193 *Evening Standard*, 24 November 1938.

194 Ibid., 21 October 1936.

195 Ibid., 13 May 1936.

196 Ibid., 14 October 1938.

197 MagColl:F/WRI/38, 23 July 1949; MagColl:F/WRI/37, 18 February 1940.

198 *Evening Standard*, 15 December 1939.

199 MagColl:F/WRI/37, 1 January 1940.

200 Ibid., December [n. d.], 1940.

201 *Evening Standard*, 2 September 1946.

202 Ibid., 7 September 1946; C. Inge to B. Liddell Hart, 27 January 1948. Captain Sir Basil Liddell Hart Papers. (Liddell Hart Centre for Military Archives, King's College, London).

203 Fox, *Dean Inge*, p. 258.

204 W. R. Inge, *The End of an Age* (London, 1948), p. 36; W. R. Inge to B. Liddell Hart, 31 August 1947; Inge, *Diary of a Dean*, pp. 153–4.

205 P. Crook, *Darwin's Coat-tails essays on social Darwinism* (New York, 2007), p. 81; *The Times*, 27 February 1954.

206 *Church of England Newspaper*, 5 March 1954; *The Times*, 27 February 1954.

207 H. Henson, *Retrospect of an Unimportant Life*, 3 vols (London, 1942–50), III, p. 66; S. Dark, *Not Such a Bad Life* (London, 1941), p. 215.

208 A. Hastings, *A History of English Christianity 1920–1985* (London, 1986), pp. 177–8.

209 Inge, *Church and the Age*, p. 22.

210 A. N. Wilson, *Penfriends from Porlock* (London, 1988), p. 183.

211 W. R. Matthews, *Memories and Meanings* (London, 1969), p. 378.

212 I. McIntyre, *The Expense of Glory: a life of John Reith* (London, 1993), p. 353.

213 C. Stuart (ed.), *The Reith Diaries* (London, 1971), p. 67; M. Leishman, *My Father: Reith of the BBC* (Edinburgh, 2006), p. 265.

214 A. Boyle, *Only the Wind will Listen: Reith of the BBC* (London, 1972), p. 36; McIntyre, *Expense of Glory*, p. 16.

215 McIntyre, *Expense of Glory*, p. 5.

216 J. Barr, *The United Free Church of Scotland* (London, 1934), pp. 83–97.

217 W. M. Clow, *Dr George Reith: a Scottish ministry* (London, 1928), pp. 66–7, 160.

218 Clow, *Dr George Reith*, p. 224.

219 'Lord Reith Looks Back', BBC Library. (Broadcast December 1967).

220 McIntyre, *Expense of Glory*, pp. 5–6.

221 J. C. W. Reith, *Into the Wind* (London, 1949), pp. 9–10.

222 McIntyre, *Expense of Glory*, p. 8.

223 Boyle, *Only the Wind*, pp. 40–41.

224 McIntyre, *Expense of Glory*, pp. 8–9; Reith, *Into the Wind*, p. 11; 'Lord Reith Looks Back'.

225 McIntyre, *Expense of Glory*, p. 13.

226 Ibid., p. 14.

227 Ibid., pp. 13–15.

228 Stuart, *Reith Diaries*, p. 22; Reith, *Into the Wind*, pp. 11–13.

229 McIntyre, *Expense of Glory*, p. 19.

230 Ibid., pp. 20, 41.

231 Reith, *Into the Wind*, p. 15; J. C. W. Reith, *Wearing Spurs* (London, 1966), p. 14; 'Lord Reith Looks Back'.

232 Reith, *Wearing Spurs*, p. 18.

233 Boyle, *Only the Wind*, pp. 51–2.

234 Ibid.

235 Reith, *Into the Wind*, p. 13.

236 McIntyre, *Expense of Glory*, p. 25.

237 Ibid., p. 25.

238 Ibid., p. 26; Stuart, *Reith Diaries*, p. 81.

239 Reith, *Wearing Spurs*, p. 22.

240 Ibid., p. 33; McIntyre, *Expense of Glory*, p. 26.

241 Reith, *Wearing Spurs*, p. 31. For following see ibid., pp. 36, 36, 65–219.

242 Ibid.

243 Ibid.

244 McIntyre, *Expense of Glory*, p. 62.

245 Ibid., p. 66.

246 Ibid.

247 Ibid., pp. 66–75.

248 Ibid., p. 72.

249 Ibid., p. 76.

250 Ibid., p. 112.

251 Reith, *Into the Wind*, p. 81.

252 Boyle, *Only the Wind*, pp. 112–13, 120.

253 McIntyre, *Expense of Glory*, pp. 84–6.

254 Ibid., p. 105.

255 Ibid., p. 116.

256 Reith, *Into the Wind*, pp. 82–8; Boyle, *Only the Wind*, p. 120.

257 A. Briggs, *The History of Broadcasting in the United Kingdom, Volume 1: The Birth of Broadcasting* (Oxford, 1995 [1961]), p. 127.

258 McIntyre, *Expense of Glory*, p. 117.

259 Reith, *Into the Wind*, pp. 89, 95.

260 Briggs, *History of Broadcasting*, I, pp. 145–7.

261 McIntyre, *Expense of Glory*, p. 123.

262 Reith, *Into the Wind*, p. 90.

263 Briggs, *History of Broadcasting*, I, pp. 141–2.

264 Reith, *Into the Wind*, p. 90.

265 McIntyre, *Expense of Glory*, pp. 127–8, 190.

266 Ibid., pp. 153, 413.

267 Stuart, *Reith Diaries*, p. 133.

268 Briggs, *History of Broadcasting*, I, p. 220.

269 Reith, *Into the Wind*, p. 98.

270 J. C. W. Reith, *Broadcast Over Britain* (London, 1924), p. 34.

271 McIntyre, *Expense of Glory*, p. 145.

272 Reith, *Into the Wind*, p. 109.

273 McIntyre, *Expense of Glory*, p. 153.

274 Vincent, *Crawford Papers*, p. 505.

275 Stuart, *Reith Diaries*, p. 169.

276 McIntyre, *Expense of Glory*, pp. 182, 199, 228; Boyle, *Only the Wind*, p. 230.

277 McIntyre, *Expense of Glory*, p. 196.

278 B. Pimlott, *The Political Diary of Hugh Dalton, 1918–1940, 1945–1960* (London, 1986), p. 121.

279 McIntyre, *Expense of Glory*, pp. 204, 223.

280 Ibid., p. 223.

281 Ibid., p. 201.

282 Ibid., p. 229.

283 Ibid., p. 234.

284 Leishman, *My Father*, p. 60.

285 Ibid., p. 206; McIntyre, *Expense of Glory*, p. 234.

286 McIntyre, *Expense of Glory*, p. 181; Boyle, *Into the Wind*, p. 310.

287 McIntyre, *Expense of Glory*, p. 228.

288 Ibid., p. 232.

289 Ibid., p. 238.

290 Ibid., p. 241.

291 Ibid., p. 242.

292 Ibid., pp. 242–3.

293 Ibid., p. 255.

294 Reith, *Into the Wind*, p. 327.

295 McIntyre, *Expense of Glory*, p. 245.

296 Reith, *Into the Wind*, pp. 351–3.

297 Ibid., p. 357.

298 McIntyre, *Expense of Glory*, p. 254.

299 Boyle, *Only the Wind*, p. 307.

300 Ibid., p. 308.

301 McIntyre, *Expense of Glory*, pp. 255, 282.

302 Boyle, *Only the Wind*, p. 311.

303 J. C. W. Reith to W. S. Churchill, 1 January 1946. BBC Written Archives (Caversham); McIntyre, *Expense of Glory*, p. 322.

304 McIntyre, *Expense of Glory*, p. 372.

305 Ibid., p. 290.

306 Ibid., p. 307.

307 Ibid., pp. 318, 335, 366.

308 Ibid., p. 362.

309 Ibid., p. 324.

310 Leishman, *My Father*, pp. 80, 115–16, 253, 270.

311 McIntyre, *Expense of Glory*, p. 392.

312 Ibid., p. 355.

313 Ibid., p. 352.

314 Reith, *Broadcast over Britain*, p. 34.

315 'Atticus' in *Sunday Times*, 19 June 1938, quoted in McIntyre, *Expense of Glory*, p. 240.

316 *Illustrated London News* (hereafter *ILN*), 13 April 1940.

317 *ILN*, 13 November 1954.

318 F. Bryant to M. Edmunds, December [n. d.], 1897. Sir Arthur Bryant Papers (Liddell Hart Centre for Military Archives, King's College, London). A/57.

319 F. Bryant to A. Bryant, 25 February 1918. Bryant Papers, B/9.

320 M. Bryant to A. Bryant, 18 February 1924. Bryant Papers, B/9; M. Bryant to

A. Bryant, 3 December 1938. Bryant Papers, B/23; P. Street, *Arthur Bryant: portrait of a historian* (London, 1989), p. 27.

321 Street, *Bryant*, pp. 35–6.

322 Mrs Mayo to M. Bryant, 3 December 1912; C. P. H. Mayo to F. M. Bryant, 15 June 1914. Bryant Papers, B/3.

323 Diary of F. M. Bryant, 5 May 1914. Bryant Papers, B/3.

324 Street, *Bryant*, p. 35; A. Bryant to F. M. Bryant, 28 January 1912. Bryant Papers, A/60.

325 C. Tyerman, *A History of Harrow School, 1324–1991* (Oxford, 2000), p. 361.

326 Street, *Bryant*, p. 49.

327 Anon. [A. Lunn], *The Harrovians* (London, 1913), pp. 243–6; C. Harman, *Sylvia Townsend Warner: a biography* (London, 1989), pp. 14–16.

328 *ILN*, 27 May 1967.

329 *ILN*, 16 September 1967; J. Stapleton, *Sir Arthur Bryant and National History in Twentieth Century Britain* (Lexington, 2005), pp. 22–5.

330 A. Bryant to M. Bryant, 18 October 1917. Bryant Papers, B/10; R. Barker, *The Royal Flying Corps in France*, 2 vols (London, 1994–95).

331 Street, *Bryant*, p. 52.

332 Capt. Wrench to Col. Warner [n. d.], Bryant papers, B/10.

333 A. Bryant to M. Bryant, 18 October 1917. Bryant Papers, B/10; *ILN*, 14 November 1936.

334 Street, *Bryant*, p. 56.

335 A. Bryant to M. Bryant, 9 September 1917. Bryant Papers, B/9.

336 A. Bryant to A. Hastings [n. d.], Bryant Papers, C/1a.

337 A. Bryant, 'Kings and Queens', *Punch*, 22 September 1920.

338 A. Bryant to M. Bryant, 25 January 1920. Bryant Papers, B/14; Stapleton, *Bryant*, p. 34.

339 Stapleton, *Bryant*, pp. 34–5; Street, *Bryant*, p. 59.

340 A. Bryant to S. Bryant, 28 April 1924. Bryant Papers, C/1a. *Daily News*, 17 May 1921.

341 L. Ford, 'Testimonial for Arthur Bryant', 6 May 1925. Bryant Papers, C/1.

342 A. Bryant to P. Bryant, 16 May 1924 and 26 December 1923. Bryant Papers, B/34.

343 *Cambridge Chronicle*, 19 April 1924; Street, *Bryant*, p. 67.

344 Bryant to S. Shakerley, 7 July 1923; Bryant to S. Shakerley [n. d.]. Bryant Papers, C/1; A. Bryant to H. Morris, 1 June 1925. Bryant Papers, C/2.

345 S. Bryant to M. Bryant, 20 April 1927. Bryant Papers, B/21; *Desert Island Discs*, 24 January 1979. British Library Sound Archives.

346 *ILN*, 20 February 1954; A. Bryant to P. Bryant [n. d.], Bryant Papers, B/34.

347 A. Bryant to S. Shakerley, 28 April 1924; A. Bryant to S. Shakerley, 7 July 1923. Bryant Papers, C/1a.

348 A. Roberts, *Eminent Churchillians* (London, 1994), p. 321; M. R. D. Foot, *Memoirs of an SOE Historian*, (London, 2008), p. 17.

349 A. Bryant to M. Bryant, 20 February 1928; A. Bryant to M. Bryant, 28 April 1927. Bryant Papers, B/21.

350 A. Bryant to J. Buchan, 23 December 1928 and 2 January 1929. Bryant Papers, C/13.

351 A. Bryant, *The Lion and the Unicorn* (London, 1969), p. 37.

352 Stapleton, *Bryant*, pp. 60–61.

353 H. Butterfield, *The Whig Interpretation of History* (London, 1950[1931]), pp. 31–2.

354 G. M. Trevelyan to A. Bryant, 20 July 1932. Bryant Papers, E/3; P. Street, *Bryant*, p. 88.

355 Street, *Bryant*, pp. 88–9.

356 Ibid., p. 89.

357 A. Bryant to S. Baldwin, 30 October 1934. Earl Baldwin Papers (University of Cambridge Library). File 169, f.50.

358 Street, *Bryant*, p. 99; Stapleton, *Bryant*, p. 72.

359 Y. Buret to A. Bryant, 20 November 1937. Bryant Papers, C1/a; S. Bryant to A. Bryant, 27 September 1937. Bryant Papers, C1/a.

360 *ILN*, 9 January 1937; ibid., 23 January 1937; D. Cannadine, *G. M. Trevelyan: a life in history* (London, 1992), pp. 124–5.

361 A. Bryant to M. Bryant [n. d.]. Bryant Papers, B/24.

362 *ILN*, 17 April 1937.

363 Stapleton, *Bryant*, pp. 128–9.

364 *ILN*, 24 April 1937; ibid., 20 February 1937; A. Bryant (ed.), *The Man and the Hour: studies of six great men of our time* (London, 1934), pp. 143–4.

365 A. Bryant to S. Baldwin, 15 April 1936. Baldwin Papers, File 169, f.50.

366 Stapleton, *Bryant*, pp. 129–30.

367 A. Bryant to H. G. Wells, 18 January 1940. Bryant Papers, C/64.

368 A. Bryant to N. Chamberlain, 21 November 1938. Bryant Papers, C/65; Stapleton, *Bryant*, pp. 107–8.

369 Stapleton, *Bryant*, p. 116.

370 A. Bryant to J. Reith, 8 December 1949. Bryant Papers, E/36; J. L. Garvin to A. Bryant, 18 December 1944. Bryant Papers, F/14.

371 Roberts, *Churchillians*, p. 288.

372 A. Bryant to R. A. Butler, 14 October 1939. Bryant Papers, C/69.

373 A. Bryant, 'Memorandum: Monday, 3 July 1939'. Bryant Papers, C/68.

374 A. Bryant, *Unfinished Victory* (London, 1940), p. xxxv.

375 Tyerman, *Harrow School*, pp. 398–9; R. Griffiths, *Patriotism Perverted: Captain Ramsey, the Right Club and British anti-Semitism, 1939–40* (London, 1998), p. 31.

376 Bryant, 'Memorandum: 13 July 1939'. Bryant Papers, C/68.

377 Roberts, *Churchillians*, p. 305.

378 A. Bryant to N. Chamberlain, 13 July 1939. Bryant Papers, B/68; Street, *Bryant*, p. 107.

379 *ILN*, 16 September 1939; ibid., 30 September 1939; ibid., 10 February 1940; Stapleton, *Bryant*, p. 145.

380 *The Times*, 7 October 1939.

381 Stapleton, *Bryant*, p. 143.

382 Ibid.

383 R. Pomaroli to A. Bryant, 28 June 1937. Bryant Papers C/64; R. Brocket to A. Bryant, 17 October 1939. Bryant Papers, C/69.

384 Griffiths, *Patriotism*, p. 211.

385 Stapleton, *Bryant*, p. 146.

386 Bryant, *Unfinished Victory*, pp. 136–7, 144–6.

387 Ibid., p. 237.

388 Stapleton, *Bryant*, p. 153.

389 *Jewish Chronicle*, 23 February 1940; Stapleton, *Bryant*, pp. 149–55.

390 A. Bryant to J. C. C. Davidson, 18 April 1941. Bryant Papers, C/57; A. Sisman, *Hugh Trevor-Roper: the biography* (London, 2010), p. 79.

391 A. Bryant to M. Bryant [n. d.]. Bryant Papers, B/24.

392 P. Bryant to A. Bryant, 8 January 1944. Bryant Papers, B/33.

393 A. Bryant to J. Junor (draft) [1968]. Bryant Papers, C/84.

394 Street, *Bryant*, p. 133; *ILN*, 8 January 1949.

395 R. Strong to W. S. Robinson, 1 May 2013; P. Street, *Bryant*, p. 34. I am also grateful to Lady Antonia Fraser, Paul Johnson and the late Kenneth Rose for sharing their memories of Bryant with me.

396 B. Brooke to A. Bryant, 29 December 1949. Bryant Papers, C/109; Roberts, *Churchillians*, p. 321.

397 R. Ollard (ed.), *The Diaries of A. L. Rowse* (London, 2003), pp. 158–9; *ILN*, 31 August 1957.

398 Roberts, *Churchillians*, pp. 287, 319.

399 *ILN*, 20 January 1965; ibid., 22 June 1963; ibid., 1 October 1966; ibid., 11 April 1970; ibid., 12 April 1958.

400 B. Cartland to A. Bryant [n. d.]. Bryant Papers, E/12; *Daily Express*, 5 February 1981.

401 B. Patterson, *The Conservative Party and Europe* (London, 2011), p. 20.

402 A. Bryant to M. Aiken, 24 June 1963. Bryant Papers, C/84.

403 A. Bryant to A. J. P. Taylor, 15 February 1970; A. J. P. Taylor to A. Bryant, 13 February 1984. Bryant Papers, E/3. H. Wilson, 'A Book in My Life', *The Spectator*, 2 October 1982.

404 *ILN*, 25 January 1969.

405 Ibid., 9 May 1964; ibid., 7 December 1968.

406 J. Reith to A. Bryant, 21 March 1954. Bryant Papers, E/63; Street, *Bryant*, p. 146; J. Betjeman to A. Bryant [1951]. Bryant Papers, E/7.

407 Street, *Bryant*, p. 169.

408 Ibid., pp. 1, 200–201, 206, 216.

409 Ibid., pp. 18, 213–14.

410 *ILN*, 25 August 1984.

411 *The Bookseller*, February 1979.

412 *ILN*, 31 July 1982; Stapleton, *Bryant*, p. 259.

413 Stapleton, *Bryant*, pp. 2–3.

414 Roberts, *Churchillians*, p. 288.

415 *The Times*, 17 May 2001.

416 Stapleton, *Bryant*, p. 4.

417 Rowse, *Historians I Have Known* (London, 1995), p. 35; A. Briggs, 'Eighty Years On', *Books and Bookmen*, April 1979.

418 Rowse, *Historians*, p. 36; J. Bishop to P. Street [n. d.]. Bryant Papers, J/14.

INDEX